T0326221

Strategic
SUPERVISION

Strategic SUPERVISION

A Brief Guide for Managing Social Service Organizations

Peter J. Pecora
Casey Family Programs and University of Washington

David Cherin
California State University, Fullerton

Emily Bruce
San José State University

Trinidad de Jesus Arguello
Tri-County Community Services, Inc.

Los Angeles | London | New Delhi
Singapore | Washington DC

For information:

SAGE Publications, Inc.
2455 Teller Road
Thousand Oaks, California 91320
E-mail: order@sagepub.com

SAGE Publications India Pvt. Ltd.
B 1/I 1 Mohan Cooperative
  Industrial Area
Mathura Road, New Delhi 110 044
India

SAGE Publications Ltd.
1 Oliver's Yard
55 City Road
London EC1Y 1SP
United Kingdom

SAGE Publications
  Asia-Pacific Pte. Ltd.
33 Pekin Street #02-01
Far East Square
Singapore 048763

Printed in the United States of America.

Library of Congress Cataloging-in-Publication Data

Strategic supervision: A brief guide for managing social service organizations/Peter J. Pecora . . . [et al.].
    p. cm.
Includes bibliographical references and index.
ISBN 978-1-4129-1543-4 (pbk.)
  1. Social work administration. 2. Human services. I. Pecora, Peter J.

HV41.S818 2010
361.0068′3–dc22   2009033563

This book is printed on acid-free paper.

09   10   11   12   13   10   9   8   7   6   5   4   3   2   1

Acquisitions Editor:	Lisa Cuevas Shaw
Editorial Assistant:	Mary Ann Vail
Production Editor:	Karen Wiley
Copy Editor:	Sheree Van Vreede
Typesetter:	C&M Digitals (P) Ltd.
Proofreader:	Jeff Bryant
Indexer:	Gloria Tierney
Cover Designer:	Arup Giri
Marketing Manager:	Stephanie Adams

Contents

Preface

M any supervision books offer general constructs that are important for conceptualizing supervision but do not include the more practical strategies and tools necessary for day-to-day supervision practice. This handbook is designed to help close those gaps by giving supervisors critical concepts, strategies, and tools that can be readily applied to providing leadership and supervision to work teams of staff members in social service agencies.

In Chapter 1 we outline the primary factors associated with organizational excellence. This outline provides a foundation on which to discuss the aspects and roles of supervision, as well as how quality supervision is essential for organizational effectiveness. It is also important for supervisors to understand that in social services, they function within larger organization and community environments. These organizational cultures shape both supervisory functioning and the structure of organizational components. Supervisors need to know how to use their knowledge of culture to both mediate between the organizational culture and the workgroup, and they need to know how to facilitate the culture of the workgroup to enable it to sustain effectiveness. Thus, Chapter 2 focuses on aspects of organizational culture and structure.

In Chapter 3, we examine value-based principles and specific laws guiding personnel management such as Affirmative Action (AA) and the Americans with Disabilities Act (ADA). These laws provide a foundation for the current implementation of many policies and procedures in social services organizations. In Chapter 4, we outline core supervisory competencies and task-based job descriptions required for employee recruitment; and in Chapter 5, we focus on strategies for staff selection.

We present an overview of the processes involved in managing project teams and other types of workgroups in Chapter 6. Integrated in these models of supervision is a focus on tasks, processes, and relationships, which are used to frame supervisory functions and roles. Together with group types, skills, and the knowledge necessary to understand and facilitate these groups, supervisors are armed with critical tools and strategies to function effectively in a team learning environment. Closely related but rarely taught are strategies for leading effective staff meetings. This material is presented in Appendix E.

In Chapter 7, we focus on designing and conducting performance appraisals, outlining methods for effective feedback, and responding to employee behavior. The final chapter moves from the discussion of providing effective feedback to addressing the concern about the behaviors of employees that detract from the goals of the organization, specifically identifying practical strategies for handling employee performance problems.

Taken comprehensively, this handbook will provide the new supervisor in a social services organization with a primer regarding the types of knowledge, skills, and abilities necessary for effective supervisory practice. For those who have been supervising for some time, this book offers a concise compendium of checklists and tools that can be used selectively, as needed.

Acknowledgments

This book was inspired by the students we have been fortunate to work with over the past years. Their questions inspired us to respond with practical content for them and the many social services staff members who are promoted to a supervisory position without much specialized training. We would like to thank the following reviewers: Geoffrey G. Yager, University of Cincinnati; Gary L. Shaffer, University of North Carolina at Chapel Hill; Patrick O. Chambers, Western Washington University; G. H. Grandbois, Creighton University; Candyce S. Russell, Kansas State University; D. Maria Elena Puig, Colorado State University; and Armand Lauffer, University of Michigan (Emeritus). The comments made by these expert reviewers helped shape and improve the book in significant ways. We also thank Delia Armendariz, Lisa Richesson, and Sarah Montgomery for contributing key editorial reviews and other administrative support. Finally, we thank our families for their support of our efforts in terms of the many nights and weekends that were required to complete this handbook.

1

Administrative Supervision Within an Organizational Context

Introduction

Supervising teams of staff members in social services organizations is demanding. It also can be personally satisfying as supervisors see workers grow in skills and confidence, and as consumers benefit from the services provided. Agency staff members with little specialized education or training in supervision, however, often are promoted to supervisory roles. Yet many management or supervision texts offer general information about administration and management, but they rarely include some of the more practical strategies and tools necessary for day-to-day supervisory practice. This handbook is designed to help address those gaps by providing supervisors with critical concepts, strategies, and tools that can be easily applied to first-line supervision with their teams.

Note. We move back and forth between workgroup and team to signify both in human services, but in many situations workgroups do not function as highly collaborative teams. However, we might say that whether we are talking about a group or a team, the supervisor's role requires the same use of tools and techniques.

In this handbook, we will focus on providing social services supervisors with materials to help them become more effective in meeting the demands of a role that requires competency in a wide variety of tasks and skills at several different levels of practice—both within and outside of the organization. These functions that require managing and coaching social services staff include, but are not limited to, (a) understanding the primary roles of a supervisor, and how professional values, ethics, law, and policy guide the supervisor;

(b) recruiting, screening, selecting, and orienting new employees; (c) designing and allocating personnel resources and job tasks; (d) supervising and coaching ongoing task performance of individuals in a changing organizational environment; (e) managing and facilitating task groups; and (f) participating in the design and implementation of agency policy, conducting performance appraisals, and when necessary, participating in decisions about employee terminations.

Many aspects of supervision could be listed, but this handbook will focus on practical strategies for being effective in what we believe is a key critical path for successful supervision.[1] In this chapter, we begin by first laying a foundation of the factors associated with organizational excellence as a platform necessary for sound supervisory practice. This foundation provides a more comprehensive context for the second section of the chapter, which discusses the aspects and roles of supervision, emphasizing how quality supervision is essential for organizational effectiveness.

COMPONENTS OF ORGANIZATIONAL EXCELLENCE

When we think about an excellent organization, what qualities spring to mind? What aspects of that organization distinguish it from others? Is excellence related to the presence of a clear focus of the service or product being delivered? Is excellence created because staff in the organization know what is expected of them and have a clear sense of what constitutes success? Are staff praised and rewarded for performance tied to those identified elements of success? Is excellence tied to the fact that consumers and/or clients are valued and respected by the organization? Is it because leadership is shared within the organization? Or is it because staff members are valued and respected by agency leaders? (See, for example, Collins & Porras, 2002; Goleman, 2000, 2008; Grant & Crutchfield, 2007; Schwartz & McCarthy, 2007.)

To deliver effective services and be considered an excellent place to work, an organization must have several of the above components in place. Workers and supervisors need to be supported in specific ways that complement the agency's mission and program objectives. Unfortunately, too many social workers and other human services practitioners work in "toxic organizational environments" characterized by unclear missions, overcrowded office space, poor supervision, low salaries, large caseloads, and troubled working relations (National Association of Social Workers [NASW], 2006; Ostroff, 2006). These poorly functioning organizations would not meet many of the administrative standards published by the national accrediting bodies, such as the Child Welfare League of America (CWLA), Joint Commission on the Accreditation of Healthcare Organizations (JCAHO), Council on Accreditation, or other accrediting organizations (CWLA, 2005; JCAHO, 2006; NASW, 2006). In contrast, leaders in several public and private agencies that have been recognized as successful operating environments have paid attention to how the following organizational, managerial, and structural components support the effective delivery of human services:

> The organization's mission and program philosophy must be clearly articulated and understood by individuals at all levels of the organization. Organizational effectiveness is also dependent on understanding the individuals, families, and communities being served. This understanding will ensure that the most cost-effective services are being provided. What bolsters and increases effectiveness over time is an organization-wide dedication to using service outcomes data through a Continuous Quality Improvement (CQI) process.

Strategic planning informs the mission in a continuous process. Can staff clearly summarize the organization's mainstream services, most effective programs, and unique client groups? What is the most cost-effective way to ensure your market share? Which organizational objectives need to be achieved in the next 2, 4, and 6 years to achieve key aspects of the organization's mission? These are just three of the many strategic questions that need to be addressed.

A clear understanding of what organizational excellence is in a particular service area, which can be clearly communicated to staff, is essential. Logic models clearly demonstrate how elements of an organization are connected and form a foundation for articulating how organizational processes work. This is the foundation for understanding and communicating excellence. "Logic models" are essential planning and management tools that help the operationalization of organizational excellence. These models outline key short-term, intermediate, and long-term processes and results to be achieved by staff, along with the identification of necessary equipment and essential resources. After identifying the components of the logic model, required costs to be incurred in order to achieve the desired outcomes need to be specified.

Organizational excellence is rooted in being an expert in the strengths and needs of your clients/consumers and what interventions or services will be most effective for meeting their needs. Excellence also involves paying attention to strategic planning, understanding your market area, as well as being focused on the well-being and the skills of your staff. Furthermore, excellence means paying attention to the outcomes achieved as an aspect of program performance and paying attention to the quality and consistency of services (e.g., Collins, 2005; Packard, 2004). Effective organizational designs and service technologies also must be implemented, including paying attention to program capacity. Balancing service capacity and quality is an additional hallmark of an excellent organization.

Developing a human resource focus, which includes a positive organizational climate and the development of staff through regular training opportunities, will produce organizational rewards. Achieving these rewards involves supporting social services staff members by treating them with dignity, maximizing professional discretion to the extent possible, and promoting a small set of key staff competencies (Glisson, 2007; Glisson & James, 2002). Reasonable caseloads and adequate clerical support are also important, which include careful personnel recruitment and selection. Social services organizations do not accomplish their work through a machine-laden manufacturing process but through the interactions between human beings and their ability to share information and learn from their supervisor and each other. Thus, personnel can make or break the effectiveness of a social services organization. Excellent service quality and outcomes are achieved with fundamental organizational commitment to providing staff with appropriate and adequate resources (Mathis & Jackson, 2006).

High-quality, ongoing coaching and monitoring of staff activities, and a strong system of supervisory capacity and supports, contribute to the creation of an excellent organization. High service quality and fidelity will be attained with adequately trained and coached supervisors who can operationalize these concepts. Note that poor supervision ranks as one of the top complaints of social services employees (Kadushin & Harkness, 2002). This handbook can provide some strategies that build staff confidence in their supervisors. For example, clear and measurable performance criteria, and clear worker appraisal methods, are crucial. This goal involves regular supervisory "check-in" sessions with staff members, and it requires realistic and adequately resourced staff development plans. Applying these methods sets the infrastructure for creating a work environment where information is shared and everyone benefits from the sharing of information to learn.

In many organizations, effective worker performance appraisal depends on having access to a larger set of organizational performance data. A system for regular collection and use of key program performance data, including performance measurement, analysis, and knowledge management, is also essential. Many organizations are drowning in data, but they are thirsty for information. Both service output and client/consumer outcomes data are important. Experts urge that a more consumer-oriented management and service delivery system be adopted, where client outcome becomes more of the program focus rather than how much service was provided (Fetterman & Wandersman, 2007).

In addition, data need to be organized and analyzed to make them accessible at multiple organizational levels and in ways that can inform program refinement decisions. Any quality organization achieves success by delineating performance expectations and then rewarding people when those performance expectations are met. This approach is not taken without a vibrant and practical management information system that has the commitment of leadership, supervisors, and staff. Performance measurement ultimately should be tied to a strong process management system, including ongoing assessment of program fidelity, outputs, outcomes, and other aspects of quality.

Organizational Standards of Quality Produce Effective Results and Minimize Liability Exposure

Performance data must be tracked over time to establish trend lines. These trends are then compared with standards of quality and key program expectations (CWLA, 2005; Fisher, 2005). Over time trend data help agency administrators, managers, supervisors, and direct staff see patterns and to not become distracted or misled by an occasional bad quarter or year.

Quality improvement and comparing agency performance with other similar organizations or client populations (benchmarking) can be informative supervisory practices that promote staff learning as well as protect both the organization and its workers from liability. Minimizing liability begins with expert knowledge of your service delivery process, strategies for risk management, and implementation of other preventive programs. Also, a political component to management of liability must not be ignored. Identifying and understanding what kinds of political support are essential to buffer a social services agency and its staff from the day-to-day controversies is prudent.

Wise Use of Technology Is Essential

Because technology can be an expensive distraction from the difficult and non-glamorous work of day-to-day service delivery and supervision, it is important to balance the need for technology versus the illogical attractiveness of this aspect of the work. In other words, a wise leader and supervisor carefully balances the kinds of technology staff need versus the kinds of technology staff want (e.g., mobile phones, fax, e-mail, portable computers, teleconference facilities, data-capturing white boards, voice-activated computers, dial-in Web-based assessment measures,[2] and all the other technological infrastructure that a social services agency could use).

The interrelationships among many of these factors are illustrated in Figure 1.1, which presents the Baldrige performance framework (U.S. Department of Commerce, National Institute of Standards and Technology [NIST]— Technology Administration, 2008). Note that although front-line supervisors are not primarily responsible for all of these areas, supervisors work within the larger context that is bounded by these parameters and illustrates how these functions are exercised.

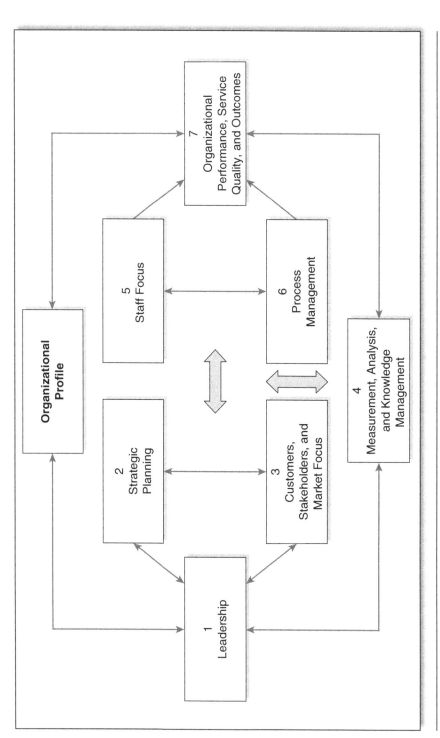

Figure 1.1 Baldrige criteria for performance excellence framework

Source: From *2008 Baldrige National Quality Program: Criteria for performance excellence* (p. iv), by U.S. Department of Commerce, NIST—Technology Administration, 2008, Gaithersburg, MD: Institute of Standards and Technology, Technology Administration. Retrieved July 27, 2008, from http://www.quality.nist.gov/PDF_files/2008_Business_Nonprofit_Criteria.pdf. Copyright 2008 by NIST, Technology Administration. Adapted with permission.

SOCIAL WORK SUPERVISION

Much attention has been focused on the dynamics of clinical supervision in social work (Munson, 2002; Shulman, 1998; Shulman & Safyer, 2007) and educational supervision of students in the process of learning social work practice (Kadushin & Harkness, 2002; Tsui, 2005). In addition, focused attention has been given to the issues critical to the overall management of social services organizations (e.g., Kettner, 2002; Patti, 2008; Perlmutter, Bailey, & Netting, 2001). With some exceptions, however, relatively little social work literature is available that provides practical strategies for the first-line supervisor in the social services agency (Austin & Hopkins, 2004). And yet business literature has many managerial and administrative concepts to offer that inform supervisory practice.

The role of supervisor in the social services organization requires a multifaceted approach to the supervisory role and a systems perspective of the organization's role in the community. The first-line supervisor is continually using a 360° view. Specifically, the supervisor is the conduit for using information gained from service delivery through and across the organization; transmitting knowledge and information up, down, and across agency levels; and even transmitting knowledge and information to those outside the agency boundaries to the community served by the agency. The supervisor here is truly a critical organizational conduit for learning and using knowledge to take action on behalf of consumers and the organization.

This supervisory role is made more complex when the organizational mission and program goals are in a state of change, influenced by shifts in local funding patterns as well as national or regional priorities. Despite these complexities, opportunities for creativity abound. One recent example is how child welfare agencies are implementing evidence-based practice models like Functional Family Therapy or Multi-Dimensional Treatment Foster Care in response to state and national emphasis on evidence-based practice in services contracts. In certain states like Illinois and California, Title IV-E Waivers are changing funding patterns to enable more funds to be spent on program innovations. Finally, supervisory management practices also are affected by regional differences in policies, funding mechanisms, multiculturalism and feminist management practices, and how privatization of services and unionization have shaped (or not shaped) certain social services and other nonprofit sectors[3] (e.g., Chaison, 2006; Connerley & Pederson, 2005; Mor Barak, 2005; Nightingale & Pindus, 1997; Van Slyke, 2003; Van Slyke & Hammonds, 2003).

EMERGING CONCEPTS IN SUPERVISION: THE LEARNING ORGANIZATION IN THE CONTEXT OF CONTINUOUS QUALITY IMPROVEMENT

Organizational transformations are often complex, and they almost always reflect how the organization responds to external forces. In this context, organizations must be dedicated to continuous efforts at improvement. Quality improvement simply means that an organization is committed to striving to understand its consumers' needs and to monitoring, analyzing, correcting, and improving actual services to meet those needs. With this approach, information derived from regular measurements of worker performance, program performance, and outcomes is used for maximizing agency success in an environment where quality and cost-effectiveness are critical. An organization that shares useful and key information about agency performance with all personnel is open and transparent. Thus, knowledge about services grows, is used to create improvements, to make change processes explicit, and to sustain quality. The supervisor is critical in facilitating these learning and improvement processes. Therefore, a renewed emphasis is placed on the important roles played by the first-line supervisor in the social services organization (Austin & Hopkins, 2004).

In an effective organization, one of the primary roles of the supervisor is to facilitate direct-line staff, sharing information in such a way members learn from the results of their interactions with each other and the environment in which they implement their practice, and conversely, the organization learns from its members. This knowledge and the reflection in action process are critical to both assuring the quality of service delivery to consumers and improving the organization at the level of service delivery. In addition, this learning process assures that not only services but also the policies and procedures that govern service provision are examined and improved. Providing an infrastructure that allows that information to be used and the knowledge gained to flow to and from first-line staff is the critical role fulfilled by direct-line supervisors.

Thus, a first-line supervisor must have the skills to facilitate this development. Senge, Kleiner, Roberts, Ross, and Smith (1994) refer to this process as creating a "learning organization." They identify five "disciplines" that are critical to a learning organization and are necessary to be adopted by the supervisor in his or her role as a facilitator in this type of organization:

Personal Mastery: This is the strategic skill in which supervisors learn to create in themselves personal goals and purposes that they can use to best affect the organization, and in which they gain mastery in the performance of tasks related to their own sphere of work.

Mental Models: The goal is for supervisors to understand their own mental models that require "continually clarifying and improving [their] internal pictures of the world" (p. 6), including the use of theoretical and more concrete management and practice frameworks. For human services professionals, this also includes investigating and understanding the mental models that have been constructed about their clients and the agency in which these models function to keep people from learning.

Shared Vision: Supervisors' use of this strategic skill facilitates a sense of group commitment that is developed and upon which individuals agree about the vision of the organization and its goals. As a group, the task team or project team needs to have a clear sense and agreement about the tasks, the goals, and the processes required to achieve the desired outcomes.

Team Learning: The goal of supervision in the learning organization is to allow an environment to encourage information sharing and reflection in order to enhance the creativity and skill of the team. Essentially, the process involves and uses sharing individual information about the task with team members to generate knowledge for action that will positively impact the organization.

Systems Thinking: In this context, supervisors model and develop their own frames of reference that recognize the interrelatedness of systems that influence language and perspective. The supervisors also must absorb and process information from the larger organizational environment.

As supervisors work to identify their own professional goals, they enhance the growth and effectiveness of the agency. In addition, engaging in that type of professional discipline can function to provide a model for supervisees and peers. Continually questioning and clarifying one's assumptions—the schema by which one navigates through issues in the organization—can help one perceive experiences more accurately without the cloud of assumptions, beliefs, and inference that often obscure the essence of the phenomena being observed.

The case example provided in Figure 1.2 illustrates how this learning process can be facilitated by a supervisor to resolve issues that may be hindering performance and, thus, hindering effective service delivery. The tool used in this example is called the ladder of inference, which illustrates how individuals, including supervisors, can leap to erroneous conclusions about situations because they have not checked out whether the validity of their assumptions is based on the facts of the situation (see Figure 1.3).

One concept that applies to this situation is *double-loop learning* (see Figure 1.4). Often as work groups explore improvement strategies and problem solving, the root cause of a problem is not, as in Figure 1.2, case example trying to teach staff about specific behavioral expectations, such as meeting attendance. When identifying behaviors that hinder effectiveness, such as tardiness to meetings, the immediate responses usually exist in the first loop of learning: understanding, identifying, and trying to resolve a problem. However, the second loop of learning involves understanding the values, beliefs, and assumptions people hold about why the behaviors occur and effective ways to intervene or alter the incentive for less than effective behaviors. In an effective organization that attempts to learn, both loops of learning are engaged, and the supervisor has to be able to facilitate the use of both learning loops to lead the organization to effectiveness. Additional opportunities for growth and development for all parties, in the context of the double loop of

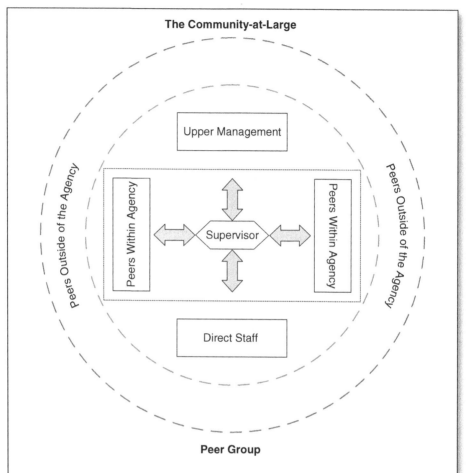

The Community-at-Large

Upper Management

Peers Within Agency

Supervisor

Peers Within Agency

Peers Outside of the Agency

Peers Outside of the Agency

Direct Staff

Peer Group

Jolynne supervises six direct staffers. Every month Marcia is late for the monthly staff meeting. Jolynne has a set of beliefs and assumptions about being late. Included in that set of beliefs and assumptions is the notion that being late to an appointment is a sign of disrespect. Jolynne finds Marcia's behavior extremely frustrating. Because Jolynne assumed the behavior was related to Marcia's time management difficulties and the low value Marcia placed on the staff meetings, Jolynne angrily confronted her during their weekly one-on-one supervisory sessions.

Marcia was shocked and hurt by Jolynne's intensity and her assumptions about her. In contrast, Marcia has a set of beliefs and assumptions about services to clients. Included in those beliefs and assumptions is the notion that service to clients is an organizational priority. Consequently, she had concluded that it should be OK for her to be a little late to a standing meeting if she was doing work on a case. After some awkward silence, Jolynne apologized for her confrontational tone and Marcia agreed that she had not communicated why she was frequently late and pledged to make a greater effort to be on time.

From their respective points of view, they are both correct. However, this is an example of an opportunity for the supervisor, the staff person, and perhaps others to consider what assumptions they bring to analyzing a situation and to learn new, more effective approaches regarding how they relate to each other.

Figure 1.2   A situation of conflicting value sets

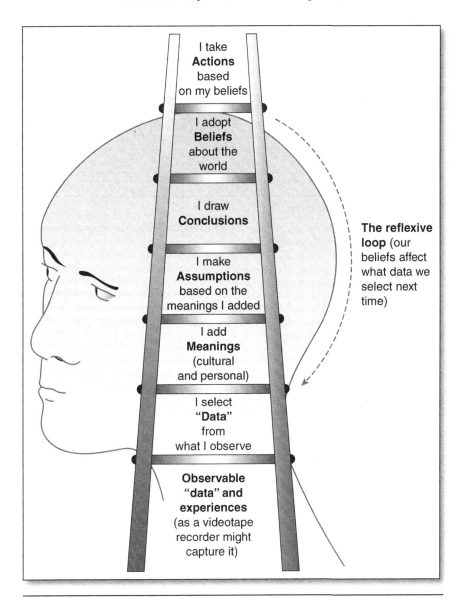

Figure 1.3   The ladder of inference

Source: From "The ladder of inference," by R. Ross. In *The fifth discipline fieldbook* (p. 243), by P. M. Senge, A. Kleiner, & C. Roberts (Eds.), 1994, London: Nicholas Brealey. Copyright 1994 by Nicholas Brealey Publishing. Reprinted with permission. Adapted from C. Argyris (1982) and C. Argyris, R. Putnam, & D. M. Smith (1985).

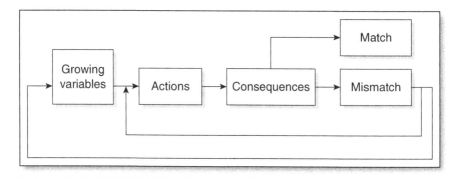

Figure 1.4   Double-loop learning

Source: From *On organizational learning* (p. 8), by C. Argyris, 1993, Cambridge, MA: Blackwell. Copyright 1992 by Blackwell. Reprinted with permission.

learning, include conducting performance appraisals, providing ongoing supervision, giving feedback, and addressing performance problems (Argyris, 1993; Smith, 2001). Essentially, problem solving involves both mitigating the immediate issue and then understanding what about the organization permitted the problem to exist. The continuous quality organization knows that to achieve effectiveness, both the cause and effect and the culture need to be explored.

In many supervisory situations, we examine performance data and other feedback to improve our performance relative to a set of work unit goals and other factors that are taken for granted. "Feedback from our performance (or 'learning from our mistakes') typically cycles immediately back into our analysis of the strategies, tactics, or techniques that led to our performance. This is important, but it is inherently limited by the environmental and cultural factors that are taken for granted and that remain unchallenged by an assessment of the performance results" (Batista, 2006, p. E1). Double-loop learning occurs when we expand our analytical frame to identify explicitly and then challenge any underlying assumptions that support our stated goals, values, and strategies. Rather than only ask, "How can we achieve our goals more effectively?" Batista encourages us to look deeper and also ask the following:

- What assumptions support our goals, values, and strategies?
- How can we test these assumptions?
- Having tested these assumptions, should we change our goals, values, or strategies?

In contrast, if we can pull back and expand the frame of our analysis, we begin to call into question some of the factors that we usually take for granted. Our performance results aren't simply used to assess the strategies that have been derived from those factors—they question the factors themselves (p. E1).

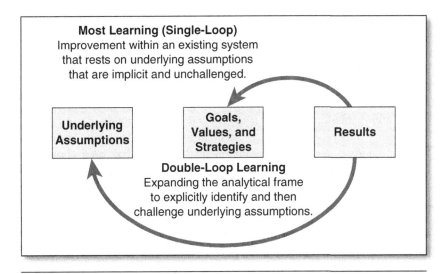

Figure 1.5   Double-loop learning as contrasted with single-loop learning

Source: From Double-loop learning, by E. Batista, 2008. Retrieved July 27, 2008, from http://www
.edbatista.com/2008/05/double-loop.html. Copyright 2008 by Ed Batista. Reprinted with permission.
Adaptation of Table 2.1. Decision Methods for Group and Individual Problems from *Leadership
and Decision-Making,* by Victor H. Vroom and Philip W. Yetton, copyright 1973. Reprinted by permission of the University of Pittsburgh Press.

Double-loop learning is both an individual counseling tool and a team
learning tool. At the individual level, double-loop learning can be a source
of personal growth and development. At the group level, double-loop learning can be used to challenge assumptions, values, and beliefs that hinder
effective service delivery. The supervisor can facilitate the learning process
specifically by providing service delivery data and by soliciting feedback
from individuals on the team to help staff understand how the values,
beliefs, and assumptions about how things are done can hinder work processes
or service delivery.

To provide a framework for the chapters that follow, we conclude this
chapter with an examination of the core functions of a supervisor.

Defining Supervision

DIMENSIONS OF SUPERVISORY LEADERSHIP BEHAVIOR

A supervisor is a staff person to whom authority is delegated to direct,
coordinate, enhance, and evaluate on-the-job performance of one or more line
staff. An effective supervisor applies leadership skills to facilitate accomplishment of agency goals through interactions with line staff. In a social services

organization, a supervisor's ultimate objective is to ensure that effective services are delivered to clients/customers in accordance with organization policies and procedures. To be effective, a supervisor also may need to challenge organization policies and procedures. Supervisors, thus, focus on the relationships with staff, the tasks to meet the organization's mission and goals, and the constant assessment of whether policies and procedures continue to meet the organization's mission and goals (Burgess, 2006; Collins, 2005).

Quality supervision includes attending to people, process, and tasks (Interaction Associates, 1997). Traditionally, leadership has been conceived around the idea that one person is firmly "in charge" while the rest are simply followers—what is termed "vertical leadership." More recent research indicates that leadership can be shared by team leaders and team members—rotating to the person with the key knowledge, skills, and abilities for the particular issues facing the team at any given moment. In fact, research indicates that poor-performing teams tend to be dominated by the team leader, whereas high-performing teams display more dispersed leadership patterns, i.e., shared leadership (Pearce, 2004; Pearce & Sims, 2002).

More specifically, at least four important types of leadership behavior can emanate from the vertical leader or be shared and distributed among the members of a team instead of residing totally with the supervisor as "vertical" leader: directive, transactional, transformational, and empowering (Ford, Heaton, & Brown, 2001; Lawler & Finegold, 2000; Pearce, 2004):

Directive leadership involves providing task-focused direction or recommendations. Directive leadership has been advocated in knowledge worker contexts as providing a much-needed structure for inherently unstructured tasks. For example, highly skilled social services workers, be they vertical leaders or other members of the team, might well find a receptive audience among less experienced or less knowledgeable members for well-meaning and constructive prescription and direction.

Transactional leadership entails influencing followers by strategically supplying rewards—praise, compensation, or other valued outcomes—contingent on follower performance. Typically the source of such rewards has been the appointed, vertical leader. However, shared transactional leadership in a team of social services workers might, for example, be expressed through collegial praise for contributions toward serving families or improving work unit outcomes. Colleagues might also award valued assignments or recommend financial or gift awards based on individual- or team-level attainment of milestones, quality targets, excellent interpersonal relationships, financial stewardship, innovations in cultural diversity, or other key performance metrics. (This kind of recognition program has been operating successfully in a child welfare agency since 2007.)

Transformational leadership adopts a more symbolic emphasis on commitment to a team vision, emotional engagement, and fulfillment of higher order needs such as meaningful professional impact or desires to engage in breakthrough achievements. On the one hand, one of the vertical leader's tasks is clarifying the vision for the team. On the other hand, social services teams might engage in shared transformational leadership through peer exhortation or by appealing to collegial desires to design better intervention approaches, locate new sources of funding, connect with key community-based resources, or some other kind of innovation.

Empowering leadership emphasizes employee self-influence rather than top-down control. In many ways, empowering leadership epitomizes the role of the designated, vertical leader under conditions of team-shared leadership. Empowering leadership can also be shared and projected laterally among peers. Examples of shared empowering leadership in a team of knowledge workers might include peer encouragement and support of self–goal-setting, self-evaluation, self-reward, and self-development. Shared empowering leadership emphasizes building self-influence skills that orchestrate performance while preserving autonomy (adapted from Pearce, 2004, pp. 53–54).

From another perspective, supervisors can tap into the power of participation and bring out the best in others by demonstrating the Seven Practices of Facilitative Leadership: (a) coach for performance; (b) celebrate accomplishment; (c) share an inspiring vision; (d) focus on results, process, and relationship; (e) optimize appropriate staff involvement; (f) design pathways to action by being aware of when to focus on problem identification and analysis, visioning, solution development, and implementation of the solutions or strategies; and (g) facilitate agreement (Interaction Associates, 1997, p. 1–14). The types of specific skills associated with the supervisory functions include administrative skills; teaching, coaching, and support; cross-cultural communication skills; and leadership skills, which are itemized in the sections that follow (Kadushin & Harkness, 2002; Casey Family Programs, 2002).

ADMINISTRATIVE SKILLS

Administrative supervision refers to leadership, the oversight of staff performance, and other personnel management tasks. These tasks include articulating a vision and mission of the organization in an ethical and forward-thinking manner. Administrative skills require a thorough grounding in key laws, ethics, and policies.

Another administrative supervisory skill is recruiting and selecting staff, which involves assessing individual capacity to succeed in a challenging culture that nonetheless encourages growth and development, both personally and professionally. As discussed in Chapters 4 and 5, recruitment and employee selection are crucial public relations functions for the organization, as it interacts with a community of persons who might have applied for positions. The process of selecting new staff must result in successfully identifying competent individuals to fill staff positions to further the work of the organization; otherwise, the organization as a whole will suffer by enduring the inadequate performance of a poorly selected staff member until that person is fired or quits.

Orienting new staff is another key aspect of administrative supervision. Orienting new employees involves planning tasks for new employees, specifying responsibilities and authority, and clarifying expected and desired outcomes to the new employee. Part of this orientation should focus on promoting cross-cultural competence. When direct line staff have clearly defined job tasks that fit into the vision, mission, and goals of the agency, not only can the supervisor provide regular reflection of the individual's effectiveness on the job, but also each staff person potentially can conduct an increasingly accurate self-assessment. This capability, of course, paves the way for a performance appraisal that accurately reflects the staff person's ability to perform his or her job.

Participating in program planning and guideline development is another closely related aspect of administrative supervision. Planning and monitoring resources is very much part of that work. It will involve advocating for staff and those who receive services from the social services organization. Coordinating the work in the program and unit includes developing task groups and leading teams. Facilitating teamwork is one of the key functions of a supervisor that is often not highlighted in generic supervision texts. However, here we devote a chapter to the leadership of work teams (Chapter 6).

Monitoring, analyzing, and evaluating work usually occurs in the context of measuring staff performance (Chapter 7) and in terms of addressing performance problems (Chapter 8). Line staff may have made commitments to personal and professional growth and development in the context of the organization; yet when concerns about performance problems occur, opportunities for learning may also be present. Finally, administrative supervision involves managing the flow of information to and from employees as well as serving as a change agent. As a middle manager, supervisors must be clear communicators and should be prepared to "manage up" by communicating staff concerns and suggestions to agency leaders (Bruce & Austin, 2000).

TEACHING SKILLS

Through the process of disseminating knowledge, supervisors help line staff learn the skills they will need to complete their jobs effectively. In the process of transferring knowledge, supervisors facilitate the accomplishment of agency goals as well as facilitate the professional development of line staff.

One of the most powerful vehicles for staff learning and reinforcement of those concepts is learning through team experience or dialogue. "Team learning" is a process designed to create a workplace that encourages and supports staff in learning from their daily experience and from each other. For example, in the case of a health care employee who has difficulty in getting health care vendors out to a patient's home, the learning environment would encourage this team member to share the information they have obtained with others in the team. This process also builds the team's knowledge about the health care vendors used by the agency. This type of individual experience and information sharing at the group level can improve overall service provision. This is what is meant by learning at the level of the group, engaging in group reflection, and then using knowledge gained for action—change or improvement.

The team learning is accomplished with other team members, rather than using traditional classroom methods of transferring knowledge. Furthermore, team learning is directed to improvement in knowledge, skills, attitudes, or other aspects of performance. The supervisor, through processes like the one above, coaches individuals on how to use information and on how to share ideas, and then he or she facilitates the group in the process of reflecting on this information and building knowledge to achieve change. In the case of the above example, the group might conclude that it needs to select better vendors or improve instructions to existing health care vendors. The team members teach and support each other in a giving and receiving environment. Team learning builds on the concept that learning is a lifelong process that does not just occur when one attends a training workshop. In addition to teaching, supervisors must model lifelong learning and be open to learning from staff.

Team learning also should be understood through the lens of quality improvement. Part of the focus of team learning is that all staff should understand how the agency's service delivery process works, the key results to be achieved, and the criteria for how things are most effectively done and with what methods. This knowledge will affect how professionals work with consumers as well as how services are documented and monitored. With a clear understanding of the work processes, the team can effectively monitor its work and gather information that will be helpful in recognizing how customers receive services and whether these services are working. Ultimately the team is exposed to the outcomes of their work and can improve, change, and strengthen what is being done. The supervisor plays an instrumental role in facilitating this team learning process by clarifying expected results, by helping the team develop the most effective work processes, and by gathering and using the performance data in discussions that engage in learning and change.

In another example of team learning, consider the situation of five pediatric social workers at the local children's hospital who are each responsible for providing services to four patients, their parents, and their entire families, when necessary. Keeping up with the mandates for accountability under managed care, as well as providing direct services, keeps these social workers very busy. The lead social worker for the pediatric unit, in consultation with the director of social work services, has created an opportunity for each of the social workers to provide the leadership for trainings at every other pediatric social work unit meeting. The trainings include content on ways to maximize efficiency, access to community resources, and new therapeutic techniques. In this example, each member has a chance to demonstrate leadership, gather data, analyze data, and share findings to the benefit of the entire team.

Supervisory promotion of employee learning is distinguished from agency-wide staff development or the in-service training processes, because a supervisor's focused knowledge/skill building opportunities are targeted to the needs of a particular employee in the context of day-to-day work. Supervisory teaching has been rated as one of the two top sources of satisfaction by employees (Kadushin & Harkness, 2002). This latter point has been validated in research studies regarding employee satisfaction in learning and nonlearning environments regarding worker motivation (Latham & Ernst, 2006). Conversely, a supervisor's failure to use effective teaching skills is one the greatest sources of frustration for supervisors and for other team members (Kadushin & Harkness, 2002).

COACHING AND SUPPORTIVE SKILLS

The coaching and supportive function of supervision is focused on helping employees meet requirements of their jobs, using several specific methods, such as the follows:

1. Scheduling regular standing times for supervision, where staff have the undivided attention of the supervisor is critical. This is one outgrowth of valuing positive working relationships between supervisors and staff.

2. Communicating staff concerns and ideas for quality improvement to management, but also respecting the confidentiality of personal information regarding employees, enhances a supervisor's capital with direct line staff and can be informative to management.

3. Ensuring that direct line staff receive necessary resources to do their job, which includes making sure that staff safety and health needs are met, elicits the confidence of direct line staff.

4. Providing regular feedback about performance through coaching sessions, much like a baseball coach would do; timely instruction and practice on a particular skill with a player are critical. This feedback also includes recognizing the achievements and competencies of staff as well as targeting attention to areas that need work.

5. Setting clear expectations regarding the job, including skills, knowledge, and attitudes necessary to perform duties and responsibilities. This encourages continuous professional growth and skill development. Setting clear expectations also motivates staff to meet the expectations. (Latham & Ernst, 2006; Rowe, de Savigny, Lanata, & Victora, 2005).

CROSS-CULTURAL SKILLS

The effective first-line supervisor must not only incorporate the above skills—increasingly, these skills must be developed and enhanced in the context of supervision in a multiethnic or multicultural workforce. Consequently, supervisors must display skills that include the critical aspects of managing cross-cultural communication and cross-cultural interpersonal dynamics, so that the respective skills and resources of an ethnically, racially, culturally, economically, and sexually diverse workforce can be brought to bear in the service of the goals of the organization. Globalization is having powerful effects on the workforce in the United States in terms of hiring practices. Thus, first-line supervisors need to be effective at supervising a multicultural group of employees and at figuring out how best to integrate these diverse workgroups to develop a cohesive work team (Laroche & Rutherford, 2006; Mor Barak, 2005).

In this context, an essential skill for first-line supervisors is the ability to model positive cross-cultural interactions. For example, effective cross-cultural communication facilitates a respectful "pluralistic perspective" with a commitment to understanding and acceptance of those with different views (Pinderhughes, 1989; Thomas & Ely, 2002). From one perspective, supervisors must be able to model this skill to staff; and from a second perspective, supervisors must pay attention to the interactions among staff in order to observe opportunities to reward staff for engaging in the process of creating and supporting an environment that recognizes and embraces "different-ness" (Thomas & Ely, 2002). From a third perspective, supervisors must ensure that no staff engages in biased behavior against any client, customer, patient, or colleague; and should it occur, they need to correct the behavior promptly. Furthermore, this correction must occur in a clear, civil, and nondenigrating manner.

Also, first-line supervisors are the key in helping managers and agency executives honestly recognize the concerns of those who are ethnically, racially, culturally, economically, and sexually different within the agency; and they must understand how differently staff who are in the minority may feel in comparison with those who have numbers and/or power and influence in the organization. This understanding throughout the agency, and specifically from management, is necessary in facilitating the organization's overall ability to provide effective and efficient services to ethnically, racially, culturally, economically, and sexually diverse clients, customers, and/or patients. This understanding may take different forms, given the variation in social services organizations in the United States.

Supervisors who can demonstrate, model, and coach these skills enhance the cross-cultural communication skills of their workgroup. Both human services organizations and businesses are beginning to recognize that cross-cultural skills are critical, particularly in terms of population demographics that are increasingly less homogeneous (Mederos & Woldeguiorguis, 2003).

If supervisors with cross-cultural skills can use a variety of approaches to demonstrate their cultural competence, they can provide staff with a variety of tools to use to enhance their effectiveness. For example, a supervisor who demonstrates open regard for her direct line staff will be more likely to establish rapport; create a safe and accepting environment for frank discussion; and to provide opportunities for all staff members to feel the confidence to be effective in their practice. The approaches to enhancing cross-cultural skills can be employed in individual supervision, as well as in group supervision, providing opportunities for the workgroup to learn from each other regarding these issues.

One caveat is that a potential result of dealing openly with difficult issues is the development of conflict. Effective resolution of cross-cultural conflicts requires addressing the issues openly and honestly. Done well, conflict resolution can increase the effectiveness of team functioning. However, these individual and group approaches to enhancing cross-cultural skill development require sensitivity. Supervisors must be careful to recognize their limits and the limits of their team, so as to not to create a more difficult situation (Hyde, 2004). Ultimately, first-line supervisors must have cross-cultural skills, knowledge, values, and sensibilities to assess the cross-cultural skills, knowledge, values, and sensibilities of staff; and they must recognize that if they do not have these skills, they need to get individual assistance and/or assistance for their workgroup.

LEADERSHIP SKILLS

The "leadership system" is one of the key areas examined by the Malcolm Baldrige Award reviewers because it places into context the importance of good management and highly skilled supervisors (U.S. Department of Commerce, NIST—Technology Administration, 2008, p. 68). Supervisory leadership functions as the process of effectively interacting with people at all levels in the organization, including superiors, peers, and subordinates, in order to influence others and bring about desired organizational outcomes (Fisher, 2005; Packard, 2004). In a secure environment that promotes increased interdependence, staff members can achieve the high levels of development and growth that allow for the formation of leadership. To create this environment, supervisors must establish cooperation and trust between themselves and their staff, as well as among the members of their staff. This sense of trust is enhanced when supervisors accurately and tactfully represent the issues of their staff members to upper management.

Assessing social, political, cultural, and other trends, and their implications for the long-term success of the organization, is another aspect of leadership. An effective leader also influences people from other departments, functions, and divisions to bring about desired organizational change. Positive and fair corrective feedback will also improve working relationships. Supervisors must engage staff in actively understanding their agency's vision, mission, and goals, while anticipating and planning for staff to change, grow, and develop in their support of these goals.

Summary

By applying the functional skills presented above, the new first-line supervisor can begin to create a climate that facilitates their own professional growth, and the professional growth and learning of those they supervise. In the organization that is open to building a dynamic environment, the supervisor is a valuable source of information so that upper management can (a) learn about the actual working conditions of those on the front line and (b) sustain the context necessary to promote service quality and effectiveness. Similarly, front-line workers in an open environment not only should understand the implications and limitations of external policy mandates on their direct practice, but also they should be encouraged to "manage up" by communicating their concerns and ideas to agency administrators through their supervisors.

Supervisors are critical in orchestrating the effective implementation of a social services organization's mission and goals. Using the various supervisory skills, supervisors function as "cross-trainers," spanning across several levels of the organization: up, down, and across the agency, working with those within the agency and with those outside of the agency (Casey Family Programs, 2002).

Similarly, a supervisor can facilitate the development of a climate where the team learns from each other and recognizes their interconnectedness to the entire system. This area is explored in more depth in our next chapter. The concept of "double-loop learning" can assist the development of this sense of interconnectedness. Essentially, supervisory excellence builds on the accomplishments of key functions, such as recruiting, selecting, and orienting new staff members; teaching, coaching, and leading; as well as utilizing and modeling effective cross-cultural communication. Thus, a progressive "building block" approach to the acquisition of supervisory skills illustrates how each skill rests on the development of a previous skill.

In the rapidly changing social services environment, supervisory skills that help staff thrive in that environment are the key. The effective supervisor in the effective social services organization responds with increased flexibility to the environment. The organization that operates in such a manner is more able to respond quickly and effectively to the changing social services needs of people and communities.

Finally, supervisors in the social services usually function within larger organizations that exist within a community environment. The organizational cultures shape both supervisory functioning and the structure of organizational components. Supervisors need to know how to use their knowledge of this culture, to both mediate between the organization and the direct staff and to mediate between individual direct-line staff and their workgroup in order to empower the staff members to sustain effectiveness in service delivery. Thus, Chapter 2 focuses on organizational culture.

Endnotes

1. Other critical ongoing supervision tasks in a social services organization include making the transition from line worker to supervisor, participating in staff development, providing clinical supervision, and understanding the interactional nature of supervision (Austin & Hopkins, 2004; Bruce & Austin, 2000; Edwards & Yankey, 2006; Kadushin & Harkness, 2002; Munson, 2002; Shulman, 1992; Tsui, 2005; Weinbach, 2008).

2. For examples of Web-based, free instant-scoring assessment tools for human services, see http://www.caseylifeskills.org.

3. Privatization does reduce the number of public employees if services formerly performed in the public sector are shifted to the private sector. But it is not clear that workers are necessarily worse off in terms of employment, wages, morale, or job satisfaction. Many examples are available of negotiated arrangements for transferring public employees to private employment or to other public agencies. Undoubtedly, though, a clear reduction in public employee members of unions is occurring, although some privatized workers may join other unions (Nightingale & Pindus, 1997, p. 1).

References

Argyris, C. (1993). *On organizational learning.* Cambridge, MA: Blackwell.

Argyris, C., Putnam, R., & Smith, D. M. (1985). *Action science* (pp. 57–58). San Francisco: Jossey-Bass.

Austin, M. J., & Hopkins, K. M. (Eds.). (2004). *Supervision as collaboration in the human services: Building a learning culture.* Thousand Oaks, CA: Sage.

Batista, E. (2006). Chris Argyris, double-loop learning and meta-work. Retrieved July 27, 2008, from http://www.edbatista.com/2006/10/chris_argyris_d.html#comment-244693250

Batista, E. (2008). Double-loop learning. Retrieved July 27, 2008, from http://www .edbatista.com/2008/05/double-loop.html

Bruce, E. J., & Austin, M. J. (2000). Social work supervision: Assessing the past and mapping the future. *The Clinical Supervisor, 19,* 85–107.

Burgess, G. J. (2006). *Legacy living.* Provo, UT: Executive Excellence Publishing.

Casey Family Programs. (2002). *A supervision model for Casey Family Programs— Working paper* [Mimeograph]. Seattle, WA: Author.

Chaison, G. (2006). *Unions in America.* Thousand Oaks, CA: Sage.

Child Welfare League of America. (2005). *CWLA standards of excellence for transition, independent living, and self-sufficiency services.* Crystal City, VA: Author.

Collins, J. (2005, July-August). Level 5 leadership: The triumph of humility and fierce resolve. *The Best of Harvard Business Review,* pp. 136–146. (Reprint R0507M; HBR OnPoint 5831)

Collins, J. C., & Porras, J. I. (2002). *Built to last: Successful habits of visionary companies.* New York: Harper Business.

Connerley, M. L., & Pederson, P. B. (2005). *Leadership in a diverse and multicultural environment.* Thousand Oaks, CA: Sage.

Edwards, R. L., & Yankey, J. A. (Eds.) (2006). *Effectively managing nonprofit organizations.* Washington, DC: National Association of Social Workers.

Fetterman, D., & Wandersman, A. (2007). Empowerment evaluation: Yesterday, today, and tomorrow. *American Journal of Evaluation, 28,* 179–198.

Fisher, E. A. (2005). Facing the challenges of outcomes measurement: The role of transformational leadership. *Administration in Social Work, 29*(4), 35–49.

Ford, R. C., Heaton, C. P., & Brown, S. W. 2001. Delivering excellent service: Lessons from the best firms. *California Management Review, 44*(1), 39–56.

Glisson, C. (2007). Assessing and changing organizational culture and climate for effective services. *Research on Social Work Practice, 17,* 736–747.

Glisson, C., & James, L. R. (2002). The cross-level effects of culture and climate in human service teams. *Journal of Organizational Behavior, 23,* 767–794.

Goleman, D. (2000, March-April). Leadership that gets results. *Harvard Business Review,* pp. 78–90. (Reprint R00204)

Goleman, D. (2008, September). Social intelligence and the biology of leadership. *Harvard Business Review, 86*(9), 74–81. (Reprint No. R08090E)

Grant, N. M., & Crutchfield, L. R. (2007, Fall), Creating high-impact nonprofits. *Stanford Social Innovation Review.* Retrieved October 17, 2008, from http://www.ssireview.org

Hyde, C. A. (2004). Multicultural development in human services agencies: Challenges and solutions. *Social Work, 49*(1), 7–16.

Interaction Associates. (1997). *Facilitative leadership workbook.* San Francisco, CA: Author. (For more information, see http://www.interactionassociates.com/)

Joint Commission on the Accreditation of Healthcare Organizations. (2006). *Revised Leadership Standards Field Review.* Joint Commission on Accreditation of Healthcare Organizations (JCAHO). Retrieved May 18, 2007, from http://www.jointcommission.org/Standards/FieldReviews/

Kadushin, A., & Harkness, D. (2002). *Supervision in social work* (4th ed.). New York: Columbia University Press.

Kettner, P. M. (2002). *Achieving excellence in the management of human services organizations.* Boston: Allyn & Bacon.

Laroche, L., & Rutherford, D. (2006). *Recruiting, retaining and promoting culturally different employees.* Newton, MA: Butterworth-Heinemann.

Latham, G. P., & Ernst, C. T. (2006). Keys to motivating tomorrow's workforce. *Human Resource Management Review, (16),* 181–198.

Lawler, E. E., III, & Finegold, D. (2000). Individualizing the organization: Past, present, and future. *Organizational Dynamics, 29*(1), 1–15.

Mathis, R. L., & Jackson, J. H. (2006). *Human Resource Management* (11th ed.). Mason, OH: Thomson South-Western.

Mederos, F., & Woldeguiorguis, I. (2003). Beyond cultural competence: What child protection managers need to know and do. *Child Welfare, 82*(2), 125–142.

Mor Barak, M. (2005). *Managing diversity.* Thousand Oaks, CA: Sage.

Munson, C. E. (2002). *Handbook of clinical social work supervision* (3rd ed.). New York: Haworth Press.

National Association of Social Workers. (2006). *Assuring the sufficiency of a frontline workforce: A national study of licensed social workers.* Washington, DC: Author. Retrieved June 16, 2006, from http://workforce.socialworkers.org

Nightingale, D. S., & Pindus, N. M. (1997). *Privatization of public social services: A background paper.* Washington, DC: Urban Institute. Retrieved May 20, 2007, from http://www.urban.org/url.cfm?ID=407023

Ostroff, F. (2006). Change management in government. *Harvard Business Review, 84,* 141–147.

Packard, T. (2004). The supervisor as transformational leader. In M. J. Austin & K. M. Hopkins (Eds.), *Supervision as collaboration in the human services: Building a learning culture.* Thousand Oaks, CA: Sage.

Patti, R. J. (2008). *Handbook of human services management.* Thousand Oaks, CA: Sage.

Pearce, C. L. (2004). The future of leadership: Combining vertical and shared leadership to transform knowledge work. *Academy of Management Executive, 18*(1), 47–57.

Pearce, C. L., & Sims, H. P., Jr. (2002). Vertical versus shared leadership as predictors of the effectiveness of change management teams: An examination of aversive, directive, transactional, transformational, and empowering leader behaviors. *Group Dynamics: Theory, Research, and Practice, 6,* 172–197.

Perlmutter, F. D., Bailey, D., & Netting, F. E. (2001). *Managerial supervision of the. human services.* New York: Oxford University Press.

Pinderhughes, E. (1989). *Understanding race, ethnicity, and power: The key to efficacy in clinical practice.* New York: Free Press.

Rowe, A. K., de Savigny, D. D., Lanata, C. F., & Victora, C. G. (2005). How can we achieve and maintain high-quality performance of health workers in low-resource settings? *Lancet, 366,* 1026–1035.

Schwartz, T., & McCarthy, C. (2007, October). Manage your energy, not your time. *Harvard Business Review, 85,* 2–9. (Reprint No. R0710B)

Senge, P. M., Kleiner, A., & Roberts, C. (1994). *The fifth discipline fieldbook.* London: Nicholas Brealey.

Senge, P. M., Kleiner, A., Roberts, C., Ross, R. B., & Smith, B. J. (1994). *The fifth discipline fieldbook: Strategies and tools for building a learning organization.* New York: Bantam Doubleday Dell.

Shulman, L. (1992). *Interactional supervision.* Washington, DC: National Association of Social Work Press.

Shulman, L. (1998). *Skills of helping individuals families, groups and communities* (4th ed.). Pacific Grove, CA: Wadsworth.

Shulman, L., & Safyer, A. (2007). *Supervision in counseling: Interdisciplinary issues and research.* San Francisco: Haworth Press.

Smith, M. K. (2001). Chris Argyris: Theories of action, double-loop learning and organizational learning. In *The encyclopaedia of informal education.* Retrieved July 27, 2008, from http://www.infed.org/thinkers/argyris.htm

Thomas, D. A., & Ely, R. J. (2002). Making differences matter: A new paradigm for managing diversity. In R. R. Thomas, D. A. Thomas, R. J. Ely, & D. Meyerson (Eds.), *Harvard Business Review on Managing Diversity* (pp. 33–66). Boston, MA: Harvard Business School Press.

Tsui, M. S. (2005). *Social work supervision: Contexts and concepts.* Thousand Oaks, CA: Sage.

U.S. Department of Commerce, National Institute of Standards and Technology [NIST]—Technology Administration. (2008). *2008 Baldrige National Quality Program: Criteria for Performance Excellence.* Gaithersburg, MD: Institute of Standards and Technology Administration. Retrieved July 27, 2008, from http://www.quality.nist.gov/PDF_files/2008_Business_Nonprofit_Criteria.pdf

Van Slyke, D. M. (2003). The mythology of privatization in contracting for social services. *Public Administration Review, 63,* 296–315.

Van Slyke, D. M., & Hammonds, C. A. (2003). The privatization decision: Do public managers make a difference? *The American Review of Public Administration, 33,* 146–163.

Weinbach, R. (2008). *The social worker as manager* (5th ed.). Boston: Allyn & Bacon.

Web-Based Resources

American Management Association: http://www.amanet.org/ (Publications and training opportunities)

American Society for Public Administration: http://www.aspanet.org/scriptcontent/index.cfm (Publications and training opportunities)

Child Welfare League of America: http://www.cwla.org/ (Practice standards, publications, and training opportunities)

National Association of Social Workers: http://www.socialworkers.org/ (Practice standards, publications, and training opportunities)

Suggested Readings

Austin, M. J., & Hopkins, K. M. (Eds.). (2004). *Supervision as collaboration in the human services: Building a learning culture.* Thousand Oaks, CA: Sage.

Brody, R. (2000). *Effectively managing human service organizations* (2nd ed.). Thousand Oaks, CA: Sage.

Edwards, R. L., & Yankey, J. A. (Eds.) (2006). *Effectively managing nonprofit organizations.* Washington, DC: National Association of Social Workers.

Perlmutter, F. D., Bailey, D., & Netting, F. E. (2001). *Managerial supervision of the human services.* New York: Oxford University Press.

Shulman, L., & Safyer, A. (2007). *Supervision in counseling: Interdisciplinary issues and research.* San Francisco: Haworth Press.

Thomas, D. A., & Ely, R. J. (2002). Making differences matter: A new paradigm for managing diversity. In R. R. Thomas, D. A. Thomas, R. J. Ely, & D. Meyerson (Eds.), *Harvard Business Review on Managing Diversity* (pp. 33–66). Boston, MA: Harvard Business School Press.

Tsui, M. S. (2005). *Social work supervision: Contexts and concepts.* Thousand Oaks, CA: Sage.

2

Organizational and Workgroup Culture

David Cherin and David Chenot

Introduction

Supervisors and their work teams in social services exist and function in a cultural sea. They are surrounded by organizational culture, the values, beliefs, assumptions, and shared behavioral norms of the organizational stakeholders and administrators that have created the policies, procedures, and structures of the organization—organizational infrastructure. Supervisors and their teams are also submerged in their own cultures: the values, beliefs, and assumptions that frame how team members see and react to each other stakeholders, administrators, and clients. Supervisors must become fluent in all aspects of culture because culture frames the professional existence of the supervisor. Existing between two cultures, organizational culture and team culture, supervisors must become experts at understanding and operating in both types of culture simultaneously.

Culture, as stated earlier, is the context of work in the organization and creates the environment in which services are conceived and delivered. This handbook provides the practitioner with a critical set of skills bounded by applied knowledge. In order for these skills to be useful and the knowledge accessible, the supervisor must understand culture and become effective in mediating the culture surrounding her team while facilitating the culture within her team. In order for supervisors to effectively accomplish the critical tasks highlighted in this handbook, they must understand how to navigate the cultural sea. This challenge includes mastering the ability to mediate between team and organizational cultures. Supervisors must learn to facilitate group culture in relationship to a host of associated and often influential organizational constituents including other work functioning groups in the organization.

Supervisors help the team achieve success concerning the group's assigned tasks while articulating issues to the administration that impact workers and clients. This exchange function is crucial in that it serves as a key link in the communication chain. Facilitation suggests that supervisors work actively within their team to engage members in communication, learning, problem solving, team-level decision making, planning, innovation, and overall improvement.

This chapter offers suggestions concerning the utilization of this knowledge to enable and empower teams in order to sustain effectiveness in service delivery. This knowledge will be provided within the context of organizational learning as discussed in the first chapter. Supervisors may develop the understanding that their active roles in mediating and facilitating culture to promote learning relates not only in their teams but at the administrative level of the organization. This is a significant point since many supervisors view the primary scope of their influence as restricted to their teams. Supervisors, however, influence both their teams and the administration by relating information from the service delivery teams to administrators while enhancing workers' abilities to learn from each other and clients in order to provide more effective services. By expanding the perspective of their roles in the organization through the acknowledgment of the pervasive and dynamic nature of their influence, supervisors can become more effective in creating a strong and sustainable learning environment that simultaneously affects their functional groups and the administration of the organization.

Culture Defined

The sections that follow provide a set of tools for the supervisor to use in mediating and facilitating culture. In this chapter, we view organizational culture as situated at the core of the organization, and it includes the shared values, beliefs, assumptions, and behavioral norms that inform all organizational dynamics and structures (Glisson, 2000). But it is important to recognize a key challenge. A pioneer in organizational culture research and literature, Edgar Schein (1992) said, "I often find that we agree 'it' (culture) exists and that 'it' is important in its effects but that we have completely different ideas of what 'it' is" (p. 12).

Culture according to Schein (1992) is defined as follows:

> A pattern of shared basic assumptions that the group learned as it solved its problems of external adaptation and internal integration, that has worked well enough to be considered valid and, therefore, to be taught to new members as the correct way to perceive, think and feel in relation to those problems. (p. 12)

What Schein (1992) highlights is the fact that organizations and teams alike, through trial and error, learn which procedures, policies, structures, activities, forms of decision making, and service delivery techniques work and adopt those as the "way things are done" in the organizational routine and in a team's pattern. The strong emphasis on learning by Schein highlights the need for a supervisor to engage administrators and workers in learning as a method to understand what they do and to help them participate in change and innovation. This is one of the major reasons this book emphasizes the concept of organizational learning as a critical method in enabling supervisors to be effective. In simple terms, culture, which by Schein's definition guides how organizations set policy and how work is carried out, is developed and implemented through shared learning at the level of the team. In practical terms, culture guides the implementation of organizational systems through the establishment of work routines. In light of the pivotal role supervisors play in establishing or changing team routines, supervisors may well be the most important players in promoting learning within organizations. For instance, supervisors in organizations or teams that experience problems must, by virtue of how the culture was formed and how it has been maintained, identify what the organization and/or team has been doing, assess how effective or ineffective past activities have been, and assist the team in learning new routines in order to affect change or produce innovation.

However, as was suggested, supervisors are situated in unique organizational positions as they function between the administration and the team. As a result, the shared learning at the team level is related to the administration by supervisors who inform structural and policy changes on the organizational level through group-level changes. Shared learning at the team level becomes shared organizational learning largely through the efforts of supervisors.

Therefore, at the organizational level, culture produces internal policies, procedures, decision-making processes, reward systems, renewal systems, and funding that impact individuals and teams. The supervisor needs to understand how these organizational systems are affecting workers and to engage in helping administrators to understand and change those systems that might be barriers to successful service delivery and to help workers articulate their concerns about organizational policies and procedures. In this manner, the effects of policies and procedures that are directly experienced by workers may be expressed clearly to those on the administrative level. On the team level, the supervisor engages with the team in helping workers understand and change routines that create difficulties in successful functioning and in adopting decision-making processes and work routines that are innovative and facilitate team successes. In essence, group/organizational learning is the key tool the supervisor may use in mediating and facilitating culture.

The conclusion of this discussion provides the supervisor with a simple, yet effective, tool that promotes an understanding of culture borrowed from Chris Argyris and Donald Schön (1974). This tool is designed to help the supervisor analyze culture and to provide a framework to assist in her articulation of how culture is impacting work and how it needs to be changed.

Espoused Theories and Theories in Action

Cultures and the routines that are developed as part of a given culture provide organizations and groups ways of talking about themselves and ways of articulating values and beliefs. For instance, we might say that a particular social services agency, Foster Care Services of Euphoria, is committed to quality improvement and invites input from families about services so that client experiences can be used by the staff and administration to evaluate the agency and its services. In essence, this statement about the agency can be viewed as their mission and as their theory about how the organization works. Argyris and Schön (1996) and Argyris (1993) would call this an "espoused theory," which means a stated operational position, process, or procedure. In this example, one could go further and suggest that this statement comes from the fact that the organization's culture is characterized by its commitment to clients in promoting quality services. If it were discovered that in fact no mechanisms were in place in the organization to gather client input (i.e., no customer surveys or suggestion boxes), there would be a *gap* between what the organization says about itself and what it truly does. The latter circumstance would be, according to Argyris and Schön (1996), the organization's theory in action. Culture in an organization is most visible when comparing espoused theories with the actual collective action or overall performance of the organization. For the supervisor, learning to measure the gap, the degree of discontinuity, between stated theory and theory in action is an important tool. In other words, the existence of a disconnect between how we say we do things and how things are done can be gauged by the size or strength of the gap. Supervisors may use this tool to help both the administration and their teams learn about issues in the organization that require attention. After the gap is clearly identified and assessed, supervisors can offer guidance toward corrective action, problem solving, or the creation of innovative new ideas. In order to be successful in these pursuits, the supervisor as mediator and/or facilitator must bring the existing gap to the surface of the organizational consciousness.

In the example mentioned above, from the Foster Care Services of Euphoria social services agency, the team is frustrated because they continually receive complaints from clients about the lack of responsiveness from the agency to requests to change agency hours in order to accommodate working parents. Workers need a means to bring this issue to the attention of the administration and to pursue change. If the supervisor has assessed the situation and realized that the organization espouses a commitment to quality and invites input from clients about services, but has limited mechanisms in place to produce quality through responsiveness to clients, they can develop a simple gap narrative about the situation and begin a dialogue with administrators concerning the problem. They can also begin to facilitate a session with the team on how they would address this situation through a problem-solving process. In this situation, a concrete resolution of difficulties with agency responsiveness has the potential to lead to the implementation of an ongoing input or feedback process for clients in which they feel that their input is valued. It is likely that such a result would lead to increased levels of client satisfaction with organizational performance.

Teams are also prone to create "culture gaps" between what they say and what is actually practiced. In the above example, regarding instituting a problem-solving process to include client input in order to improve agency services, a team may share the belief that they are inclusive in engaging everyone in the team in problem solving, otherwise known as shared engagement. Although this may be the existing view, the actual problem-solving process may become limited, as it does in many groups. Often, senior group members or those who are skilled in argumentative techniques unduly influence the problem-solving process, excluding new workers or those who may choose their words carefully and are comparatively circumspect about their interjections to the group. In this situation, the theory in action suggests that the problem-solving process is less than inclusive and is based on other, less socially responsive criteria. The supervisor in this situation can create a gap narrative for the group and may want to use specific examples to highlight the espoused theory of inclusiveness and the reality of exclusiveness that seems to exist in the problem-solving process. Nothing is more powerful than bringing a group together and facilitating a process for addressing situational realities. This type of facilitation will be discussed in the following sections of this chapter.

Gauging the Gap: A Tool for Cultural Narratives

We conclude this section by offering the supervisor the use of an old friend as a method for creating gap narratives, the process recording. Those who have taken courses as social workers at either the bachelor's or the master's level have used this device to discern how they performed during engagement with clients. A paper is divided in half with the actual events of a situation recorded on the one side and the recorder's thoughts and emotions recorded in columns on the other side. This device offers a helpful tool for reviewing actions and accompanying thoughts and feelings. One might view these elements as some of the essentials of the personal culture that frames a situation. In the case of gap analyses in organizations, a supervisor can use this simple method to record on the one side of the paper the stated or espoused beliefs of the organization or the team. On the other side of the paper, the supervisor then records actual events. In the group problem-solving example, the information recorded might include the topics discussed, solutions identified, and how congruent they are with the organizational culture. One might also record who talked during the session, how many people remained silent and who remained silent, how often questions were asked to engage the entire group, and how many inclusive statements were made.

Supervisors may also use a similar tool in a group exercise format to elicit information about shared perceptions or variations in perceptions concerning the gap between espoused culture and actual culture by members of the team. The gap may be measured by each participant with the inclusion of a narrow column to the right of the second column. In this column, supervisors can ask group members to rate the gap on a scale of 1 to 10 with 1 representing the least separation and 10 representing the greatest divide between stated culture and lived culture. Variations of 2 to 3 points on this subjective scale would be considered small, 4 to 6 moderate, and 7 to 10 strong. A simple average of the group scores provides an overall indicator of the team's perception of the gap. If changes are implemented to address the gap once it is identified, this process can be repeated post-change efforts and the averages before and after the implementation of changes compared to indicate progress toward closing the gap.

For those supervisors who wish to invite ideas from group members about closing the gap, a column or separate piece of paper may be devoted to proposed solutions. A brainstorming process may be used to allow the airing of all possible ideas prior to narrowing the focus to realistic, practical solutions. It is important, however, when transitioning from brainstorming to a solution focus, for supervisors to clarify that feedback concerning solutions must take the form of practical steps that may realistically be implemented. (The S.M.A.R.T. model can be used to facilitate this goal by specifying measurable, agreed upon, realistic, and timed objectives. See #4 on page 38 in the *Facilitation* section.)[1] When this process culminates in proposed solutions that are actually chosen for implementation, timelines should be set for reevaluation of the gap subsequent to solution application. In this case, the tool recommended above may be divided into the columns already suggested with the addition of a column devoted to timeframes for the completion of proposed solutions and a narrow column used for a post-solution rating of the gap. The gap gauging tool may then be used to evaluate implementation of proposed solutions and progress toward closing the gap (see Table 2.1). A process such as the one detailed above may be useful in teams or organizations that wish to increase a sense of participatory decision making.

As will be related at the end of this chapter, the authors recommend that supervisors primarily maintain a task- or goal-oriented approach with the team when addressing identified gaps. However, in some situations, supervisors may want to adopt an approach that is more process oriented. Since the tool described in Table 2.1 offers a great deal of flexibility, it can also provide a way

Table 2.1 Gauging the Gap

Espoused beliefs	Actual practice	Pre-change ratings	Proposed solutions	Post-change ratings

to process thoughts and feelings about gaps in espoused and realized culture. Assuming primarily shared views of the gap exist among group members, the process recording tool provided above may be used to elicit thoughts and feelings about the gap. The paper can simply be folded or divided into four major columns (with a narrow column devoted to the gap rating). The first two columns are devoted to highlighting the gap with the exercise mentioned above, and the third major column can be used to record thoughts about the gap. The fourth major column can be used to list feelings about the gap.

The types of narratives produced by the processes mentioned above result in data that allow for an initial assessment of the gap, measurement of the gap over time, and (if the supervisor chooses to process group perceptions) team thoughts and feelings about the gap. This information may be used by the supervisor to begin to facilitate issues or problems in groups or to mediate issues between a team and the organizational administration. Mediation and facilitation are "learning techniques" that promote awareness and change with regard to the culture. Discussions of mediation and facilitation are provided in the following sections.

Mediation and Facilitation as Aspects of Organization Culture

Differentiation between mediation and facilitation may be clarified through a discussion of organizational culture and team culture as they relate to the supervisor's position in the organization. The supervisor may provide input to agency executives and, as such, plays an advisory role in impacting the overall organizational culture. A supervisor in playing this role is said to be a mediator. A supervisor has a more direct effect on his or her team than anyone else in the organization and, therefore, can be a coach or mentor to the team in problem solving and "group learning." In other words, the supervisor can directly impact the team culture and act as a "direct" agent of change and improvement within the team. A supervisor in playing this role is said to be a facilitator. See Figures 2.1 and 2.2 for depictions of the supervisor's role in mediation and facilitation processes. These illustrations are intended to highlight for supervisors the flow of their roles in the organization when it comes to culture.

MEDIATION

In actual organizational practice, the supervisor is charged with mediating the impact of culture on his or her team. Mediation, then, is understanding and assisting the team to make sense of organizational policy, procedures, and decisions. However, the supervisor is also responsible for communicating the needs of the team and information from the team to the administration. In each of these roles, various skills are required. At the organizational level, the supervisor has to be skillful in bringing issues before the administration and providing information necessary for the administrative group to use that knowledge to take action. Through this function, the supervisor acts as a mediator, between the administrative group and the team. This type of mediation

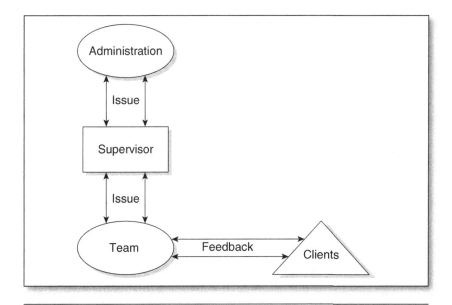

Figure 2.1   Mediation process flow

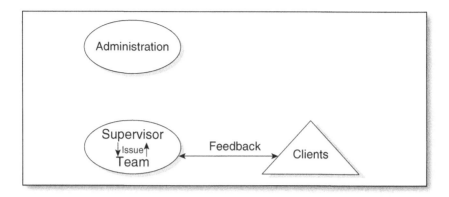

Figure 2.2   Facilitation process flow

role can be very difficult and requires that the supervisor learn to present information in a manner that can be understood through both the espoused and the
actual cultures represented within the administration.

In order to aid mediation efforts, we recommend the application of a technique developed by Donald Schön and Martin Rein (1994) called *frame reflection*. Frame reflection adopts the perspective that policy stances, procedural
regulations, or actions taken are bounded by the values, beliefs, and assumptions of individuals (mental models, etc.). Schön and Rein state:

> We see policy positions as resting on underlying structures of belief, percep-
> tion and appreciation, which we call "frames." We see . . . controversies as
> disputes in which the contending parties hold conflicting frames. (p. 23)

Recall the client input example from the Foster Care Services of Euphoria social
services agency. The supervisor may wish to engage their senior managers in discussion about the need for outreach to clients to elicit their opinions about services. It
may in fact be important to emphasize that clients provide continuous feedback to
members of the team and have expressed their unhappiness with the hours services
are currently provided. Although the supervisor may well be tempted to use a direct
approach, believing that the need for client input in the face of a stated organizational
value ("we welcome client input") is obvious, it is best to understand the frame that
is currently active and has kept this value from being operationalized in the past.
Engaging the senior manager may mean mediating the circumstance as opposed to
confronting the circumstance. For instance, inquiring why there are no surveys or
suggestion boxes to solicit client input may initiate a discussion about effective ways
to gather client input. A discussion prompted by such questions can easily transition
to the supervisor communicating information gained from clients by the team.

This type of positive or appreciative inquiry (Shani and Lau, 2000) is an
attempt to begin to understand the value frame held by the administration and

to communicate the dissimilar value frame exhibited by the team to the administration. It would be useful for the supervisor to frame the issue from the team's perspective. For instance, it may be that service providers are concerned about retaining clients, and about the organization being perceived as a quality organization. The members of the team take pride in the public's perception of their organization. This type of frame reflection engages the parties in discussion and is designed to avoid putting anyone, including administrators, on the defensive, while attempting to bring the discussion of issues to the level of the values (organizational culture) that hold them in place. Raising issues to this level through frame reflection provides optimal opportunities for successful change attempts. In order to use frame reflection effectively, we suggest a few simple notions:

1. Reflect on an issue before bringing the issue to the level of dialogue. Try to understand the values, beliefs, and assumptions that have created the problem. With this understanding, construct a brief narrative that outlines your understanding of the issue.

2. Reflect on the values, beliefs, and assumptions of the team regarding the issue. Attempt, as much as possible, to understand why team members see the issue as a problem that must be addressed. Engage in a discussion with members of the team about their assumptions to clarify their perspectives. This is critical in representing their point of view to the administration.

3. Create a frame around the issue that takes into consideration group members' values, beliefs, and assumptions concerning the issue at hand. In other words, construct a statement about the issue that is a synthesis of the individual frames represented in the team as a shared team frame.

4. Employ open-ended questions that are designed to open dialogue and do not threaten group members or encourage defensiveness.

5. Remain open to possible solutions that you have not considered. In other words, understand your own value frame and be willing to have your assumptions, values, and beliefs challenged.

6. Begin a dialogue with the administration using positive or appreciative inquiry. Use tentative openings to questions or statements, such as "I was wondering if . . ."

Supervisors will need to practice engaging in frame reflection. The most helpful perspective in this regard is to maintain a focus on the values, beliefs, assumptions, and behavioral norms that drive the actions of individuals, groups, and organizations. Gauging the gap between espoused theories and theories in action can be a very useful tool to enhance frame reflection. While attending to actions or routines within the organization, supervisors should develop theories that explain the behavioral norms that are shared in the organization. Having gained an understanding of the value frame surrounding a circumstance, the next step is to learn to inquire in a way that will get the discussion "ball rolling."

Supervisors must also learn to frame questions as a positive inquiry, which means asking questions designed to promote understanding, not designed to espouse a particular point of view. This skill is among the most difficult ones to master, but it is essential in filling the role of a true mediator. The simple practice of initiating questions in the positive inquiry "tense" takes practice. Essentially, questions must be framed in a manner that promotes learning. In the example offered above, concerning client input in the Foster Care Services of Euphoria social services agency, one might begin the discussion by asking, "When we say we solicit client input, we don't! Why?" This approach may get to the point but most likely would prevent or stall further dialogue. Using positive inquiry, the question might be framed as follows: "I am hearing from clients that they would like to have a way of expressing their views of our program in a way that would be helpful, is that possible?" This question is framed as genuine inquiry and avoids creating a defensive reaction on the part of the administrator by not emphasizing the gap between stated values and actual practice initially. Another sample of an inquiry designed to initiate dialogue with an administrator that includes a tentative opening statement might be as follows: "I was wondering if we have ever considered using some sort of client survey to gather input about their views of our services?"

This type of inquiry method may also be helpful for the supervisor in dialogue with her own team. Effective mentors and coaches learn to approach problems, issues, or situations in the team through frame reflection with an attitude of genuine inquiry. In a learning organization, there is no stronger method of modeling learning behavior than the approach to interactions with the team suggested above. This approach might be summarized as a "learning frame perspective." This approach will be discussed in the next section of this chapter.

FACILITATION

Although team culture is shaped in large part by organizational culture, teams develop their own set of dominant values, beliefs, and assumptions concerning all facets of the team, including supervisors, coworkers, and the clientele. This culture shapes how teams interact with other teams and constituents within the organization and external to the organization as well. The greatest impact of team culture, though, is on service provision to clients by team, relationships between group members, and relationships between group members and supervisors. Unlike the mediation role supervisors fulfill concerning organizational culture, supervisors are direct facilitators of team culture, a capacity in which they play a very active role. Supervisors essentially guide their team by fulfilling the positions of role model, coach, and mentor. Some aspects of facilitation require that the supervisor become action oriented and engaged. This type of engagement was defined by Cherin (2000) as leading the team in communications processes, learning, and work. In fact, "organizational engagement" may be understood as the place where team culture and service delivery (processes and outcomes) interact. In the case of organizational culture, the team's values, beliefs, assumptions, and shared behavioral norms impact and shape the value placed on outcomes, perceptions of clients, and the team approach to all work-related tasks. Supervisor facilitation takes place at the point of engagement where culture and task fulfillment interact (Cherin, 2000). This point of engagement is depicted in Figure 2.2.

It is important for supervisors to understand, however, that for the facilitating team, the focus needs to be on the tasks of the teams, and not on culture. All too often when problems originate in working groups, the supervisor gathers the team and they process the issue at hand by attempting to address the values, beliefs, and assumptions of individuals in the team. This approach has the potential to put individual workers on the defensive and stall the productive resolution of problems or issues. It may be instructive to return to our example about offering clients the opportunity to provide team members feedback about the quality of services they receive from an agency. Is the idea here to process the team's feelings about being confronted by clients when the administration has created a problem that the team must frequently deal with? Processing would be a legitimate activity, but would it conclude with the creation of a solution (e.g., an input system for clients within the agency)? The facilitative supervisor may well want to help the team process feelings about being confronted by clients, but this can be handled most effectively while engaging the group in a discussion concerning communication of the issue to the administration. The conversation guided by supervisorial facilitation centers on attempts to create solutions to the issue. Within a task-oriented dialogue, the value frames of individuals and the group will emerge and can be discussed in the context of solving a work-based problem.

Rather than attempting to focus on culture, then, the goal of the successful supervisor is to involve the group in problem solving about a relevant issue and, within that context, allow the value-laden aspects of the team, the cultural frame, to emerge. In this manner, processing may occur as a secondary function, whereas the goal of proposing solutions is considered to be primary. This facilitation approach may be viewed as the depth and breadth of effective supervisory action. Facilitation can be used to work with groups to improve communication, help groups reveal and discuss work flow issues, and focus the group on improving outcomes.

Concerning the client input/quality-of-service example, the discussion needs to be facilitated with a focus on proposing an effective system that will allow client input into the quality of services provided by the team. A facilitation focus may, for instance, produce suggestions of creating a survey that workers can give clients at the end of a visit or subsequent to a series of interactions. However, the survey in this situation may emphasize the services provided by the team rather than by the organization. This task-oriented solution proposed by the group allows the supervisor to assist the group in framing an issue for the administration regarding the group's position in the organization and articulating that the group represents the direct interface between the agency and clients. The supervisor can then bridge facilitation with mediation by suggesting to the team that the survey approach would provide excellent data that would inform dialogue with administrators about client input and the quality of services. This would also provide a natural impetus to suggest further that a simple survey approach could be routinely used to provide direct feedback from the team on issues concerning service provision to the administration. In this instance, the team has proposed a task-oriented solution and targeted key organizational culture issues (client input and the quality-of-service provision). However, although the team focused on a practical solution, they were also included in communications to the administration concerning client feedback. The net effect of the bridged facilitation and mediation processes for the team in this example is as follows: the proposed solution, inclusion of team members in significant communications with the administration about issues that are important to them and their clients, and the generation of perceptions that the team's views are received and respected through the process.

We offer the following ideas to aid supervisors with facilitation:

1. When issues develop in teams, examine the actual work processes or tasks that are being undertaken. Focus on the issue at hand and identify its connection to the values, beliefs, and assumptions of the team.

2. As mentioned in Chapter 1, this is group learning in the first and second loop simultaneously. The second loop of learning in a group integrates the values, beliefs, and assumptions that drive how the group works and solves problems. In order to get the group to address second-loop issues, those that encourage effective working and learning, engage the group in the first loop of learning, with a focus on the problem immediately at hand.

3. Avoid leading discussions; facilitate them instead. Supervisors can initiate the inquiry process but allow the members of the team to take over the discussion with minimal guidance. Model appreciative inquiry questioning, and add your voice on occasion to reframe questions or issues or to invite a worker who is not speaking to contribute to the discussion.

4. When encouraging the group to propose solutions, always guide the group through S.M.A.R.T. statements of resolution: Proposed solutions that are Specific, Measurable, Agreed upon, Realistic, and Timed are the most helpful. In other words, make the solution development task oriented, while attending to the process aspects of the task within the team in an indirect manner.

5. Always focus on and facilitate the task at hand. The task is a behavioral manifestation of culture, and through a focus on the task, cultural issues will emerge for discussion. There is no need to focus directly on culture in an attempt to change values, beliefs, assumptions, or shared behavioral norms. They are extremely difficult to alter directly.

Summary

Our focus in this chapter has been to introduce the concept of culture and explore the manner in which it forms the frame or background for all organizational dynamics. The supervisor must understand how culture impacts her team and how the team, to revisit our nautical metaphor, is awash in culture. This chapter provides supervisors with a sense of culture and offers insights and tools that can help the supervisor operate effectively in the cultures of their organizations.

The remaining chapters of this book explore in detail the tools and techniques that the supervisor can use to facilitate and support a learning culture. The critical methods provided include leading team, performance appraisal, working with staff experiencing job performance difficulties, and meeting facilitation. Master these skills with the help of the tool set offered in these pages, and you will become successful supervisor.

Endnotes

1. S.M.A.R.T. solutions have the characteristics of effective objectives. When applied, the acronym provides guidance that can sculpt proposed solutions into effective recommendations for change that target organizational needs with Specific language. Proposals must include a format that lends itself to Measurable change with plans for initial baseline assessments and subsequent evaluation spelled out. Proposed change needs to be Agreed upon by the major constituents in order to go forward with implementation. Proposals need to be Realistic concerning many factors (including projected resource commitments, i.e., financial, staff time and energy, etc.) in order for there to be a fair chance that they will be accepted, implemented, and potentially effective. Finally, proposals should be Timed, with dates set as goals for the fulfillment of intermediate objectives and final completion of proposed solutions.

References

Argyris, C. (1993). *Knowledge for action: A guide to overcoming barriers to organizational change.* San Francisco: Jossey-Bass.

Argyris, C., & Schön, D. A. (1974). *Theory in practice: Increasing professional effectiveness.* San Francisco: Jossey-Bass.

Argyris, C., & Schön, D. A. (1996). *Organizational learning II: Theory, method, and practice* (Rev. ed.). Reading, MA: Addison-Wesley.

Cherin, D. A. (2000). Organizational engagement and managing moments of maximum leverage: New roles for social workers in organizations. In M. Barak, E. Michàl, & D. Bargal (Eds.), *Social services in the workplace: Repositioning occupational social work in the new millennium* (pp. 29–46). New York: Hayworth Press.

Glisson, C. (2000). Organizational climate and culture. In R. J. Patti (Ed.), *The handbook of social welfare management* (pp. 195–218). Thousand Oaks, CA: Sage.

Schein, E. H. (1992). *Organizational culture and leadership* (2nd ed.). San Francisco: Jossey-Bass.

Schön, D. A., & Rein, M. (1994). *Frame reflection: Toward the resolution of intractable policy controversies.* New York: Basic Books.

Shani, A. B., & Lau, J. B. (2000). *Behavior in organizations: An experiential approach* (7th ed.). Boston: Irwin, McGraw-Hill.

Web-Based Resources

Outline of Schein's classic material: http://www.tnellen.com/ted/tc/schein.html

Organizational culture articles and other resources: http://www.businessperform
.com/html/organizational_culture_articles.html

Practical Web site for assessing organizational culture and climate: http://leo.oise
.utoronto.ca/~vsvede/culture.htm

Organization dedicated to offering courses and support on culture: http://www
.justculture.org/

Suggested Readings

Schein, E. H. (2004). *Organizational culture and leadership* (3rd ed.). San Francisco: Jossey-Bass.

Shani, A. B., & Lau, J. B. (2000). *Behavior in organizations: An experiential approach* (7th ed.). Boston: Irwin, McGraw-Hill.

3

Value-Based Principles and Laws Guiding Personnel Management

Introduction

KEY VALUES AND ETHICS

What standards should organizational leaders articulate and reinforce with regard to ethical behavior for direct line staff? We believe that first-line supervisors are in the best position to do this selection and reinforcement. Ethics have been articulated by many professional groups that work in a variety of social services areas, including public administration, social work, and psychology, all of which help to establish a framework within which to guide practice (Haynes, Corey, & Moulton, 2003; Khurana & Nohria, 2008; Lencioni, 2002; Menzel, 2007; National Association of Social Workers, 2006; Strom-Gottfried, 2008). Ethics is a complex and high-stakes area of professional practice. Too often when practitioners think of ethics, they think of an abstract or lofty philosophical discussion far removed from the challenges of their daily work lives. But ethical behavior is about making decisions and fulfilling other professional duties in proper ways that adhere to a professional code of conduct that requires *moral courage:*

> Moral courage is the ability to put ethics into action. It means standing up and standing out in defense of principle, even when others are standing aside. Ethical action is more than whistle blowing. It involves daily acts of integrity, carried out with dignity, in which individuals stand up for what is right and encourage others to do the same. (Strom-Gottfried, n.d.).

Professional codes of conduct provide direction where there often is a lack of clarity in the differential demands of consumers and agency policies (Reamer, 2005, 2006). Providing clarity involves balancing the needs of the supervisee with practicality, efficiency, and maintenance of organizational systems. This balance requires a fit between the job responsibilities and the knowledge and skills of the staff person, ensuring for each person that there are the resources and tools necessary to accomplish the job, being alert to help staff balance their aspirations and opportunities, and clarifying expectations in terms of performance criteria *and* professional ethics.

In the broader field of human services supervision, this mandate also applies to a broad set of professional groups in the human services arena (e.g., social work, public administration, psychology, and health care). Cohen (1987) and Haynes et al. (2003) have applied some of those principles as they have discussed the need for supervisors to provide a model of the helping relationship—but not a model that duplicates the therapeutic relationship between service provider and consumer. Instead a supervisor establishes a structure for the worker–supervisor relationship that is bounded by the performance contract. A good contract clarifies what is expected of both parties and lessens the potential of abuse of power by the supervisor. Currently, some human services agencies spell out the terms of these contracts not only in position descriptions (see Chapter 4), but also in the performance development plans that outline what the employee is expected to accomplish by when, and with what supports provided by the supervisor and by the agency, as a whole (see Chapter 7 and Hugman, 2003). Supervisors also model ethical practice in how they provide advice and support to staff in times of stress or crisis, as well as in how they make decisions and support teamwork (see Chapter 6).

What other values should undergird our work as supervisors?

- Cooperation, collaboration, and competition can be good and/or bad depending on the context.
- Incentives and rewards do not result in as much competition when there are different (or fewer) incentives and rewards, but it is a real challenge to coach people to win and achieve without creating animosity.
- Recognizing the different abilities and sources of power that each person brings to the table creates a more fully informed set of relationships, allowing teamwork to develop.
- It is not always clear how to focus on enhancing the values of your employees through an understanding of the key laws that guide employee recruitment, selection, and ongoing supervision.

For the social services supervisor, values are the context in which we operate and laws can be seen as operationalizations of those values in ways that make concrete and explicit those values. In a way, laws are the grammar of behavior, articulating what is meant by values, beliefs, and assumptions.

Key Laws Guiding the Personnel Management Aspects of Supervision

In the United States, supervision is a management process that is guided by numerous laws, regulations, and administrative policy, some of which are specific to a particular state or service field. Many of those laws and policies are translated into personnel or human resource policies, as summarized in Table 3.1.

Table 3.1   Typical Table of Contents for a Social Services Agency: Personnel Manual

Introduction
    Organization philosophy and mission
    Major organizational goals and objectives
    Organizational programs or types of service
 	
1. **Employment**
    Hiring authority
    Nondiscrimination and Affirmative Action policies and safeguards (includes safeguards as mandated by Equal Employment Opportunity Commission [EEOC], Affirmative Action [AA], and Americans with Disabilities Act [ADA])
    Types of employment (full time, part time, temporary, volunteer)
    Probationary period procedures
    Maintenance and access to personnel records
 	
2. **Working hours and conditions**
    Work schedule and office hours
    Flexible time
	Overtime or compensatory time
	Types of absence
	3. **Salaries and wages**
	    Wages and salary structure and rationale
	    Paydays
	    Deductions
	    Raises (merit and cost of living) guidelines and rationale
	    Compensation for work-related expenses
	    Employee access to current salary schedule
	4. **Employee benefits**
	    Leaves and absences
	    Vacations
	    Holidays
	    Sick days
	    Personal days
	    Family and maternity leave
	    Paternity leave
	    Leave of absence
	    Other excused absences
	    Insurance
	    Social Security

(Continued)

Table 3.1 (Continued)

Medical insurance	Telephone
Life insurance	Travel
Disability insurance	Personal property
Unemployment insurance	**9. General office practices and procedures**
Worker's compensation	
Pension or retirement plans	Client confidentiality and Health Insurance Portability and Accountability Act (HIPAA)
5. Employee rights and responsibilities	
Employee responsibilities	Office coverage by staff
Employee rights	Smoking
Grievance procedures	Use and care of equipment
6. Performance and salary review	E-mail and Internet usage
Procedures	Dress code
Timing	**10. Termination**
Use of probation periods or suspension	Grounds of dismissal
	Resignation
Promotion policies and procedures	Retirement
	Release
7. Staff development	Reduction in force
Orientation of new employees	Appendixes
Planning process for in-service training and related activities	Organizational chart
	Salary ranges by position
Educational programs and conferences	Equal Opportunity guidelines on sexual harassment
8. General policies and procedures	Conflict of interest policies
Outside employment	Personnel evaluation procedures and forms
Office opening and closing	

Sources: Cox, F. M. (1984); Helfgott, K. P. (1991); NASW (1991); Pecora, P. J. & Wagner, M. in R. Patti (2000); and Wolfe, T. (1984).

Several federal laws provide a legal framework for supervisory actions. Among the most significant are those governing Affirmative Action (AA), Equal Employment Opportunity Act of 1972 (enforced by the Equal Employment Opportunity Commission [EEOC]), and Americans with

Disabilities Act (ADA), as well as those specific civil rights laws that are intended to guard against sexual harassment. Regulations from The Occupational Safety and Health Administration (OSHA) also may apply to many work settings.

We will focus first on the specific laws that focus on equal employment options for minorities, women, and those with disabilities. Next to be examined are the laws that specifically address sexual harassment. AA, Equal Employment Opportunity, and ADA guidelines have become fundamental to management practice, so much so that employers and employees should be very familiar with the concepts and regulations governing the implementation of these laws. *But before reading any further, and as part of our commitment to share useful tools, give yourself a pre-test to assess your knowledge of this area by completing the quiz in Figure 3.1.* The answers to the quiz are in Appendix B. After taking this quiz, review the federal statutes and legal interpretations that influence current personnel management practice outlined subsequently in this chapter.

According to current law and/or EEOC policy:

1. It is permissible for you to keep on file information concerning your employee's race, color, religion, sex, or national origin.

   T ___ F ___ Don't know ___

2. If your department is charged with one form of discrimination and the EEOC's investigation finds the charge to be untrue, the EEOC may find you guilty of another form of discrimination even if you were not charged with it.

   T ___ F ___ Don't know ___

3. You may use the fact that a job applicant has a long arrest record as a reason for not hiring him/her.

   T ___ F ___ Don't know ___

4. You may require a pregnant woman to take a leave of absence at a specified time before her delivery date.

   T ___ F ___ Don't know ___

5. An employer must give a woman who has been off for maternity leave her *same* job and salary, and guarantee no loss of seniority when she is ready to return to work.

   T ___ F ___ Don't know ___

Figure 3.1 *(Continued)*

(Continued)

---

6. If a job applicant's religious faith requires that he/she be off on a normal work day, you may refuse to hire him/her.

   T ___ F ___ Don't know ___

7. Even if your department has few or no racial minorities, it is permissible for you to refuse to hire a racial minority because he or she failed an employment test.

   T ___ F ___ Don't know ___

8. This decision is permissible: John is 60. Bill is 38. You choose Bill because he is younger and, therefore, will be able to devote more years to the department before retirement.

   T ___ F ___ Don't know ___

9. You may terminate or refuse to hire a person because of a conviction record.

   T ___ F ___ Don't know ___

10. You may discharge a male for refusing to cut his long hair.

    T ___ F ___ Don't know ___

11. An applicant may be refused employment because of a poor credit rating.

    T ___ F ___ Don't know ___

12. It is permissible to refuse employment to someone without a car.

    T ___ F ___ Don't know ___

13. General questions about high school or college degrees may be asked during an interview even though that educational degree is not necessary to perform the job.

    T ___ F ___ Don't know ___

14. You may ask an applicant's age or date of birth.

    T ___ F ___ Don't know ___

15. An employer may ask an applicant if he or she is a citizen, or ask for place of birth so as not to violate immigration laws.

    T ___ F ___ Don't know ___

16. It is permissible to ask applicants if they have any mental or physical handicaps that relate to their fitness to perform a particular job.

    T ___ F ___ Don't know ___

17. Applicants may be asked whether they are married.

    T ___ F ___ Don't know ___

Figure 3.1 Skills application exercise for Equal Employment Opportunity

Source: Abstracted from materials developed by Gloria J. Rendon, Training Section, Personnel Administration, University of Utah, Salt Lake City.

AFFIRMATIVE ACTION

Legislation for AA and Equal Employment Opportunity continues to affect the recruitment, screening, and selection of employees in both for-profit and nonprofit organizations.[1] The distinctive components of EEOC laws are based on Title VII of the 1964 Civil Rights Act and other laws, including the Age Discrimination in Employment Act of 1967; Sections 503 and 504 of the Rehabilitation Act of 1973, as amended; the Vietnam Era Veterans' Readjustment Assistance Act of 1974 (amended in 2000; P.L. 106–419); and the Equal Pay Act of 1963.[2] With few exceptions, Title VII (Equal Employment Opportunity) prohibits employers, labor organizations, and employment agencies from making employee or applicant personnel decisions based on race, color, religion, sex, or national origin. Although it originally applied only to private employers, the concern of Equal Employment Opportunity was extended to local and state governments by 1972 amendments to the 1964 Civil Rights Act.[3]

Equal opportunity laws reflect a management approach to reducing discrimination against employees by ensuring that equal opportunity is implemented in all employment actions. These laws require nondiscrimination, which involves the elimination of all existing discriminatory conditions, whether purposeful or inadvertent. Because of their tax-exempt status and because they may depend on government contracts, social services organizations must carefully and systematically examine all their employment policies. They cannot operate to the detriment of any individuals or groups on the grounds of race, color, religion, national origin, sex, age, or status as a person with a disability, disabled veteran, or veteran of the Vietnam era. These organizations must also prevent and eliminate biases related to gay, lesbian, bisexual, or transgender employees. Federal and state laws and regulations often specify that managers of those who are responsible for matters of employment, including supervisors, must ensure that practices are nondiscriminatory.

In contrast, AA requires that many organizations take steps to ensure proportional recruitment, selection, and promotion of qualified members of groups, such as members of ethnic and racial minority groups and women, who historically have been excluded. Most employers, unions, and employment agencies are required to plan and document, through written AA programs (AAPs), the steps they are taking to reduce the under-representation of women as well as ethnic and racial minority groups. Most public and private organizations that provide goods and services to the federal government and their subcontractors must comply with the AA provisions described in Executive Order No. 11246. Guidelines for working with AAPs are found in Title 41, Part 60–2 (known as "Revised Order No. 4") of the Office of Federal Contract Compliance (Office of Federal Compliance Programs, 2006).

Both Equal Employment Opportunity and AA seek to eliminate discrimination in employment both substantively and procedurally. The safeguards and improvements mandated by these guidelines vary regarding practices for recruiting, screening, selecting, and promoting employees. For example, Equal

Employment Opportunity organization guidelines suggest the type of questions that can be asked on an employment application or in an interview to avoid any perception of discrimination. These guidelines emphasize the use of screening or interviewing committees that include people of color and a mixture of men and women. These types of changes are procedural changes. In contrast, a mental health organization may develop an outreach process to recruit and hire more female supervisors. These types of changes in approach are substantive changes.

There are four major EEOC concepts to keep in mind:

1. *Equal employment.* Employment that is not affected by illegal discrimination.

2. *Blind to differences.* Differences among people should be ignored, and everyone should be treated equally.

3. *AA.* Employers are urged to hire groups of people based on their race, age, gender, or national origin to make up for historical discrimination.

4. *Protected class.* Individuals within a group identified for protection under equal employment laws and regulations (Mathis & Jackson, 2006, pp. 98–99).

Knowledge of Equal Employment Opportunity and AA guidelines is essential for designing employment application forms and interviewing protocols that avoid the use of illegal questions.[4] However, court cases such as *Hopwood v. Texas* (1996) and the legislation passed in some states, such as Proposition 209 in California and Proposition 200 in Washington, may alter what is permissible under Equal Employment Opportunity and AA guidelines (California State Office of the Secretary of State, 1996; Holland, 1999; Washington State Office of the Secretary of State, 1998). In fact, some of these state laws have limited the usage of AA efforts (Alger, 2003). Government updates and legal consultation are important resources for assessing the adequacy of procedures.

EQUAL EMPLOYMENT OPPORTUNITY, CIVIL RIGHTS ACT OF 1991, AND THE CLASSIFICATION OF JOBS

In addition to banning certain types of questions for candidates on applications or in interviews, Equal Employment Opportunity guidelines forbid any selection process that has an adverse impact on any social, ethnic, or gender group, unless the procedure is validated through the analysis of jobs or research on the selection of employees. Descriptions and notices of positions that delineate knowledge, skill, ability, education, or other prerequisites require a determination of whether the prerequisites are genuinely appropriate for the job. Some requirements, such as years of experience, certificates, diplomas, and educational degrees, may be considered unlawful on the basis of previous court decisions for a particular position. Specifically, proscriptions against discrimination in employment demand that any requirement, such as education or experience, that is used as a standard for decisions about employment must be directly relevant to the job in question.[5]

The use of standards that disqualify women, certain racial or ethnic groups, or other groups at a substantially higher rate than other applicants would be unlawful unless they could be shown to be significantly related to the successful performance of a job and otherwise necessary for the safe and efficient operation of the job for which they are used (e.g., height and strength criteria that are demonstrably related to an individual's capacity to perform the job tasks). Educational requirements are defined as a test by the federal government and must be validated in accordance with EEOC's testing guidelines. In addition, if an organization validates its selection criteria, Equal Employment Opportunity guidelines require it to demonstrate that no suitable alternative with a lesser adverse impact is available.

The Civil Rights Act of 1991 requires employers to show that an employment practice is *job related for the position* and is consistent with *business necessity*. The act clarifies that the plaintiffs bringing the discrimination charges must identify the particular employer practice being challenged and must show only that protected-class status played *some role*. For employers, this requirement means that an individual's race, color, religion, sex, or national origin *must play no role* in their employment practices.

The Civil Rights Act of 1991 also addressed other issues. Briefly, some of the key issues and the provisions of the act are as follows:

- *Race norming:* The act prohibited adjusting employee test scores or using alternative scoring mechanisms, depending on the race or gender of the test takers. The concern addressed by this provision is the use of different passing or cutoff scores for members of protected classes.
- *International employees:* The act extended coverage of the U.S. Equal Employment Opportunity laws to U.S. citizens working abroad, except where local laws and customs conflict.
- *Government employee rights:* Congress extended Equal Employment Opportunity law coverage to employees of the Senate, presidential appointees, and previously excluded state government employees (Mathis & Jackson, 2006, pp. 103–104).

When an adverse impact can be demonstrated with regard to a screening instrument or process (e.g. a test or structured interview), employers should use alternative measures that are equally valid but produce a less adverse impact. Other than background screening for assuring educational qualifications, medical screening, and a criminal background check (Beginner's Guide Staff, 2005), a modest amount of progress has been made in identifying and using screening procedures for skills and attitudes as alternatives to educational and experience qualifications (Thomson, Inc., 2001). Nonprofit organizations should carefully analyze their jobs and clearly define their tasks in terms of requisite knowledge, skills, and abilities.

Certainly, information establishing an individual's minimum qualifications for various positions is essential to certify that the person can be recruited or selected. Table 3.2 provides a concise summary, based on Equal Employment Opportunity and AA regulations, of what is acceptable and unacceptable to use in application forms and as interview questions. Note that the guidelines for people who have physical disabilities are being revised, and that questions must be carefully considered with the implementation of the ADA.

AMERICANS WITH DISABILITIES ACT[6]

The ADA, enacted July 26, 1990, provided broad civil rights protection to an estimated 43 million Americans with disabilities. The act contains four

Table 3.2   Guide to Lawful or Pre-Employment Inquiries

Subject	Acceptable inquiry	It may be discriminatory to inquire about:
1. Name	"Have you ever used another name?" /or/ "Is any additional information relative to change of name, use of an assumed name, or nickname necessary to enable a check on your work and education record? If yes, please explain."	Maiden name.
2. Residence	Place of residence.	"Do you own or rent your home?"
3. Age	Statement that hiring is subject to verification that applicant meets legal age requirements. "If hired, can you show proof of age?" "Are you over 18?" "If under 18, can you, after employment, submit a work permit?"	• How old are you? (age) • What year were you born? • Birth date. • Dates of attendance or completion of elementary or high school. Questions that tend to identify applicants over 40.
4. Birthplace/ citizenship	"Can you, after employment, submit verification of your legal right to work in the United States?" /or/ Statement that such proof may be required after employment.	• Birthplace of applicant, applicant's parents, spouse, or other relatives. • "Are you a U.S. citizen?" or • Citizenship of applicant, parents, spouse, or other relatives.

Subject	Acceptable inquiry	It may be discriminatory to inquire about:
5. Language or national origin	Language applicant speaks, reads, or writes.	• Questions as to nationality, lineage, ancestry, national origin, descent, parentage of applicant, applicant's parents, or spouse. • "What is your native or mother tongue?" • "Language commonly used by applicant?" • "What language is used at home?" • How applicant acquired ability to read, write, or speak a foreign language.
6. Height and weight		• Any inquiry into height or weight of applicant unless it is a qualification clearly required by the position.
7. Sex, marital status, or family composition	• Name and address of parent or guardian if applicant is a minor. • Statement of company policy regarding work assignment of employees who are related.	• "Are you married?" (marital status) • Questions that indicate the applicant's sex. • Number or ages of children or dependents. Provisions for child care. • Questions regarding pregnancy, child bearing, or birth control. • Name or address of relative, spouse, or children of adult applicant. • "With whom do you reside?" /or/ "Do you live with your parents?"
8. Race or color		• Questions as to the applicant's race or color. • Questions regarding applicant's complexion or color of skin, eyes, or hair. • "Where do your parents come from?"

(Continued)

Table 3.2 (Continued)

Subject	Acceptable inquiry	It may be discriminatory to inquire about:
9. Physical description, photograph	Statement that photograph may be required after employment.	• Questions about applicant's height and weight. • Require applicant to affix a photograph to application. • Request applicant, at his or her option, to submit to a photograph. • Require a photograph after interview, but before employment.
10. Physical limitations, condition, or handicap	• Statement by employer that offer may be made contingent on applicant's passing a job-related physical examination. • "Do you have any physical condition or handicap that may limit your ability to perform the job applied for? If yes, what can be done to accommodate your limitation?"	• "Do you have any physical disabilities or handicaps?" • Questions regarding applicant's general medical condition, state of health, or illness. • Questions regarding receipt of worker's compensation, such as, "Have you ever filed for workman's compensation?" • Any recent operations, treatments, or surgeries and dates.
11. Relatives	Names of any relatives already employed by employer.	• Name and/or address of any relative on application, including whom to contact in terms of emergency.
12. Education	• Training applicant has received, if related to the position. • Highest level of education (if a certain level of education is validated as job related.)	• Date of high-school graduation.
13. Religion or creed	Statement by employer of regular days, hours, or shifts to be worked.	Questions regarding applicant's religion. • Applicant's church, parish, mosque, or synagogue. • Religious holidays observed /or/ "Does your religion prevent you from working weekends or holidays?"

Subject	Acceptable inquiry	It may be discriminatory to inquire about:
14. Arrest, criminal record, or connections	"Have you ever been *convicted* of a felon or (within a specified time period) a misdemeanor that resulted in imprisonment?" (Such a question must be accompanied by a statement that a conviction will not necessarily disqualify the applicant for the job applied for.)	• Arrest record /or/ "Have you ever been arrested?" • Convictions that would *NOT* be job related.
15. Bonding	Statement that bonding is a condition of hiring.	Questions regarding refusal or cancellation of bonding.
16. Military service	• Branch of military served in and ranks attained. • Question regarding relevant skills acquired during applicant's U.S. military service, such as type of education or training.	• General questions regarding military service, such as dates of service, service record, and type of discharge. • Questions regarding service in a foreign military.
17. Financial or economic status		• Questions regarding applicant's current or past assets, debts, liabilities, or credit rating, including bankruptcy or garnishment.
18. Organizations, activities	"Please list any job-related organizations, clubs, professional societies, or other associations to which you belong—you may omit those that indicate your race, religious creed, color, national origin, ancestry, sex, or age."	"List all organizations, clubs, societies, and lodges to which you belong."

(Continued)

Table 3.2 (Continued)

Subject	Acceptable inquiry	It may be discriminatory to inquire about:
19. References	• "By whom were you referred for a position here?" • Name of persons willing to provide professional or character references for applicant.	• Questions of applicant's former employers or acquaintances that elicit information specifying the applicants race, color, religious creed, national origin, ancestry, physical handicap, medical condition, marital status, age, or sex. • Political affiliations and contacts.
20. Notification in case of emergency	Name and address of person to be notified in case of accident or emergency.	Name and address of relative to be notified in case of accident or emergency.

Sources. Adaped from California Department of Fair Employment and Housing, n.d. Retrieved March 17, 2008, from http://www.dfeh.ca.gov/publications/publications.aspx. From "How to hire the right person for the job," by J. Jensen, 1981, *Grantsmanship Center News, 9*(3), pp. 28–29. Copyright 1981 by The Grantsmanship Center. The Grantsmanship Center (TGC) publishes a magazine and has archived articles online that may be of use. See http://www.tgci.com/. From *Human resource management* (11th ed.), by R. L. Mathis & J. H. Jackson, 2006, Mason, OH: Thomson Southwestern.

major sections: employment (Title I), state and local government services (Title II), public accommodations provided by private entities (Title III), and telecommunications (Title IV). The ADA is neither preemptive nor exclusive; stricter requirements of state or federal law will continue to apply (see http://www.ada.gov; http://www.usdoj.gov/crt/ada/adahom1.htm). Becker (2008) provided a current context for why the ADA is important:

The U.S. Census Bureau's 2002 Survey of Income and Program Participation (SIPP) found that there are 51.2 million people with disabilities in the United States. To put that number into perspective, the 2002 SIPP indicates that the U.S. population's percentage of people with disabilities is 18.1%. That is larger than the percentage of Hispanics in the U.S. population (13.3%), the country's largest ethnic, racial, or cultural minority group. Almost 21 million American families have at least one member with a disability (Becker, 2008, p. E1).

The purpose of the act is to:

- Provide a clear and comprehensive national mandate for the elimination of discrimination against individuals with disabilities (including those coping with obesity)
- Provide clear, strong, consistent, enforceable standards addressing discrimination against individuals with disabilities
- Ensure that the federal government plays a central role in enforcing the standards established in this act on behalf of individuals with disabilities
- Invoke the sweep of congressional authority, including the power to enforce the 14th Amendment and to regulate commerce, in order to address the major areas of discrimination faced every day by people with disabilities

The ADA is not an AA law. It is an Equal Employment Opportunity law because it addresses discrimination in hiring, accommodation of a disabled person on the job, and access of people with disabilities to public and private facilities. Even if a person has a disability, she still must be qualified under the act. A qualified individual with a disability is one who, with or without reasonable accommodation, can perform the essential functions of the job that the person holds or desires (see Table 3.3). Becoming qualified under the provisions of the ADA is a two-step process that (a) identifies the essential functions of the job and (b) then determines whether the individual seeking the position can perform the functions with or without a reasonable accommodation.

Job requirements should always be expressed in terms of actual job duties and skill requirements and should never be expressed in terms of an applicant's or employee's limitations. An employer should not focus on whether a candidate or employee has a disability or is protected under the act. Rather, an employer should focus on the essential functions of the position and whether a candidate or employee, with reasonable accommodation, is able to perform the essential functions of the job. An applicant should *not* be asked about the existence, nature, or severity of a disability but may be asked whether he or she is able to perform each essential job function.

Table 3.3   Conditions Considered Disabilities by the ADA[a]

ADA definition
The term "disability" means, with respect to an individual: 1. A physical or mental impairment that substantially limits one or more of the major life activities of such individual   2. A record of such an impairment   3. Being regarded as having such impairment

(Continued)

Table 3.3 (Continued)

Some of the conditions considered disabilities by the ADA[b]:	
Deafness	Blindness
Wheel chair use	Epilepsy
Mental illness	Diabetes
Cancer	Heart disease
Learning disabilities	HIV/AIDS
Recovering alcoholism	Recovering drug abuse
Multiple sclerosis	Back injury or vulnerability to injury
Obesity[c]	
Conditions specifically excluded by the act:	
Kleptomania	Pyromania
Psychoactive substance abuse disorders	Voyeurism

a. From the Americans with Disability Act. 2008. Web site materials. See http://www.ada.gov. For the original act, see http://www.ada.gov/pubs/ada.htm#Anchor-49575. From "Avoiding charges of discrimination against the handicapped," by P. Perry, 1993, *Law Practice Management, 34*, pp. 35–38.

b. It is not possible to include a list of all the specific conditions, contagious and non-contagious diseases, or infections that would constitute physical or mental impairments because of the difficulty of ensuring the comprehensiveness of such a list, particularly in light of the fact that other conditions or disorders may be identified in the future. However, the list of examples in paragraph (1)(ii) of the definition includes orthopedic, visual, speech and hearing impairments, cerebral palsy, epilepsy, muscular dystrophy, multiple sclerosis, cancer, heart disease, diabetes, mental retardation, emotional illness, specific learning disabilities, HIV disease (symptomatic or asymptomatic), tuberculosis, drug addiction, and alcoholism. The phrase "symptomatic or asymptomatic" was inserted in the final rule after "HIV disease" in response to commenters who suggested the clarification was necessary. (See http://www.ada.gov/reg2.html).

c. "U.S. says Disabilities Act may cover obesity," 1993, *New York Times*, p. Y17.

Employers are still free to hire the most qualified candidate for any particular job. Qualifications of all applicants should be reviewed without regard to their disabilities. If the applicant with a disability is the most qualified, then an employer should evaluate whether the disability limits or precludes the performance of an essential function of the job and, if so, whether reasonable accommodation will permit the person to perform the essential functions of the job.

Duty of Reasonable Accommodation

The concept of reasonable accommodation is the new, unique distinguishing characteristic of employment practices under the ADA. The concept is not well defined. A reasonable accommodation is an action taken by an employer that assists a person with a disability to perform the essential job functions. In determining whether a person is qualified for a position, any individual with a disability must be evaluated assuming all reasonable accommodations will be provided (i.e., the agency would incur undue hardship). If the individual is then not qualified for the position, he or she may be rejected.

Accommodations Provided by Private Entities

Title III of the ADA prohibits discrimination against individuals with disabilities "in the full and equal enjoyment of goods, services, and facilities, of any place of public accommodation by any person who owns, leases (or leases to) or operates a place of public accommodation." A public accommodation is broadly defined and includes some places of lodging; restaurants and bars; theaters and stadiums; auditoriums, convention centers, or other places of public gathering; sales or retail establishments; service establishments such as banks, insurance offices, hospitals, and medical offices; public transportation stations; places of recreation; private educational facilities; social services establishments such as day care centers, homeless shelters, food banks, adoptions agencies, and senior citizens centers; and places of exercise or recreation such as gymnasiums, spas, and golf courses.

The alterations and new construction provisions of the ADA also apply to commercial facilities intended for nonresidential use whose operations affect commerce. These facilities include office buildings, to the extent they are not covered by the public accommodations provisions of the act, factories, and warehouses.

Discrimination

The ADA requires that services be provided to individuals with disabilities in the most integrated setting, appropriate to the needs of the individual. It is discriminatory to deny a person with a disability the opportunity to participate in or benefit from the goods, services, facilities, privileges, advantages, or accommodations offered by an entity or to provide such opportunity in a manner that is not equal to that afforded to other individuals. An entity may provide a service that is different or separate from that provided to other individuals only if such action is necessary to provide a service that is as effective as that provided to others.

WORKPLACE SAFETY

Although we will not have space to discuss issues of workplace safety regulations and age discrimination, these also are important aspects of personnel management (i.e., the Age Discrimination in Employment Act of 1967). This legislation and the other policy requirements are summarized in Table 3.4.

Table 3.4   Legislation, Court, and National Labor Relations Board Decisions
                 Affecting Personnel and Human Resource Management

Act/issue addressed	Year	Key provisions
Broad-based discrimination		
Title VII, Civil Rights Act of 1964	1964	Prohibits discrimination in employment on basis of race, color, religion, sex, or national origin
Executive Orders 11246 and 11375	1965 1967	Require federal contractors and subcontractors to eliminate employment discrimination and prior discrimination through AA
Executive Order 11478	1969	Prohibits discrimination in the U.S. Postal Service and in the various government agencies on the basis of race, color, religion, sex, national origin, handicap, or age
Vietnam Era Veterans' Readjustment Assistance Act	1974	Prohibits discrimination against Vietnam-era veterans by federal contractors and the U.S. government and requires AA
Civil Rights Act of 1991	1991	Overturns several past Supreme Court decisions and changes damage claim provisions
Congressional Accountability Act	1995	Extends Equal Employment Opportunity and Civil Rights Act provisions to U.S. congressional staff
Race/national origin discrimination		
Immigration Reform and Control Act	1986 1990 1996	Establishes penalties for employers who knowingly hire illegal aliens; prohibits employment discrimination on the basis of national origin or citizenship
Gender/sex discrimination		
Equal Pay Act	1963	Requires equal pay for men and women performing substantially the same work
Pregnancy Discrimination Act	1978	Prohibits discrimination against women affected by pregnancy, childbirth, or related medical conditions; requires that they be treated as all other employees for employment-related purposes, including benefits

Act/issue addressed	Year	Key provisions
Age discrimination		
Age Discrimination in Employment Act (as amended in 1978 and 1986)	1967	Prohibits discrimination against persons over age 40 years and restricts mandatory retirement requirements, except where age is a bona fide occupational qualification
Older Workers Benefit Protection Act of 1990	1990	Prohibits age-based discrimination in early retirement and other benefit plans
Disability discrimination		
Vocational Rehabilitation Act and Rehabilitation Act of 1974	1973 1974	Prohibits employers with federal contracts over $2,500 from discriminating against individuals with disabilities
Americans with Disabilities Act	1990	Requires employer accommodations for individuals with disabilities

Source: From Mathis, R. L., & Jackson, J. H. (2006), p. 188. Reprinted with permission.

PROTECTION RELATED TO SEXUAL ORIENTATION

Few protections have been regulated in relation to employment for gay, lesbian, bisexual, and questioning individuals. Some states and cities have passed laws prohibiting discrimination based on sexual orientation or lifestyle, but protections are not comprehensive or consistent across states: "Even the issue of benefits coverage for 'domestic partners,' whether heterosexual or homosexual, has been the subject of state and city legislation. No federal laws of a similar nature have been passed. Whether gays and lesbians have rights under the Equal Protection Clause of the 14th Amendment to the U.S. Constitution has not been decided by the Supreme Court" (Mathis & Jackson, 2006, pp. 111–112). Much work is needed to clarify the employment and benefits rights for this group of people.

SEXUAL HARASSMENT

Sexual harassment is a form of employee behavior that violates ethical standards and that has significant potential for worker grievance. Sexual harassment is recognized as one of the most sensitive employee situations. Agency supervisors and managers, as well as the organization, are legally liable for damages and penalties when found by local and federal courts to have failed to address problems of sexual harassment (O'Connor & Vallabhajosula, 2004; U.S. EEOC, 1980, 2007).

Sexual harassment involves unwelcome sexual advances, requests for sexual favors, and other verbal or physical conduct of a sexual nature. The official EEOC guidelines are listed in Figure 3.2. Harassment can take many forms, including verbal, visual, and physical harassment. For example, visual harassment involves constant leering, suggestive ogling, offensive signs and gestures, or open display of pornographic and/or other offensive materials. Verbal harassment takes the form of dirty jokes, sexual suggestions, highly personal innuendos, and/or explicit propositions. Examples of physical harassment are "accidentally" brushing up against the body, patting, squeezing, pinching, kissing, fondling, forced sexual assault, and/or rape.

The Equal Employment Opportunity Commission (EEOC) has issued official guidelines that define sexual harassment as a form of sex discrimination under Title VII of the Civil Rights Act of 1964. The guidelines of Section 1604.11 Sexual harassment are reprinted below:

TITLE 29—LABOR

CHAPTER XIV—EQUAL EMPLOYMENT
OPPORTUNITY COMMISSION

PART 1604—GUIDELINES ON DISCRIMINATION BECAUSE OF SEX

Table of Contents

Sec. 1604.11 Sexual harassment.*

(a)   Harassment on the basis of sex is a violation of section 703 of title VII. Unwelcome sexual advances, requests for sexual favors, and other verbal or physical conduct of a sexual nature constitute sexual harassment when (1) submission to such conduct is made either explicitly or implicitly a term or condition of an individual's employment, (2) submission to or rejection of such conduct by an individual is used as the basis for employment decisions affecting such individual, or (3) such conduct has the purpose or effect of unreasonably interfering with an individual's work performance or creating an intimidating, hostile, or offensive working environment.

(b)   In determining whether alleged conduct constitutes sexual harassment, the Commission will look at the record as a whole and at the totality of the circumstances, such as the nature of the sexual advances and the context in which the alleged incidents occurred. The determination of the legality of a particular action will be made from the facts, on a case by case basis.

(c)   [Reserved]

(d)   With respect to conduct between fellow employees, an employer is responsible for acts of sexual harassment in the workplace where the employer (or its agents or supervisory employees)

Figure 3.2 *(Continued)*

knows or should have known of the conduct, unless it can show that it took immediate and appropriate corrective action.

(e) An employer may also be responsible for the acts of non-employees, with respect to sexual harassment of employees in the workplace, where the employer (or its agents or supervisory employees) knows or should have known of the conduct and fails to take immediate and appropriate corrective action. In reviewing these cases the Commission will consider the extent of the employer's control and any other legal responsibility which the employer may have with respect to the conduct of such non-employees.

(f) Prevention is the best tool for the elimination of sexual harassment. An employer should take all steps necessary to prevent sexual harassment from occurring, such as affirmatively raising the subject, expressing strong disapproval, developing appropriate sanctions, informing employees of their right to raise and how to raise the issue of harassment under title VII, and developing methods to sensitize all concerned.

(g) Other related practices: Where employment opportunities or benefits are granted because of an individual's submission to the employer's sexual advances or requests for sexual favors, the employer may be held liable for unlawful sex discrimination against other persons who were qualified for but denied that employment opportunity or benefit.

Figure 3.2   Federal EEOC guidelines related to sexual harassment

Sources: From the Code of Federal Regulations, Title 29, Volume 4 [Revised as of July 1, 2001]. From the U.S. Government Printing Office via GPO Access. CITE: 29CFR1604.11, pp. 186–192.

Note: *The principles involved here continue to apply to race, color, religion, or national origin.

At the request of the U.S. Congress, the Merits Systems Protection Board conducted a landmark study of sexual harassment in the federal workplace in 1980, with follow-up studies in 1987 and 1995 (U.S. Merit Systems Protection Board [USMSPB], 2004). In the 1980 survey, participants reported whether they had received "any forms of uninvited and unwanted sexual attention" from a person or persons with whom they worked during the 24-month period of the study (pp. 26–37). The forms of behavior identified were as follows:

- Actual or attempted rape or sexual assault
- Pressure for sexual favors
- Deliberate touching, leaning over, cornering, or pinching
- Sexually suggestive looks or gestures
- Letters, phone calls, or materials of a sexual nature

- Pressure for dates
- Sexual teasing, jokes, remarks, or questions

Approximately 42% of the women and 15% of the men reported being sexually harassed during this period. Only 1% reported the severest form (i.e., actual or attempted rape or sexual assaults). But that 1% means that nearly 12,000 employees in the federal workforce were victimized in a severe manner during that period (USMSPB, 1981). The proportion of men who categorized uninvited sexual remarks by coworkers as sexual harassment rose from 42% in 1980 to 64% in 1994. For women, the figures were 54% and 77%, respectively. The percentage of men who believed that pressuring a coworker for sexual favors is sexual harassment rose from 65% in 1980 to 93% in 1994. For women the figures were 81% and 98%, respectively. Researchers believe this increase is due to sexual harassment education (USMSPB, 1995, pp. 5, 7).

Thus, although the pattern of harassment has not changed significantly, employees' attitudes have changed. Federal employees seem to be more willing to recognize a broad range of behaviors as sexual harassment. Sexual harassment was also identified as letters, e-mails, phone calls, pressure, touching, while sexual teasing, jokes, and suggestive gestures were also included as sexual harassment. Sexual harassment seems to occur more than once for each victim (Antecol & Cobb-Clark, 2004).

More recent statistics are available from the EEOC based on the total number of charge receipts filed and resolved under Title VII alleging sexual harassment discrimination as an issue. In fiscal year (FY) 2006, the EEOC received 12,025 charges of sexual harassment. About one in six (15.4%) of those charges were filed by males. The EEOC resolved 11,936 sexual harassment charges in FY 2006 and recovered $48.8 million in monetary benefits for charging parties and other aggrieved individuals, not including monetary benefits obtained through litigation (EEOC, 2007).

The overall findings from these surveys are that sexual harassment is widespread and occurs regardless of a person's age, marital status, appearance, sex, ethnicity, occupation, or salary level. Based on the above studies, it is apparent that many people are treated unequally, are discriminated against, or are abused severely.

Emotional and Economic Effects of Sexual Harassment

Victims report a wide range of effects, including feelings of anger, guilt, depression, emotional stress, anxiety, and even physical problems (Boland, 2007; Schneider, Swan, & Fitzgerald, 1997; Sexual Harassment Support, 2006). Besides emotional effects, there are costs to the employer associated with individual and group productivity, as well as employee replacement and training costs. The total estimated cost of sexual harassment to the government was $327.1 million across these four areas:

- Job turnover ($24.7 million)
- Sick leave ($14.9 million)
- Individual productivity ($93.7 million)
- Team productivity ($193.8 million) (USMSPB, 1995, p. 27)

In addition, federal employees lost $4.4 million in wages from 1992 to 1994 because of sexual harassment (USMSPB, 1995, p. 27). This does not include what national governments, local governments, and U.S. businesses are paying for the thousands of sexual harassment claims filed every year.

Legal Issues

The law regarding sexual harassment is unclear and evolving. Nevertheless, supervisors and agencies can be held responsible and sued. In one of the landmark court cases (*Miller v. Bank of America*, 1976), the U.S. Court of Appeals held the employer liable for the sexually harassing conduct of its supervisors, even when the company had a policy against sexual harassment. (See Clark, 2004, and the EEOC Web site, for other cases.)

Some courts have argued that it is not the unwelcome sexual advances or overtures, by themselves, that constitute sexual harassment, but it is the retaliatory measures taken by the perpetrators, once the advances are refused, that violate the law. Sexual harassment is partly dependent on individual perceptions of the event. However, employers are in violation of Title VII of the Civil Rights Act even if harassment does not result in the loss of tangible work benefits. So if managers allow a discriminatory work environment to exist, they are liable because of a broad definition of sexual harassment in the workplace. Workers have won suits without having to prove that the offensive behavior left them psychologically damaged or unable to do their job. (See the EEOC Web site; Greenhouse, 1993.) Finally, government agencies may be more liable than private employers due to federal laws. However, much of the case law has resulted from corporate suits that are primarily individual in nature and not class action (Towns & Johnson, 2003).

ORGANIZATIONAL AND SUPERVISOR STRATEGIES FOR PREVENTING AND ADDRESSING DISCRIMINATION

To reduce the incidence of sexual harassment and other forms of discrimination, the damage to staff, and supervisor or organizational liability, supervisors working with and through their organizations should do the following:

1. *Take proactive and preventive approaches.* For example, issue a policy statement defining and condemning sexual harassment as a prohibited behavior. This policy must have the strong endorsement of management and be publicized widely: posted on bulletins, reprinted in newsletters, and placed in employee and manager handbooks. Identify the most cost-effective approaches to vigilant detection

of this behavior (Bell, Cycyota, & Quick, 2002). This may include conducting an employee survey about the types and extent of sexual harassment, assuring employee anonymity and confidentiality. The survey should be worded carefully to cover the whole range of behavior and consequences. The results should be posted and reprinted and used to develop educational and training programs.

2. *Provide special training for managers and staff.* The training, which will use information gained through the employee survey, as well as other material, should explain fully the agency stance on sexual harassment and emphasize the outcomes such behavior could have on the perpetrators, the victims, and other employees. This training should also inform managers about the legal liabilities involved and how to be alert for this kind of behavior. Efforts to end sexual harassment that rely primarily on reporting by victims are believed by some as less likely to be successful because most targeted persons do not report their experiences. Thus, one alternative mechanism for controlling sexual harassment—"observer intervention"—is being actively explored (Bowes-Sperry & O'Leary-Kelly, 2005). This training may take the form of discussions about sexual harassment at employee meetings and during orientation sessions for new employees. Advise employees not only of the agency policy on sexual harassment and the grievance channels available to them, but also advise them on what constitutes sexual harassment and the ramifications that may occur from both appropriate and inappropriate allegations. An example of what might result from improper allegations is the $23.7 million lawsuit filed by a Clark University professor against two faculty members and three other women who accused him of sexual harassment. Contending that the charges were "false and malicious" and ruined his reputation, he sued each woman for millions of dollars.

3. *Establish an investigative or ombudsman procedure, either as part of an existing program or as a special process.* The first step in such an investigation is to assure the victim that his or her job is not in jeopardy and that all efforts will be made to protect the victim's identity and position in the agency. Advise the victim to document all incidents relating to the alleged harassment. The supervisor also might do a careful search for other victims, particularly if the alleged harasser has a history of high turnover among subordinates of the opposite sex. In some cases, it may be advisable to consider the use of an outside consultant or investigator to enhance credibility and provide needed expertise. Offer both the victim and the harasser use of an agency or external counseling program, if available. Counseling may be a means of correcting harassment and comforting victims.

4. *Set out a progressive disciplinary agenda, and if the allegations are found to be true, punish the perpetrator.* Punishment could range from verbal reprimand to warning letters, transfer, denial of a bonus or promotion, poor performance appraisals, suspension or probation, or ultimately, dismissal. Take care to ensure the perpetrator's due process. If no evidence of harassment is found, be sure that the allegation is not publicized and that there is no retaliation against the complainant. To the extent possible, confidentiality should be maintained.

5. *Treat all complaints consistently and fairly.* The key to a successful preventive program lies in a prompt, documented response and in the credibility of the responsible individual or department handling the complaint. Although many

of the techniques and procedures developed for race and sex discrimination cases apply, the emotional and hierarchical nature of sexual harassment make it a unique situation in the workplace, with serious and potentially devastating implications for management. (Adapted from Howard, 2007; Neugarten & Miller-Spellman, 1983, pp. 286–287).

In addition to a clear response by the supervisor, workers should be informed that there are several strategies that they can individually employ to discourage or respond to sexual harassment and other forms of discrimination. These strategies include indicating to the person that the behavior is inappropriate and will not be tolerated. Harassing behavior is often repeated even when the victim clearly communicates that the behavior is unacceptable. In addition, staff should begin to keep a private record documenting their interactions with the perpetrator in order to prepare a formal grievance (i.e., documenting who, what, where, when, how, and witnesses to the offenses).

Staff members who perceive discrimination may want to talk with fellow staff members to determine whether others have been victimized and how they have handled the situation. Finally, staff should be encouraged to complain officially. Sexual harassment and other forms of discrimination are a serious personnel problem that often goes unrecognized or, at least, not addressed formally until serious disciplinary measures become necessary. Following some of the preventive measures outlined above can reduce the likelihood of discrimination and allow supervisors to address the problem without resorting to employee dismissal.

Summary

In review, we have outlined four key personnel policy areas that require the ongoing attention of first-line supervisors: AA regulations, Equal Employment Opportunity regulations, ADA regulations, and regulations regarding how to respond to allegations of sexual harassment.

These ethical issues are critical in the management of social work and other human services agencies, and the related personnel laws and guidelines are essential to address because of the organization's legal liability and obligation for accurate implementation of these policies. The values embodied by the Social Work Code of Ethics (NASW, 2006) include service, social justice, dignity of the person, importance of human relationships, integrity, and competence. These values clearly have implications for first-line supervisors in the learning organization, particularly in promoting and modeling the values of integrity and competence for direct line staff. In that regard, the review of current developments in AA rules and regulations is important, as are the parameters of the Equal Employment Act. In addition to AA and Equal Employment Opportunity rules, the developments regarding discrimination against those with disabilities and sexual harassment are relatively recent. With increasing direction being provided by court decisions, the implementation of the protections against discrimination in all quarters is becoming a standard component of the personnel infrastructure in social work agencies and social services organizations. Human resources staff can be invaluable sources of training and ongoing consultation. The next chapter illustrates how staff recruitment and selection can be effective in attracting a talented and diverse workforce while adhering to these personnel laws and policies.

Endnotes

1. AA is based on Executive Order No. 11246, as amended. Guidelines for handling AAPs are found in the Office of Federal Contract Compliance Program's Title 41, Part 60–2 (also known as "Revised Order N0.4"). Also see The Equal Employment Opportunity Act of 1972, P.L. 93–380, 88 Stat. 514, 2–0 USC 1228 (1976). Executive Order No. 11246, in general, applies to an organization if they have a government contract or subcontract exceeding $10,000. A written AAP is required by this Executive Order (see also 503/38 U.S.C. 2012) if the organization has 50 or more employees and a contract in excess of $50,000.

2. Tests as screening devices continue to be used rarely in social services but more so in business (Anderson, 2003) For example, cognitive ability (measuring an individual's thinking, memory, reasoning, verbal, and mathematical abilities), physical ability (strength, endurance, and muscle movement), and situational judgment (measuring a person's judgment in work settings) tests are being used (Mathis & Jackson, 2006, pp. 237–239). In addition, personality tests that measure various aspects such as conscientiousness, agreeableness, openness to experience, emotional stability, extroversion, and honesty are used, but with some concerns about their validity with certain jobs. Furthermore, psychological testing research has shown that certain types of tests (i.e., those testing cognitive ability) are valid predictors of successful job performance across jobs and settings (see Zedeck & Cascio, 1984, pp. 484–485), but there are large differences across racial groups (Outtz, 2002; Salgado et al., 2003).

3. See the Civil Rights Act of 1964, P.L. 88–352, 78 Stat. 241, 28 USC §1147 (1976). Several laws also support equal opportunity in relation to such factors as age (Age Discrimination Employment Act of 1967, as amended); handicap status (Sections 503 and 504 of the Rehabilitation Act of 1973, as amended); Vietnam veterans (38 USC 2011–2014, Vietnam Era Veterans' Readjustment Assistance Act of 1974); and equal pay (Equal Pay Act of 1963).

4. See, for example, various articles in the *Labor Law Journal*. Additional resources include the manuals published by the following organizations, which are regularly updated:
   - Commerce Clearing House, Inc.: Employment Practices, Equal Employment Opportunity Commission Compliance Manual, and Office of Federal Contract Compliance Program Manual.
   - Bureau of National Affairs: Affirmative Action Compliance Manual for Federal Contractors.
   - Prentice Hall, Inc.: Equal Employment Opportunity Compliance Manual.
   - Federal Programs Advisory Service: *Handicapped Requirements Handbook*.

5. See the landmark document, "Uniform guidelines on employee selection procedures" by the EEOC (1978) for original guidance in this area. More specifically,

these are EEOC's Uniform Guidelines on Employee Selection Procedures (designated as UGESP (1978) Sections 1–18). These guidelines are incorporated into the official regulations of the EEOC, 29CFR 1607; Office of Federal Contract Compliance Program, 41CFR 60–3; Department of Justice, 28CFR 50.14; and the former Civil Service Commission, 5CFR 300.103(c).

    6. The ADA section draws material from the following sources: ADA Web site: http://www.ada.gov/, Bruyére (2000), Davis-Wright-Tremaine Law Firm (1992), Pardeck (1998), Perry (1993), and the *New York Times* article, "U.S. says Disabilities Act may cover obesity" (1993).

References

Age Discrimination in Employment Act, P.L. 101-433 (1967).

Alger, J. (2003). What's ahead for affirmative action? *Change, 35*(3), 34–35.

Americans with Disabilities Act, 42 U.S.C. §§12101-12213 (1990).

Anderson, N. (2003). Applicant and recruiter reactions to new technology selection. *International Journal of Selection and Assessment, 2*, 121–136.

Antecol, H., & Cobb-Clark, D. (2004). The changing nature of employment-related sexual harassment: Evidence from the U.S. government, 1978–1994. *Industrial and Labor Relations Review, 57*, 443–461.

Becker, G. C. (2008). Prepared Remarks of Grace Chung Becker Acting Assistant Attorney General ADA Business Connection Leadership Meeting Contemporary Resort, Disney World Lake Buena Vista, Florida, January 7, 2008. Retrieved April 4, 2009, from www.usdoj.gov/crt//speeches/gcb_ada_leadership_mtg.pdf

Bell, M. P., Cycyota, C. S., & Quick, J. C. (2002). An affirmative defense: The preventive management of sexual harassment. In D. L. Nelson & R. J. Burke (Eds.), *Gender, work stress, and health* (pp. 191–210). Washington, DC: American Psychological Association.

Beginner's Guide Staff. (2005). *What is employment screening?* Retrieved April 12, 2006, from http://beginnersguide.com/human-resources/employment-screening/what-is-employment-screening.php

Boland, M. L. (2007). *Sexual harassment in the workplace*. Naperville, IL: Sphinx.

Bowes-Sperry, L., & O'Leary-Kelly, A. M. (2005). To act or not to act: The dilemma faced by sexual harassment observers. *Academy of Management Review, 30*, 288–306.

Bruyère, S. M. (2000). Civil rights and employment issues of disability policy. *Journal of Disability Policy Studies, 11*(1), 18–28.

California State Office of Secretary of State. (1996). *Proposition 209: Text and analysis.* Retrieved April 7, 2006, from http://vote96.ss.ca.gov/bp/209analysis.htm

Civil Rights Act, 42 U.S.C. §1981 (1991).

Civil Rights Act, Title VII, 42 U.S.C. §2000e (1964).

Civil Service Commission, 5 CFR 300.103(c) (1981).

Clark, M. R. (2004). Ruling allows defense in harassment cases. *HR Magazine, 49*, 30–32.

Cohen, B. (1987). The ethics of social work supervision revisited. *Social Work, 32*, 194–196.

Congressional Accountability Act, 2 U.S.C. 1301 (1995).

Cox, F. M. (1984). Guidelines for preparing personnel policies. In F. M. Cox et al. (Eds.), *Tactics and techniques of community practice* (2nd ed., p. 275). Itasca, IL: F.E. Peacock.

Davis-Wright-Tremaine Law Firm. (1992). *ADA summary* [Mimeograph]. Seattle, WA: Casey Family Programs.

Department of Justice, Guidelines on Employee Selection Procedures, 28 CFR 50.14 (1979).

EEOC, Uniform Guidelines on Employee Selection Procedures, 29 CFR 1607(1978).

Equal Employment Opportunity Act, P.L. 92-261 (1972).

Equal Employment Opportunity Commission. (1978). *Uniform guidelines on employee selection procedures.* Retrieved on April 7, 2006, from http://www.uniformguidelines.com/uniformguidelines.html

Equal Pay Act, 40 U.S.C. §206(d) (1963).

Executive Order No. 11246, Equal Employment Opportunity, 30 F.R. 12319 (1965).

Executive Order No. 11375, Equal Employment Opportunity, 32 F.R. 14303 (1965).

Executive Order No. 11478, Equal Employment Opportunity, 34 F.R. 12985 (1969).

Greenhouse, L. (1993). Court, 9-0, makes sex harassment easier to prove. *New York Times,* Wednesday, November 10, 1993. Retrieved April 15, 2009, from http://www.nytimes.com/1993/11/10/us/court-9-0-makes-sex-harassment-easier-to-prove.html

Haynes, R., Corey, G., & Moulton, P. (2003). *Clinical supervision in the helping professions: A practical guide.* San Anselmo, CA: Brooks Cole.

Health Insurance Portability and Accountability Act, Public Law 104-191 (1996).

Helfgott, K. P. (1991). *Preparing a personnel policy manual.* Washington, DC: Child Welfare League of America.

Holland, R. (1999). *Implementing Initiative 200—Keeping faith with the voters.* Seattle: Washington Policy Center. Retrieved April 7, 2006, from http://www.washingtonpolicy.org/ECP/PNKeepingFaithWithVoters99–06.html

Hopwood v. Texas, 78 F.3d 932 (5th Cir. 1996).

Howard, L. G. (2007). *The sexual harassment handbook.* Franklin Lakes, NJ: Career Press.

Hugman, R. (2003). Professional ethics in social work: living with the legacy. *Australian Social Work, 56*(1), 5–15.

Immigration Reform and Control Act, 8 U.S.C. §1364 (1986).

Immigration Reform and Control Act, 8 U.S.C. §1182 (1990).

Immigration Reform and Immigrant Responsibility Act, 8 U.S.C. §1324 (1996).

Khurana, R., & Nohria, N. (2008, October). It's time to make management a true profession. *Harvard Business Review.* (Reprint No. R0810D)

Kuncel, N. R., Thomas, L. L., & Crede, M. (2005). Beyond the big test: Noncognitive assessment in higher education [Book review]. *The Review of Higher Education, 28,* 439–440.

Lencioni, P. M. (2002, July). Make your values mean something. *Harvard Business Review,* pp. 113–117. (Reprint No. R0207S)

Mathis, R. L., & Jackson, J. H. (2006). *Human resource management* (11th ed.) Mason, OH: Thomson Southwestern.

Menzel, D. C. (2007). *Ethics management for in public administrators.* Armonk, NY: M.E. Sharpe.

Miller v. Bank of America, 418 F. Supp. 233 (1976).

National Association of Social Workers. (2006). Code of ethics. Retrieved April 8, 2006, from http://www.socialworkers.org/pubs

Neugarten, D. A., & Miller-Spellman, M. (1983). Sexual harassment in public employment. In S. W. Hays & R. C. Kearney (Eds.), *Public personnel administration: Problems and prospects.* Englewood Cliffs, NJ: Prentice Hall.

O'Connor, M., & Vallabhajosula, B. (2004). Sexual harassment in the workplace: A legal and psychological framework. In B. J. Cling (Ed.), *Sexualized violence against women and children: A psychology and law perspective* (pp. 115–147). New York: Guilford Press.

Office of Federal Compliance Programs. (2006). Code of Federal Regulations Pertaining to U.S. Department of Labor, Title 41, Public Contracts and Property Management, Office of Federal Contract Compliance Programs, Equal Employment Opportunity, Department of Labor. Retrieved April 12, 2006, from http://www.dol.gov/dol/allcfr/Title_41/Chapter_60.htm

Office of Federal Contract Compliance Program, Uniform Guidelines on Employee Selection Procedures, 41 CFR 60-3 (1978).

Older Workers Benefit Protection Act, 29 U.S.C. §623 (1990).

Outtz, J. L. (2002). The role of cognitive ability tests in employment selection. *Human Performance, 15*(1-2), 161–172.

Pardeck, J. T. (1998). *Social work after the Americans with Disabilities Act: New challenges and opportunities for social service professionals.* Dover, MA: Auburn House.

Pecora, P. J., & Wagner, M. (2000). Managing personnel. In R. Patti (Ed.), *Handbook on social welfare management* (pp. 395–423). Thousand Oaks, CA: Sage.

Perry, P. (1993, Jan/Feb). Avoiding charges of discrimination against the handicapped. *Law Practice Management, 34,* 35–38.

Pregnancy and Discrimination Act, 42 U.S.C. §2000e(k) (1978).

Reamer, F. G. (2005). Ethical and legal standards in social work: consistency and conflict. *Families in Society, 86,* 163–169.

Reamer, F. G. (2006). *Social work values and ethics.* New York: Columbia University Press.

Salgado, J. F., Anderson, N., Moscoso, S., Bertua, C., de Fruyt, F., & Rolland, J. P. (2003). A meta-analytic study of general mental ability validity for different occupations in the European community. *Journal of Applied Psychology, 88,* 1068–1081.

Schneider, K. T., Swan, S., & Fitzgerald, L. (1997). Job-related and psychological effects of sexual harassment in the workplace: Empirical evidence from two organizations. *Journal of Applied Psychology, 82,* 401–515.

Sexual Harassment Support. (2006). Sexual harassment, trauma, and PTSD. Retrieved August 7, 2008, from http://www.sexualharassmentsupport.org/TraumaPTSDand SexualHarassment.html

Strom-Gottfried, K. (2008). *Straight talk about professional ethics.* Chicago: Lyceum Books.

Strom-Gottfried, K. (n.d.). Moral courage. Retrieved August 9, 2008, from http://for moralcourage.com/

Thomson, Inc. (2001). Inside employee screening. Retrieved April 12, 2006, from http://www.apesma.asn.au/women/articles/inside_employee_screening_feb_01.asp

Towns, D. M., & Johnson, M. S. (2003). Sexual harassment in the 21st century: e-harassment in the workplace. *Employee Relations Law Journal, 29*(1), 7.

U.S. Equal Employment Opportunity Commission. (1980). *Final guidelines on sexual harassment in the workplace.* Washington, DC: U.S. Government Printing Office. [Electronic version available at http://www.uniformguidelines.com/questionand answers.html]

U.S. Equal Employment Opportunity Commission. (2007). Sexual harassment. Retrieved June 10, 2007, from http://www.eeoc.gov/types/sexual_harassment.html

U.S. Merit Systems Protection Board (USMSPB). (1981). *Sexual harassment in the federal workplace: Is it a problem?* Washington, DC: U.S. Government Printing Office.

U.S. Merit Systems Protection Board. (1995). *Sexual harassment in the federal workplace: Trends, progress, continuing challenges.* Washington, DC: Author. Retrieved

August 9, 2008, from http://www.mspb.gov/netsearch/viewdocs.aspx?docnumber =253661&version=253948&application=ACROBAT

U.S. Merit Systems Protection Board. (2004, Summer). Sexual harassment in the federal workforce problems persist despite increased awareness. *Issue of Merit*, p. 5. Retrieved August 8, 2008, from http://www.mspb.gov/netsearch/viewdocs.aspx? docnumber=255805&version=256094&application=ACROBAT

"U.S. says Disabilities Act may cover obesity." (1993, November 14). *New York Times*, p. Y17.

Vietnam Era Veterans' Readjustment Assistance Act, 38 U.S.C. § 4212 (1974).

Vocational Rehabilitation Act and Rehabilitation Act, 29 U.S.C. §794d (1974).

Washington State Office of the Secretary of State. (1998). Washington State initiative 200. Retrieved April 7, 2006, from http://www.secstate.wa.gov/elections/1998/ i200_text.aspx

Wolfe, T. (1984). *The nonprofit organization: An operating manual* (pp. 63–64). Englewood Cliffs, NJ: Prentice Hall.

Zedeck, S. & Cascio, W. F. (1984). Psychological issues in personnel decisions. *Annual Review of Psychology, 35*, 461–518.

Web-Based Resources

American Management Association: http://www.amanet.org/ (Publications and training opportunities)

Stop Violence Against Women: http://www.stopvaw.org/Effects_of_Sexual _Harassment.html (Information on women's rights world-wide, publications, and other issues)

U.S. Equal Employment Opportunity Commission: http://www.eeoc.gov/ (Information on EEOC publications, court decisions, and other issues)

West HR Advisor: http://advisor.west.thomson.com.mathis (Information on recent human resources developments)

Suggested Readings

Bell, M. P., Cycyota, C. S., & Quick, J. C. (2002). An affirmative defense: The preventive management of sexual harassment. In D. L. Nelson and R. J. Burke (Eds.), *Gender, work stress, and health* (pp. 191–210). Washington, DC: American Psychological Association.

Lencioni, P. M. (2002, July). Make your values mean something. *Harvard Business Review*, pp. 113–117. (Reprint No. R0207S)

4

Recruiting Effective Employees

Introduction

Recruitment, screening, and selection of staff members is one of the most important aspects of a supervisor's job. The employee selection process requires both analytical and interpersonal skills, as well as knowledge of Affirmative Action (AA), Equal Employment Opportunity Commission (EEOC), and other rules (see Chapter 3). In terms of analytical skills, supervisors need to specify the major job tasks for each position. Task-based job descriptions must be developed, key job parts must be designated, and essential worker "competencies" (i.e., knowledge, skills, abilities, and attitudes) must be identified. Well-developed interpersonal skills are required for interviewing job candidates in a courteous and professional manner. This chapter outlines the key tasks and strategies for designing job descriptions and other tools for recruiting and screening new employees.

Recruitment, screening, and staff selection are part of a larger set of responsibilities of supervisors and other mid-managers:

1. *Recruitment* involves generating an applicant pool that provides the employer an opportunity to make a selection, which will satisfy the needs of the organization. This process is important for all agencies that are attempting to overcome a history of discrimination against women, racial or ethnic minorities, or other groups. When combined with broad-based recruiting, it allows the agency to develop a large and diverse pool of applicants.

2. *Selection* is concerned with reviewing qualifications of job applicants in order to decide who should be offered the position.

3. *Placement* involves assigning the new employee to the position and orienting them properly so that they can begin working (Arthur, 2004).

4. *Compensation management* relates to the impact that staff salaries and benefits have on attracting and retaining highly skilled employees.

5. *Training and development* program quality affects the ability to attract skilled recruits who are committed to further skills development.

6. *Employment relations* refers to how an organization treats its employees. Although it affects the image of the organization, more importantly, a healthy organizational culture increases your ability to attract high caliber applicants, as well as lowers worker turnover and produces higher job satisfaction.[1]

7. *Performance evaluation* is the process of assessing how well an employee has performed functions as a means to guiding personnel actions (e.g., employment, termination, and advancement), rewarding personnel, assisting with personal development, identifying training needs, and integrating human resource planning with coordination of other personnel functions (DelPo, 2007).

The major steps involved in recruitment and selection are presented in a checklist form in Figure 4.1. This important supervisory function begins with creating a job description that contains information regarding the minimum prerequisite qualifications for the position. The hiring team then develops and posts position announcements in the local newspapers through their online and possibly paper editions, various list-serves, with professional societies, and other forms of external advertising. This is followed by screening job applicants using application forms, resume reviews, checklists, and tests (when appropriate).

Step 1: Developing a Job Description and Minimum Qualifications

   A. Does the job description contain clear and specific task statements that describe the essential duties of this position?

   B. Are the required knowledge, skills, abilities, educational degrees, and years of related job experience specified anywhere?

   C. Do the required minimum qualifications for the job match the work to be performed; that is, can the connections between the education and experience required and the tasks of the job be subsidized?

Step 2: Employee Recruitment

   A. Do the job announcements include the necessary details of the position?

   B. Are the announcements clearly worded?

   C. Is the application deadline realistic, given the usual delays in dissemination and publication; that is, does the deadline allow the applicant sufficient time to respond to the announcement?

   D. Has the announcement been distributed to enough community, professional, or other groups? Have both formal and informal networks been used to publicize this position?

Figure 4.1 *(Continued)*

E. Is a record being kept of how and where the position was advertised or posted, including personal recruitment efforts?

Step 3: Screening Job Applicants Using Application Forms and Tests (if Appropriate)

A. Does the application form provide information that helps in determining whether the applicant has related education, training, and experience?

B. Does the application form contain questions that are illegal according to Equal Employment Opportunity laws?

C. Can the advertisements and application form be structured so that applicants are asked to submit a cover letter or other summary statements to highlight how their training and experience qualify them for the position?

Step 4: Conducting the Screening Interview

A. Have the interviewers been trained in the basic phases and principles of the selection process?

B. Has a list of standard questions to be asked of each applicant been developed? (Ideally each subset of questions is asked by the same interviewer.)

C. Has a quiet place been set aside for the interview? Have phone or other interruptions been prevented?

D. Has a person been chosen to lead the interview through the opening, information gathering, and closing phases?

E. Has a timeline for the selection process been established; and is there a plan for who, during the interview, will inform each applicant of how and when he or she will be notified?

Step 5: Reference and Background Checks

A. Have a sufficient number of applicants' references been contacted?

B. Have other background checks been made (if appropriate)?

Step 6: Selecting the Person and Notifying the Other Applicants

A. Has the committee weighed carefully all the information gathered to determine the most qualified and committed applicant?

B. Has a firm commitment from the primary candidate been made before notifying the other applicants?

C. Is the letter notifying the other applicants worded sensitively to ease their disappointment and to thank them for their interest in the position?

Figure 4.1 Summary checklist for recruiting, screening, and selecting employees

Source: From "Recruiting and selecting effective employees," by P. J. Pecora. In R. L. Edwards and J. A. Yankey (Eds.), *Skills for effective management of non-profit organizations*, 1998, Washington, DC: National Association of Social Workers. Copyright 1998 by National Association of Social Workers. Adapted with permission.

Telephone and in-person screening interviews are often the next step in the process—with some of the prescreening done by human resources staff in many organizations as they check to make sure applicants meet the minimum qualifications for the position. The final phases of this process involve checking the reference materials of the finalist(s) and making background reference checks. The successful candidate is then selected, and the other applicants are promptly notified. As discussed later in this chapter, caution needs to be taken in conducting reference checks for the finalists and in communicating with candidates who were not selected for the position.

The skills involved in recruitment and selection include being able to work collaboratively with agency staff to develop common expectations for positions and to develop a common set of interview questions. Equally important is the ability to reach an agreement on what constitutes acceptable responses to interview questions and how to rate them. The staff members involved in the process must also be able to interview job applicants in a professional and courteous manner. (For additional information on various aspects of employee selection, see Chaneski, 2001; Frase-Blunt, 2001; Harvard Business School, 2006; Penttila, 2005).

The employment selection process should be considered an important investment of staff time. If this process is not carried out properly, supervisory staff and other managers will spend valuable time and energy unnecessarily in monitoring marginal work performance, addressing increased organizational conflict, and dealing with the stress involved in transferring or terminating staff.

Although many local, state, and federal laws affect recruitment, three major sets of law and policy described in Chapter 3 help shape what is effective and legal practice in this area: (1) AA, (2) Equal Employment Opportunity, and (3) Americans with Disabilities Act (1990). Although state policies, agency accreditation standards, and other factors affect minimum qualifications and other aspects of employee recruitment, these laws remain important.

Specifying Job Tasks and Position Descriptions

POSITION DESCRIPTIONS ARE
ESSENTIAL TOOLS FOR SUPERVISORS

Supervisors pay attention to the details of human services work not only for staff recruitment but in other areas as well. For example, the greater the job clarity, the greater the potential for staff members to understand their work and what is expected to be accomplished. As worker understanding is increased, there is greater opportunity to connect observations and feedback about job performance with the position. As clarity and feedback are increased, worker autonomy can also be increased. And as clarity, feedback, and autonomy are increased, there seems to be more opportunity for job enhancement and job enlargement.

Job enhancement relates to adding or changing components of the job to further worker growth and development. Job enlargement involves expanding authority, autonomy, and responsibility to carry out increasingly more complex and sophisticated functions. Both processes have been linked with higher employee motivation, productivity, and employee satisfaction (Baard, Deci, & Ryan, 2004), as well as less burnout (Zunz, 1998). One of the basic tools necessary for increasing job clarity is an accurate position description.

Position descriptions take on greater importance when a job vacancy is being advertised and when a new worker appears on the job for the first time. Even at these critical points in the recruitment, selection, and orientation process, some human services practitioners pay very little attention to the position description. There may be several reasons for this. First, position descriptions tend to be written in vague terms because inadequate time is set aside to consider job responsibilities and activities carefully. Second, the job might also be defined primarily in terms of the person filling the position or the description is based on the assumption that everyone with a BSW or MSW "ought to know" how the job is to be performed. Third, the position description may be purposely vague so that other tasks not in the job description can be added on a later date. Finally, position descriptions are viewed as administrative documents to be filed away and retrieved only when necessary.

The above assumptions undermine effective supervision. Position descriptions can be crucial to establish wages, salary ranges, and grades, and to help inform performance evaluations (O'Leary, 2002). Position descriptions also specify what skills and background are necessary to perform the job. They should be viewed as management tools for helping workers grow on the job and for evaluating job performance. In addition, they help map what work employees perform and how employees are interconnected in delivering services. Job descriptions play a major role in program planning and implementation, as well as in defining quality service delivery.

BENEFITS OF A POSITION DESCRIPTION

An up-to-date position description facilitates several crucial supervisory functions because it:

1. Ensures that any recruitment process is job related and not necessarily worker specific so that it provides continuity during staff turnover.

2. Provides a basis for clarifying job expectations with workers, since the job descriptions are often vague and incomplete.

3. Provides guidelines for oversight regarding work demands and is a resource for assessing staffing needs, and for requesting additional staff support based on tasks performed in the unit.

4. Enhances worker performance reviews, since there is specific information about job tasks and competencies necessary for assessing outcomes; this provides a structure for monitoring the relationship between the work performed by staff and program outcomes. An up-to-date position description also provides profiles that are useful in identifying training needs of workers.

5. Provides consistency of approach across range of workers in a unit and can serve as a tool for ensuring equitability of work performed and equity in salary levels. (See Appendix C for a sample position description.)

One approach to developing task-based position descriptions is to focus on the role and functions of the worker (Fine & Cronshaw, 1999; Harvard Business School, 2006). This can be a fairly informal process of sitting down with incumbents and identifying their key job responsibilities (what some personnel experts call "key job parts"), or it could involve a more formal job analysis process that uses a set of steps to analyze the job tasks and requirements (Serumola, 2001).

When creating job-specific tasks and position descriptions, care should be given to the use of excessive requirements. The use of these tactics has been found to have a negative effect on the recruitment process of ethnic minorities and may also violate Equal Employment Opportunity laws. Special attention should be given to the use of concrete action verbs to describe the activity required for the position in job descriptions.

DESIGNING AND USING TASK STATEMENTS[2]

Although several technologies are used to describe work, the task statement described in the task-based job analysis approach is perhaps most useful to human services personnel (Fine & Cronshaw, 1999; Mathis & Jackson, 2006). The technology is useful because activities are always linked with expected outcomes, which helps everyone in the agency see how job performance is linked to outcomes and keeps the focus on continuous improvement. In an industrial setting, the *expected results* of replacing a defective part in a machine are obvious, but in the human services setting, the expected results of "discussing personal problems with a walk-in client" might not be quite as obvious and might be different in different settings. For an intake worker in protective services, the expected results would be to "assess the family situation for evidence of abuse or neglect," whereas in a psychiatric hospital, the expected results of the same activity might be to diagnose the case for referral to the appropriate specialist. Therefore, it is not only the *activity* that is important in analyzing human services work but also the *expected results*.

For supervisors and workers, the basic unit of analysis for describing jobs is the *task* ("ask the client questions and write answers on standard intake form to record basic client demographic information"). A job is composed of a series of tasks. Supervision of worker performance is frequently based on how well the assigned tasks are performed. In-service training is often designed to enable staff to perform a series of tasks on the job. The action related to the task may be primarily *physical* such as operating computer hardware; primarily *mental* such as analyzing a case record; and/or primarily *interpersonal* such as counseling with a client. The two most important elements of a task statement are as follows: (1) the *action* that the worker is expected to perform (e.g., asks questions and listens to responses), and (2) the *result* expected of the worker action (e.g., in order to complete the client intake process). Fine and Cronshaw (1999) have identified five major questions that need to be answered in order to write a task statement:

1. *Who? (Subject)*

> The subject of a task statement is understood to be simply the "worker." The task statement does not define what kind of worker.

> Example: A task statement contains no subject because it is always assumed to be "worker."

2. *Performs what action? (Action verb)*

> A task statement requires a concrete, explicit action verb. Verbs that point to a process (such as develops, prepares, interviews, counsels, evaluates, and assesses) should be used only to designate broad processes, methods, or techniques, which are then broken into explicit, discrete action verbs.

> Action: Asks client questions, listens to responses, and writes answers on standard intake form.

3. *To accomplish what immediate results?*

> The purpose of the action performed must be explicit so that (a) its relation to the objective is clear, and (b) performance standards for the worker can be set.

> Result: To record basic client demographic information (e.g., items 1–8 on intake form). The resultant objective is to establish a client information system that enables workers to locate clients quickly and efficiently.

4. *With what tools, equipment, or work aids?*

> A task statement should identify the tangible instruments that workers use as they perform a task, for example, telephone, word processor, pencil/paper, checklists, and written guides.

> Tools: Computer skills.

5. *Under whose instructions, guided by which agency rules?*

> A task statement should indicate what parts of the task are prescribed by a superior and what is left to the worker's discretion or choice.

> Prescribed content: Following standard intake form.

> Discretionary content: Exercising some leeway regarding sequence of questions (pp. 50–51).

An example of a task statement that includes all of these components might read as follows:

> Evaluates and assesses clients with the SCL 90 and other measures, based on state policy and DSM IV categorizations, in order to provide professional treatment planning, consultation, or referral assistance.

One way of reviewing the components of a task statement is to turn to Appendix C, a tool to assist you with action-oriented task statements, and circle all the action verbs that appear at the beginning of each task statement listed in the Mental Health Specialist position description. This process helps to underscore the importance of selecting action verbs that describe specific activities. For example, "participates" in staff meetings is a better action verb than "attends" staff meeting. The action or activity is more clearly defined. In a similar fashion, return to Appendix C and circle all of the "in order to" phrases. This process helps to underscore the role of the outcome statement and its relationship to the action verb.

If it is difficult to develop outcome statements to accompany the main activity of the task statement, you probably need to reassess the value of the task. When drafting outcome statements for the first time, there is a general tendency to overload these statements. For example, the task statement, "Counsels client in order to help a client secure a job," includes a very large outcome statement. Alternatively, it might be useful to isolate several counseling tasks with more modest and feasible outcomes, such as "in order to acquire job search skills," "in order to increase client's self-confidence," or "in order to share information about jobs and careers."

Writing task statements requires practice. First efforts will feel clumsy and awkward, but with practice, the process becomes much easier. When starting with no existing job description, you may want to use the following steps:

1. List all the various job activities or specific responsibilities of the position.

2. Divide the job into four to six major components, which become the basis of defining broad areas of responsibility.

3. Distribute all the major activities under each of the components or responsibility areas, adding additional activities as they are identified. (Agencies sometimes attach a percentage weighting to each of the responsibility areas and check to see that the total for combining the weighted percentages equals 100%.)

4. Use the activity statements, such as "drive clients to clinic," and convert them into task statements (e.g., transport clients to clinic in order to assist them to secure prenatal care for their young children).

In building a new, undefined position description, it is useful to share the process with a colleague. For example, if you are a supervisor working on your own position description, it is important to involve your immediate supervisor.

This collaborative process can begin with discussions about the weighting of major responsibilities as well as sharing drafts of specific task statements. It may be helpful to build on an existing position description even if it is out-of-date. Similarly, if you are a supervisor seeking to update, revise, or entirely redesign the position description of a subordinate, it is important to approach the process as a collaborative effort. Position descriptions can also be built by using a task bank developed by specialists in the field (see the *Dictionary of Occupational Titles:* http://www.oalj.dol.gov/libdot.htm).

In reviewing the job tasks in Appendix C, it should be apparent that they reflect considerable specificity. Therefore, it is important to clarify the objectives for selecting tasks. For example, if the job is designed for a person with a bachelor's degree in the social sciences without specialized training in the human services, it might be necessary to include 8 to 10 specific task statements in order to delineate what tasks are appropriate for these workers. (See, for example, Rittner & Wodarski, 1999.)

In summary, not only do the position descriptions provide the foundation for job announcements, but the task statements also provide a vehicle for the supervisor to identify performance standards. A major challenge in human services agencies is the development of performance standards that are meaningful to workers. Performance standards linked to a task or cluster of tasks provide a basis for ongoing worker self-assessment and for supervisory "troubleshooting" when workers do not meet a minimum standard of performance. (See Chapters 7 and 8.)

Use of Competency Statements in Supervision and Personnel Management

OVERVIEW

A competency can be defined as any knowledge, skill, or attribute, observable in the consistent patterns of an individual's behavior, interactions, and work-related activities over time, which contributes to the fulfillment of the mission and accomplishment of the strategic objectives of the organization. Through the understanding and incorporation of both core (organization-wide) and domain (job-related) competencies, organizations are able to:

- Identify concrete valued behaviors within the organization.
- Recruit and select new employees.
- Assess and enhance staff levels of contribution to the organization's effectiveness, as well as assess and enhance the level of contribution of those whom staff supervise or team with.
- Focus and manage one's professional development and growth, including setting reasonable goals (Mathis & Jackson, 2006).

USING COMPETENCIES

To recruit effective staff, clarity is needed about the job, as well as clarity about the knowledge, skills, and abilities (i.e., competencies) necessary to perform that work. A competency-based approach can help with this process. But to use a competency platform effectively in your personnel program and practices, every major system needs to have competencies successfully embedded in it. For example, some social services organizations followed the example of several corporations by adopting core competencies for recruiting, supervising, training, and recognizing staff members. (See Appendix D; Bristow, Dalton, & Thompson, 1996; and for a public health example, see Council on Linkages Between Academia and Public Health Practice, 2005.)

A competencies approach can be linked with a framework for viewing levels of contribution that staff members can make. In the fields where employee learning and constant innovation are essential, these are being referred to as "levels of knowledge work":

- *Level one: Acquiring knowledge.* The knowledge acquired is in the form of ideas, theories, methods, principles, skills, and information about the organization, the work of the organization, and its consumers. The Level One contributor seeks and acquires knowledge from two primary sources:
  1. From supervisors and coworkers (by seeking information, advice, guidance, and feedback)
  2. From the codified sources of knowledge in the organization (i.e., systems, guidelines, work manuals, operating procedures, and policies)
- *Level two: Applying knowledge.* Level Two contributors use acquired knowledge to plan and complete independently value-added work for the organization. They exercise judgment to make their own decisions, rather than deferring those decisions to others. Unless new knowledge is used, it adds little or no value for the organization. By exercising confidence and initiative, Level Two contributors turn previously acquired knowledge into a value-added resource for the organization. (A way to think of Level Two knowledge workers is as the "solid performers" in most organizations. "Star" status is usually only conferred on those knowledge workers who contribute at Levels Three, Four, and Five.)
- *Level three: Creating knowledge.* The Level Three contributor creates new knowledge by pushing the boundaries of existing knowledge:
  o Asks "What if" questions
  o Takes the risk of doing things that have never been done before
  o Solves critical problems that have no predetermined solutions
  o Invents new products, processes, technologies or work methods
- *Level four: Developing knowledge in others.* The Level Four contributor grows intellectual capital in several different ways:
  o Shares knowledge directly with others
  o Helps other apply new or existing knowledge to their work

o Provides people with useful feedback
o Motivates others to create and apply new knowledge
o Communicates a sense of direction and purpose
o Facilitates the face-to-face transfer of knowledge between others

- *Level five: Leveraging knowledge.* Level Five contributors help define what the organization does and how it does it. They often do this by transforming the knowledge in people's heads into systems that are "owned" by the organization; systems that accelerate the transfer and application of knowledge across the organization. These systems are referred to as structural capital. Although Level Five contributors may not create this structural capital, they convince a critical mass of the organization to accept and use the new structural capital. This structural capital could include any of the following:

o New business or technology strategies and directions
o New work methods and expert systems
o New people systems or organization structures
o New training, communication, or information systems (Bristow, 1999, pp. 5–6; also see Bristow, 2005.)

In summary, part of defining a position and developing the skills of staff members includes paying attention to the key competencies that are required and how an employee can grow and contribute to the organization in different ways over time.

Recruitment and Selection Phases and Strategies

RECRUITING EMPLOYEES

The next step in the hiring process is to prepare announcements of the position to (a) officially publicize the availability of the position, (b) describe the tasks of the job, (c) attract a wide range of qualified candidates to improve the pool of candidates and maximize compliance with the legislative intent of both Equal Employment Opportunity and AA, and (d) inform interested persons of the minimum qualifications and the process involved in applying for the position.

Note that the recruitment and selection of employees is a form of public relations. The quality of recruitment materials and the respect and professionalism shown to applicants shape the image of the agency—including the many applicants who were *not* selected. The way the recruitment and screening process is carried out can improve or damage the reputation of the agency. If unsuccessful applicants are treated fairly in a well-organized professional screening process, they may be disappointed, but their level of respect for the organization will increase. Future case referrals or the agency's community image may therefore depend on the people not hired.

This "public relations" aspect of recruitment has implications for how the other steps in the process are carried out. For example, the announcement of the position should be as detailed as possible to allow potential applicants to determine whether the position would fit their qualifications, current interests, and career goals. Communication with job applicants and screening interviews should be handled carefully. To meet AA laws and regulations, the job announcement should include the following information:

A. Job title, classification, and salary range, although salary ranges in some organizations are listed as "open" and "negotiable"

B. Location of job (i.e., geographic and organizational unit)

C. Description of duties

D. Minimum qualifications

E. Starting date for the position

F. Application procedures (i.e., what materials should be sent to whom)

G. Closing date for the receipt of applications (Klingner & Nalbandian, 2003)

A typical announcement of a position is shown in Figure 4.2. Various forms of this basic announcement can be distributed to a variety of organizations, placed as newspaper advertisements, listed in professional newsletters or Web sites, posted at regional or national universities, and distributed at conferences or other events to reach potential applicants. Many organizations make special efforts to recruit women or ethnic minorities by contacting community organizations, churches, university departments and placement centers, minority newspapers, radio shows, and other community groups. Other special efforts may be necessary if economic or other factors are affecting the labor market and the availability of qualified applicants.

Check to see that the announcement contains the necessary details of the position and is clearly worded. Make sure that the application deadline is realistic,

POSITION ANNOUNCEMENT
Family Preservation Services Specialist
Children's Services Society
Seattle, Washington

Function and Location

Provides intensive in-home services to families considering out-of-home placement for one or more members. Is on-call 24 hours per day to provide crisis intervention and other family services with problem resolution. Will work out of the Wallingford social services office.

Figure 4.2 *(Continued)*

Duties and Responsibilities (Partial List)

1. Provides in-home, crisis-oriented treatment and support to families in which one or more family members are at risk of being placed outside the home in foster, group, or institutional care to prevent unnecessary child placement.**

2. Works a 40-hour nonstructured workweek (including evenings and weekends) to be responsive to the needs of families.*

3. Provides family education and skills training as part of a goal-oriented treatment plan to prevent the recurrence of or to reduce the harmful effects of the maltreatment of children.*

4. Advocates for family members with schools, courts, and other social services agencies to help family members obtain financial assistance, housing, medical care, and other services.*

Qualifications

Master's degree in social work, psychology, educational psychology, or psychosocial nursing is required. Graduate degree in social work preferred. Experience in counseling families and children is required. Knowledge of crisis intervention social casework, communication skills, and family therapy techniques is also required. Knowledge of cognitive-behavioral interventions, group work, and functional family therapy is desirable. Must have reliable transportation. Required to live in county served. Salary range: $29,000–$35,000.

Application Procedures and Deadline

An agency application form, résumé, and cover letter describing related education and experience must be submitted. Position closes April 25, 2005. Starting date is tentatively scheduled for May 25, 2005. Please send application materials to

Annette Jandre

Program Supervisor

Children's Services Society
4601–15th Avenue, NW
Seattle, WA 98103
(206) 263–5857

AN EQUAL OPPORTUNITY EMPLOYER—ALL QUALIFIED INDIVIDU-ALS ARE ENCOURAGED TO APPLY

Figure 4.2 Sample position announcement
*Key job parts.

given the usual delays in the dissemination of announcements and the response of applicants. Consider also whether the announcement has been distributed to a sufficient number of communities, professionals, or other groups. Both formal and informal networks are useful for publicizing the position, especially among communities of color; the gay, bisexual, transgendered, and lesbian community; and other groups that an agency may desire to contact in order to maximize staff diversity. Finally, keeping a record of how and where the position was advertised and a record of individual recruitment efforts is a strategic way to document the efforts made in the process. This strategy also can be used to track those individuals who have expressed interest in the organization, and who might be good candidates for future openings. When an immediate selection decision cannot be made, the agency or institution has the responsibility to communicate with those applicants who have been included in the recruitment process, and inform them about the status of their application.

Summary

This chapter has presented an overview of the recruitment process of staff in special services organizations. It has outlined key tasks and practical strategies for designing job descriptions and other tools for recruiting new employees. Supervisory and agency excellence is determined, in a large part, by the staff's compatibility with and commitment to the program's mission. Sound recruitment and screening practices help ensure that effective staff is hired, and that a minimum number of people are released during the probationary period. Although this process requires organizational, analytical, and interpersonal skills, it is critical for obtaining high-quality personnel. The next chapter discusses the characteristics of strategies for screening résumés and interviewing conduct.

Endnotes

1. Organizational culture has been documented as crucial to effectiveness. For example, Glisson (2007), Glisson and James (2002), and Yoo and Brooks (2005) have found that certain organizational factors, like how workers are treated, supervisor support, good organizational routines, and other factors predict more positive service outcomes.
2. Adapted from Pecora and Austin (1987, pp. 27–30).

References

Americans with Disabilities Act, 42 U.S.C. §§12101–12213 (1990).
Arthur, D. (2004). *The employee recruitment and retention handbook*. New York: Amacom Books.

Baard, P. P., Deci, E. L., & Ryan, R. M. (2004). Intrinsic need satisfaction: A motivational basis of performance and well-being in two work settings. *Journal of Applied Social Psychology, 34*, 2045–2068.

Bristow, N. (1999). *The new leadership imperative.* Orem, UT: Targeted Learning. Retrieved March 21, 2008, from http://www.targetedlearning.com

Bristow, N. (2005). *Flying the coop: Breaking free of the beliefs that limit our potential and rob us of fulfillment.* Orem, UT: Targeted Learning. Retrieved from http://www.targetedlearning.com

Bristow, N., Dalton, G., & Thompson, P. (1996). *The four stages of contribution* [Mimeograph]. Orem, UT: Novations.

Chaneski, W. S. (2001, March). *Replacing that key employee-recruitment process.* Retrieved February 14, 2006, from http://findarticles.com/p/articles/mi_m3101/is_10_73/ai_71838940

Council on Linkages Between Academia and Public Health Practice. (2005). *Core competencies for public health professionals.* Retrieved August 10, 2008, from http://www.phf.org/link/competency-directions.pdf

DelPo, A. (2007). *The performance appraisal handbook: Legal and practical rules for managers.* Berkley, CA: Nolo.

EEOC, Uniform Guidelines on Employee Selction Procedures, 29 CFR 1607 (1978).

Fine, S. A., & Cronshaw, S. F. (1999). *Functional job analysis.* Mahwah, NJ: Lawrence Erlbaum.

Frase-Blunt, M. (2001). Peering into an interview: Peer interviewing can reveal the perfect candidate for your team—if it's done right. Agenda: Recruitment—Brief article. Retrieved February, 14 2006, from http://www.findarticles.com/p/articles/mi_m3495/is_12_46/ai_81393640/print

Glisson, C. (2007). Assessing and changing culture and climate for effective services. *Research on Social Work Practice, 17*, 736–747.

Glisson, C., & James, L. R. (2002). The cross-level effects of culture and climate in human service teams. *Journal of Organizational Behavior, 23*, 767–794.

Harvard Business School. (2006). *Hiring smart for competitive advantage.* Boston, MA: Harvard Business School Press.

Klingner, D. E., & Nalbandian, J. (2003). *Public personnel management: Context and strategies* (5th ed.). Upper Saddle River, NJ: Prentice Hall/Simon & Schuster.

Mathis, R. L., & Jackson, J. H. (2006). *Human resource management* (11th ed.). Mason, OH: Thomson Southwestern.

O'Leary, T. (2002). Using your team for recruiting—A retention strategy for the human resources professional. Retrieved March 17, 2008, from http://humanresources.about.com/library/weekly/aa022402a.htm

Pecora, P. J. (1998). Recruiting and selecting effective employees. In R. L. Edwards and J. A. Yankey (Eds.), *Skills for effective management of non-profit organizations.* Washington, DC: National Association of Social Workers.

Pecora, P. J., & Austin, M. J. (1987). Personnel management for human service agencies. Newbury Park, CA: Sage.

Penttila, C. (2005, Jan). Peering in: Peer-to-peer interviews give you a closer look at how prospective employees will get along with your staff-but be careful whom you introduce them to. Retrieved February 14, 2006, from http://www.findarticles.com/p;/articles/mi_m0DTI/is_1_33/ai_n8688091/print

Rittner, B., & Wodarski, J. S. (1999). Differential uses for BSW and MSW educated social workers in child welfare services. *Children and Youth Services Review, 21*, 217–238.

Serumola, P. (2001, March). *Job task analysis*. Retrieved February 23, 2006, from http://web.syr.edu/~deseryel/FEA/task.html

Yoo, J., & Brooks, D. (2005). The role of organizational variables in predicting service effectiveness. *Research on Social Work Practice, 15*, 267–277.

Zunz, S. J. (1998). Resiliency and burnout: Protective factors for human service managers. *Administration in Social Work, 22*(3), 39–54.

Web-Based Resources

Chaneski, W. S. (2001). *Replacing that key employee—recruitment process*. Retrieved March 21, 2008, from http://findarticles.com/p/articles/mi_m3101/is_10_73/ai_71838940

Frase-Blunt, M. (2001). *Peering into an interview: Peer interviewing can reveal the perfect candidate for your team—if it's done right. Agenda: Recruitment—Brief article*. Retrieved April 21, 2008, from http://www.findarticles.com/p/articles/mi_m3495/is_12_46/ai_81393640/print

O'Leary, T. (n.d.). *Using your team for recruiting—A retention strategy for the human resources professional*. Retrieved August 17, 2008, from http://humanresources.about.com/library/weekly/aa022402a.htm

Suggested Readings

Baard, P. P., Deci, E. L., & Ryan, R. M. (2004). Intrinsic need satisfaction: A motivational basis of performance and well-being in two work settings. *Journal of Applied Social Psychology, 34*, 2045–2068.

Harvard Business School. (2006). Workforce wisdom: Insights on recruiting, hiring, and retaining your best people. Cambridge, MA: Harvard Business School Press.

5

Screening and
Interviewing for Selection

Introduction

The applicant screening process involves a crucial set of steps (see Figure 5.1). The purpose of screening applicants is to narrow your pool of finalists to those individuals who qualify for the position and who would fit in with the organization. Some applicants may lack the appropriate educational degree, adequate professional certification, or job experience. Prompt attention to communication with those screened out at this stage assists the organization as well as the prospective applicant who is not qualified. The process helps those individuals who do not qualify for the position to seek appropriate job opportunities elsewhere.

THE APPLICATION FORMS AND TESTS

Use of Application Forms

If properly designed, the application form can provide a significant amount of information about the applicant's qualifications. The application form should gather objective data about the applicant's previous work history. Other aspects of the screening can include the applicant's cover letter. Although the application form reveals objective data about the applicant, the cover letter often provides additional information about the applicant's interpersonal skills. This skill set can be assessed by directing the applicant to fill out the form in full as well as submit a letter of interest. The applicant's response will demonstrate his or her ability to think creatively or to follow directions. Application forms typically require the following information:

- Name, address, and phone number(s)
- Educational degrees and related course work.

- Employment history (i.e., positions, places of employment, major duties of employment, reason for leaving, and former supervisor's names)
- Veteran status (this information may be required—some agencies give "points" for employment tests or special consideration to veterans)
- References
- Any disabilities that would interfere with performing the particular job
- Adult convictions for a Class A misdemeanor or felony
- Affirmative Action (AA) information, such as ethnic group, sex, age, and any disability (this information is detached from the application and is kept on file for AA analysis)

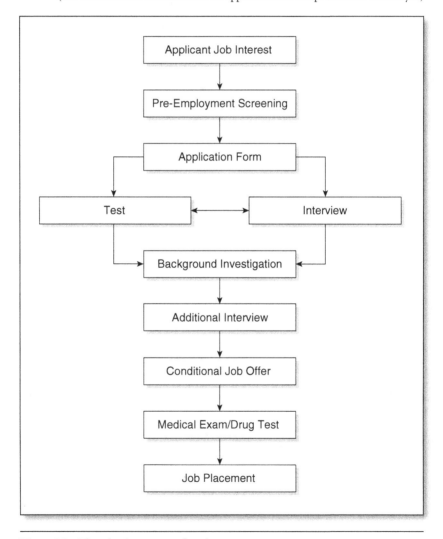

Figure 5.1   The selection process flowchart

Source: Human resources management (11th ed., p. 230), by R. L. Mathis & J. H. Jackson, 2006, South-Western, a part of Cengage Learning, Inc. Reproduced by permission. www.cengage.com/permissions.

In addition, some agencies require applicants to complete a questionnaire where they indicate their knowledge and skills for major tasks of the job and provide contact information for references. The agency's application should not contain questions that violate AA guidelines. (See Chapter 3.)

Use of Tests

The use of tests to screen and select candidates in social welfare organizations is limited due to the lack of appropriate tests that are adequately validated, as well as the controversy surrounding such tests (American Psychological Association, 1996; Keller, 2004). Opponents of testing argue that tests are rarely powerful predictors of job performance, and there are large test score differences across racial groups (see Chapter 3).

But given the lack of alternatives for screening a large number of applicants, tests may continue to be used in certain social welfare agencies as screening devices. Nearly all states use a standard examination for license as a social worker, which was developed by the Association of State Social Work Boards to test qualifications at both the BSW and MSW levels (Association of Social Work Boards, 2005). These licenses are required for some positions and may encourage the development of tests for screening applicants for social services and other nonprofit organization jobs nationwide. The Harvard Business School (2002, pp. 52–55) and Holly (2003) offer the following guidelines for using tests as devices to select employees: (a) Specify carefully the job requirements in terms of values and behavior and then make sure the test is related to the position in question; (b) tests should not have an adverse impact on protected classes; (c) consider more than one test to cross-validate; (d) experts should administer and score the tests; and (e) tests that are clinically oriented, such as psychological assessments that measure intelligence, potentially violate the Americans with Disabilities Act (1990) and should not be used.

PRELIMINARY SCREENING

Preliminary screening of résumés, cover letters, applications, and test scores is the traditional process used to remove unqualified individuals during the first phase of the hiring process. But this process should be carefully implemented so that any bias in applicant selection will be avoided. A preliminary screening of applications should be conducted by a small committee of administrators, supervisors, and staff to eliminate applications that clearly do not meet the minimum standards, and to help select a group of applicants to be interviewed.

To facilitate this process, a "screening grid" may be used (see Table 5.1). Each application is reviewed in relation to the minimum qualifications and the applicant's competencies or experience in certain areas (i.e., the degree of training in mental health services, the number of years of direct practice experience

Table 5.1   Applicant Screening Grid for a Child Mental Health Supervisor Position

Applicant name	MSW or MA in one of the social sciences (Yes/No)	Years of experience in mental health	Specialized training in child therapy	Years of supervisory experience	Special characteristics or qualifications

in child mental health, and the number of years of supervisory experience). Expansion of space on the spreadsheet is a useful way to record information about the "special characteristics" of certain applicants.

Methods for selecting personnel also use technology such as the following:

- Use of online applications and screening tools that allow applicants to provide information through the Web.
- Use of a job Web site so applicants can download and print a copy of the application.
- Use of Web-based forms so candidates can complete applications online or send them in as e-mail attachments.
- Use of e-mail for communications about job postings and confirming job interviews.
- Employer "skill banks" for applicants. This makes it possible for employers to access applicants made to order based on skills needed for the required position.
- Computerized application testing with immediate scoring (Lavigna, 2005).

The usefulness of the screening grid and the application-review process depends on the amount of information provided by the applicant. Clearly, the ability to assess the applicant's qualifications, beyond adherence to minimum qualifications, is dependent on the application form, résumé, and any other information that is gathered. Therefore, a cover letter describing how their education, training, and experience qualify them for a particular job provides additional information. Detailed cover letters and screening grids facilitate the initial screening process, especially when the screening committee may have to consider 10 or more applicants.

The screening committee needs to ensure that the job application form provides information that will help them determine whether the applicant has the required education, training, and experience to meet the job qualifications. In addition, the committee needs to check that the application form does not contain questions that are illegal according to Equal Employment Opportunity laws (Equal Employment Opportunity Act, 1972). The following types of information cannot be requested in either an application form or a job interview: maiden name, type of residence, proof of age, verification of birthplace and citizenship, language and national origin, photographs, physical condition, religion, criminal record, military service, or organizational affiliations (see Chapter 3).

The committee must be prepared to encounter some fellow staff members who are not aware of what questions are illegal or improper to use in application forms and interviews. Chapter 3 discussed how AA and Equal Employment Opportunity regulations affect this work and may assist staff in understanding how and why these guidelines came into existence. Individuals who do not meet the education, training, or experience minimum qualifications, or who do not possess the required knowledge, skills, abilities, education certificates, or academic training should be immediately eliminated from the application pool and notified respectfully that they will not be considered for the position.

INVOLVING OTHER EMPLOYEES AND TEAM MEMBERS IN THE HIRING PROCESS

Using a cross-functional team approach in the hiring process fosters employee growth and development. Team members' involvement in the hiring process creates a work atmosphere and culture that values a collaborative process. This approach enhances individual and team commitment, and it reinforces collaborative organizational values and employee cohesiveness.

To foster a successful team environment, clear communication must be provided, expectations must be spelled out clearly, and collaboration among employees must be an organizational norm. Not only must executive leadership provide the impetus to foster teamwork, but most importantly, teamwork must be positively rewarded and recognized. For individual employees, the experience of being involved in the hiring process emphasizes the feeling of belonging to a team, and creating a feeling of being part of the larger picture and a sense of contributing to the overall success of the institution. This type of involvement makes individuals feel unique, while helping them feel connected to each other. The involvement of employees in the hiring process can also be used as a practical training tool for the development of interviewing skills. Finally, when team members and other employees work with new hires, stronger working relationships are forged (O'Leary, 2002).

PURPOSES OF THE INTERVIEW

An interview serves various functions related to both providing information to and gathering information from the individual being interviewed: (a) selecting applicants who best meet the job requirement; (b) advertising the institution's positive qualities; (c) developing good public relations; (d) providing information about the organization; (e) establishing rapport; and (f) educating the individual being interviewed. To achieve the most positive outcome during the recruitment process, two issues should be kept in mind and simultaneously addressed:

1. Securing the most qualified individual for the position.

2. Communicating realistic expectations about the position and the organization to the most promising candidates for the position. Excellent clarity of communication between interviewers and the prospective employee will result in a lower rate of turnover among new hires.

CONDUCTING THE SCREENING INTERVIEW

The discussions about the EEOC, AA, and the Americans with Disabilities Act in Chapter 3 and in this chapter provide a technical backdrop to the hiring process. Due to the challenges of conducting applicant testing, many nonprofit organizations have traditionally relied on the employment interview as a screening device. Once the applicant or applicants have been selected for the interview, a setting such as a conference room that offers minimal distraction needs to be chosen. Ensure that the interview committee consists of more than one interviewer from each of the departments that will most interact with the new employee. Preferably each interviewer will be a representative for his or her department.

Information gathered from the interview should address four major questions. First, does the applicant have the necessary knowledge, skills, values, and abilities to do the job? Second, does the person have the motivation, attitude, and initiative to do the job well? Third, will the individual be compatible with the other employees in that unit and the agency as a whole? This question requires learning about the applicant's work style and personality, to some degree through the interview process and later through a check of references, if legally possible. Fourth, when can the desirable candidates start if offered the position (Tvrdik, 2007).

PREDICTIVE VALUE OF INTERVIEWS

Some researchers argue that interviews, as typically conducted, are of limited predictive value (Kirkwood & Ralston, 1999). Despite the lack of conclusive empirical evidence in this regard, interviews are the most widely used means of selecting personnel. Additionally, some evidence is available that properly conducted interviews may yield information that is valid for predicting an applicant's performance of a job (Mathis & Jackson, 2006).

Furthermore, a growing body of practice wisdom (see Evers, Anderson, & Voskuijl, 2005) and some research (Kirkwood & Ralston, 1999) provide useful guidelines for interviewing applicants. For example, guidelines are available that spell out steps to train interviewers so as to improve the selection and hiring process, interviewing techniques, and methods for combining various sources of information to evaluate applicants (Tyler, 2005).

The successful interviewing of applicants involves preparation in several areas. Clearly, each member of the selection committee should be familiar with the duties, responsibilities, and qualifications of the job. Interviewers should evaluate the applicant by carefully reading the application form, résumé, cover letter, and letters of reference before the interview. They should be prepared to check out inconsistencies or gaps in the interview and possibly later when contacting references. Finally, to standardize the areas covered in the interview, the staff should monitor each member of the screening committee to ensure that the same job-related questions are asked of each applicant. This consistency is because applicants may respond differently to the same questions when asked by different interviewers if multiple applicants are being interviewed. If at all possible, the same members of the interview committee should participate in all the interviews.

These facets are important so interviewers can gather information to answer the following two basic questions:

1. *Can the applicants do the job?* To assess the applicants' potential to perform specific tasks, the interviewers should examine their previous work experience, training and education, and actual behavior during the interview.

2. *Will the applicants do the job?* Interviewers may overlook the applicant's willingness to perform key responsibility areas. This part of the information-collecting involves examination of applicants' preferences for and interest in the nature of the work to be done, their preferences for conditions of employment (such as salary, hours, and travel), and the compatibility between their career goals and the organization's career opportunities (Goodale, 1989, p. 316).

Given the importance of this aspect of the hiring process, the design and process of the interview demands excellence on the part of the selection committee. In general, it is most useful to select open-ended questions that cannot be answered with a simple "yes" or "no" but require information or explanations. In other words, interviewers should start their questions with *what, why, where, when,* and *how* rather than with *can, did,* or *have.* Do not hesitate to ask the applicant to provide more details. It is also important to establish a comfortable, confidential, supportive, and nonthreatening atmosphere to reduce the applicant's nervousness or hesitancy to talk. In this regard, you should divert or hold all calls and visits, avoid interviewing from behind a desk that is stacked high with books and papers, have all the necessary materials (i.e., applicant's résumé, application form, note-taking equipment, and description of the position) ready, and set aside adequate time for the interview and between interviews.

MINIMIZING INTERVIEWER BIAS IN THE SELECTION PROCESS

According to Equal Employment Opportunity Commission (EEOC) laws, recruiting methods that favor individuals of a particular ethnic minority group, gender, age, or religion are prohibited unless the methods being used by the institution can be justified as valid practice of success in job performance. Title VII of the Civil Rights Act of 1964 specifically documents the prohibition of discrimination on the basis of race, religion, sex, or national origin (see Chapter 3).

The law was extended to protect those individuals within age groups that had been discriminated against by the Age Discrimination in Employment Act of 1967. This section of the law prohibits discrimination against an individual because of age (e.g., enforcing mandatory retirement) unless it can be revealed that age is a justifiable qualification of the job. Under the Vocational Rehabilitation Act of 1973, Section 504, it is illegal to discriminate against qualified disabled individuals on the basis of their handicap. See Figure 5.2 for examples of poor interviewing practices.

Some job applicants have encountered interviewers who act in inappropriate ways that may violate EEOC regulations:

- Interviewers asked the following questions:
  - "How many children do you have?"
  - "What would your spouse think of you taking this job?"
  - "Would you consider dating someone you worked with?"
  - "What do your mother and father do for a living?"
  - "What will your boyfriend think of you working long hours?"

Some people we have worked with in workshops report interviews where:

- There were constant interruptions from phone calls.
- People came in and out of the office.
- It was obvious that the interviewer was reading their résumé for the very first time in the midst of the interview.
- One or more members on the interview team read e-mails on their phones during the interview process.

Figure 5.2   Examples of poor interview practices

VIDEO-CONFERENCE INTERVIEW

Using a video-conference interview can be an option for the interview process. With Skype, Breeze, or similar resources, the interviews can be held at little cost to the agency; or applicants can go to a video-conferencing facility to be interviewed. This is a time-saving approach to reviewing the pool of applicants. One disadvantage is that a few applicants are skeptical of that approach (Strauss, Miles, & Levesque, 2001).

Phases of the Interview

The guidelines discussed above are designed to maximize the effectiveness and fairness of selection committees. Preparation alone is not sufficient; the interview should be conducted in a smooth, directed, professional manner and be led by one spokesperson for the group. An efficient and effective hiring process follows a definite pattern. There are essentially four phases to an effective interview: the opening, the process of gathering information from the applicant, responding to the applicant's questions, and the closing. Each phase is critical in gathering the proper information and for providing applicants with the necessary details of the screening process.

During the *opening or introductory phase,* the interviewer uses small talk to relax the applicant and to help him or her settle into the interview setting. This phase may last anywhere from 2 to 10 minutes, depending on the overall length of the interview. At the start of the interview, introduce the committee. Follow this introduction by explaining the nature of the interview to the applicant. Discuss confidentiality issues as well as format and length of the interview. Ask permission to take notes during the session, and make sure to document the responses from the interviewee. The lead interviewer may then briefly review information about the agency and the nature of the position.

The transition from this phase to the *information-gathering phase* is usually accomplished by an introductory statement that may take the following form:

> We're glad you could meet with us today. We will have the next 60 minutes to discuss the position and your qualifications. Members of our committee will be asking you questions and possibly taking some notes. After that, you will have an opportunity to ask questions about the position and our agency.

In the *information-gathering phase,* the interviewers provide direction without talking too much, certainly no more than 30% of the time. Job-related and follow-up questions should help the applicant describe his or her qualifications more clearly. It is also important to assess the degree of a match among the applicant's career goals, the position, and the work unit/organization's culture. An example of some general and selected diversity-related interview questions are presented in Figures 5.3 and 5.4.

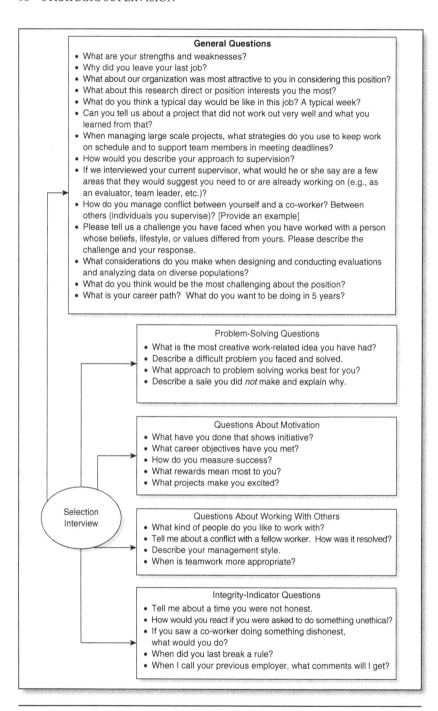

General Questions

- What are your strengths and weaknesses?
- Why did you leave your last job?
- What about our organization was most attractive to you in considering this position?
- What about this research direct or position interests you the most?
- What do you think a typical day would be like in this job? A typical week?
- Can you tell us about a project that did not work out very well and what you learned from that?
- When managing large scale projects, what strategies do you use to keep work on schedule and to support team members in meeting deadlines?
- How would you describe your approach to supervision?
- If we interviewed your current supervisor, what would he or she say are a few areas that they would suggest you need to or are already working on (e.g., as an evaluator, team leader, etc.)?
- How do you manage conflict between yourself and a co-worker? Between others (individuals you supervise)? [Provide an example]
- Please tell us a challenge you have faced when you have worked with a person whose beliefs, lifestyle, or values differed from yours. Please describe the challenge and your response.
- What considerations do you make when designing and conducting evaluations and analyzing data on diverse populations?
- What do you think would be the most challenging about the position?
- What is your career path? What do you want to be doing in 5 years?

Problem-Solving Questions

- What is the most creative work-related idea you have had?
- Describe a difficult problem you faced and solved.
- What approach to problem solving works best for you?
- Describe a sale you did *not* make and explain why.

Questions About Motivation

- What have you done that shows initiative?
- What career objectives have you met?
- How do you measure success?
- What rewards mean most to you?
- What projects make you excited?

Selection Interview

Questions About Working With Others

- What kind of people do you like to work with?
- Tell me about a conflict with a fellow worker. How was it resolved?
- Describe your management style.
- When is teamwork more appropriate?

Integrity-Indicator Questions

- Tell me about a time you were not honest.
- How would you react if you were asked to do something unethical?
- If you saw a co-worker doing something dishonest, what would you do?
- When did you last break a rule?
- When I call your previous employer, what comments will I get?

Figure 5.3 Questions commonly used in selection interviews

Source: From *Human resource management* (11th ed., p. 246), by R. L. Mathis & J. H. Jackson, 2006, South-Western, a part of Cengage Learning, Inc. Reproduced by permission. www.cengage.com/permissions.

- Please tell us a challenge you have faced when you have worked with a person whose ethnicity, religious beliefs, lifestyle, or values differed from yours. Please describe the challenge and your response.
- What does valuing diversity mean to you?
- Please discuss your thoughts about the value of diversity in working with a range of consumers and stakeholders.
- How would you define cultural competence? Please give an example of when you were performing in a culturally competent manner.
- Describe the most difficult challenge you have faced involving a conflict of culture, religious beliefs, values, and lifestyles.

Figure 5.4 Additional questions to consider when addressing diversity, antiracism, and cultural competence

To signal the end of this phase and movement into the third phase *(answering applicant questions)*, the lead interviewer might discuss the next steps and timeline for recruitment, and then say, "Now that we have had the opportunity to discuss your experience, do you have any questions for us?" This statement invites the applicant to ask any questions he or she may have other than "What happens next?" This part of the interview is important because superior candidates often have thoughtful or challenging questions about the agency. However, some candidates (e.g., those who represent certain cultural communities or are of a different economic group) may not feel comfortable asking challenging questions. If questions are asked that you cannot answer at that time, offer to later phone the applicant with the answer.

The last phase of the interview process is *the closing*. Here, interviewers share their appreciation for the applicant's participation while providing information about the closing date of the position and how the lead interviewer can be contacted. In this phase, the lead interviewer, if it has not been mentioned, explains the timeline for the final selection, along with any additional steps that must be taken (i.e., contacting references, a possible follow-up interview, the date when the decision will be made, and how the applicant will be notified). Finally, the applicant is thanked for his or her interest in the position.

At the end of the interview session, provide information about how the applicant can follow up on his or her interview at a later date or to ask any additional questions. Make sure the committee meets soon for a post-interview conference to evaluate the interviewee and settle any discrepancies from the session.

AVOIDING INTERVIEWING MISTAKES

During the interview, try to avoid the following mistakes:

- Not establishing rapport due to a hurried interview, allowing frequent interruptions, not using "active listening" techniques, or making sarcastic or critical remarks. (These problems impede communication by making candidates uncomfortable. The absence of an interview strategy with preplanned questions can also produce incomplete information about the applicant.)
- Dominating the interview with details about the organization, jumping in to fill a pause in the conversation, and not allowing the applicant to present his or her qualifications.
- Deliberately putting the candidate under significant stress. Deliberate or inadvertent stress interviewing is a "high-risk approach" for an employer, as it can destroy rapport, cause resentment, and inhibit the open sharing of information (Mathis & Jackson, 2006, p. 244). However, a realistic, job-related, role-play simulation, although slightly stressful, is a bona fide method for assessing an applicant's skills and abilities.
- Forming a premature judgment about the applicant based on the applicant's unusual physical appearance, mannerisms in speech, or other characteristics. This judgment biases the interviewer's acceptance of important information later in the interview (Koen, 2004).

At the close of the interview, some organizations conduct a tour of the agency to familiarize applicants with the organization. These tours provide applicants a more complete picture of the nature of the organization and the job. These tours may also lead to additional questions or comments from the applicant that can be used in selecting the appropriate employee. (Other agencies reserve these tours for the 1–2 finalists to save staff time.) An exercise with which to practice interviewing skills appears in Figure 5.5.

TWO PRACTICAL INTERVIEWING STRATEGIES

Two techniques may help you maximize the validity, reliability, and usefulness of the interview process. One technique is the Patterned Behavior Description Interview (PBDI), in which a special set of questions is incorporated into the interview process, allowing the interviewers to move beyond asking general questions, and to instead focus on what applicants have actually done in situations similar to ones they will face on the job (Klehe & Latham, 2005). For example, an interviewer might ask an applicant how he or she

Members of a selection committee or graduate students can practice these interviewing skills by dividing into small groups to develop a set of interview questions for a position. One member of each group becomes an "applicant" for the other group, whereas the other members choose who will lead the interview and which persons will ask what questions. The "applicants" from each group switch and are then interviewed by the other group.

After the interview, the applicant and the group debrief by discussing what went well and what aspects of the process could be improved. This interviewing simulation allows members of a selection committee to pilot a set of interview questions and practice interviewing skills.

Materials needed include a detailed position description, flip charts to help the teams to draft possible interview questions, and small private rooms to hold the simulation interviews.

Figure 5.5 Skills application exercise regarding interviewing skills

responded to a hostile client, what circumstances were involved, and how the applicant handled the situation. The answers to this question reveal the specific choices the applicant made in the past. Long-standing patterns of behavior are highly predictive of future behavior.

A second related technique is the *situational interview,* which poses hypothetical questions to applicants, such as "What would you do if . . . ?" and is one of the few approaches to interviewing based on any type of theory, in this case, goal-setting theory (Latham, 1989). Goal-setting theory states that intentions or goals are the immediate precursors to a person's behavior. "The purpose of the situational interview is to identify a potential employee's intentions by presenting that person with a series of job-related incidents, and asking what he or she would do in that situation" (1989, p. 171). The technique involves devising ways of scoring an applicant's response to a "what if" question in relation to what interviewers think would result in effective job performance. Interviewers then use the scoring criteria to rate each applicant. Results from several studies have shown relatively high levels of reliability and validity (see Cohen, 2001, and Christina & Latham, 2004, for specific guidelines regarding how to use this technique). Using both of these interviewing strategies may be useful.

In summary, during the interview phase, train your interviewers regarding the basic phases and principles of the selection process. Develop a list of questions to be asked of each applicant by the same interviewer. The committee should set aside a quiet place for the interview, with phone calls or other interruptions prevented. Choose a person to lead the interview through the opening, information-gathering, response to applicant queries, and closing phases. Finally, establish a realistic timeline for the selection process and inform each applicant of how and when he or she will be notified. Soon after the closing of the interviews, schedule a meeting with the search committee to share and record their impressions of the candidates.

Completing the Employee Selection Process: Reference Checks and Notifying Other Applicants

REFERENCE AND BACKGROUND CHECKS

Once the final candidates have been interviewed, their references may be called to clarify questions or issues that have originated during the interview. Before making an offer of employment, many organizations review the applicant's letter of reference and contact his or her professional references. Note that in some states, the threat of lawsuits and accurate reference information from previous employers limits the organization's ability to screen out undesirable applicants. Criminal background checks are, however, often required. Contact your state labor department for guidance on checking references.

In carrying out this step in the selection process, administrators should be careful to contact a sufficient number of applicant references. Reference checks can be important for obtaining information on how the applicant interacted with his or her fellow employees; exploring questions left unanswered during the interview; and determining work habits, attendance, and other criteria of performance. The most cost-effective approach is to phone references, especially if you use open-ended and nondirective questions that seek to confirm the facts of the person's position (i.e., date of hire, job responsibilities, relationships with colleagues, and rapport with children or parents being served). (See Figure 5.6 for some practical guidelines for checking applicant references.)

People most experienced in checking references should avoid sounding too eager to hire the person. One of the most important questions to ask is whether the reference person would hire this candidate again. This question may elicit information that is valuable for screening candidates. Do not reveal information obtained in reference checks to the candidate. If the person is not hired, state that the person who was selected most nearly met the qualifications of the position. Divulging information from references is a violation of confidentiality, and many organizations are, therefore, becoming wary of releasing information. In fact, as mentioned, many human services agencies and other nonprofit agencies are being advised to only provide information regarding the title, duration, and salary of the former employee's employment. In other words, no information will be provided unless the screening agency can provide a signed *Release of Information* from the applicant, or unless the employee, upon leaving that agency, had signed a release form authorizing the disclosure of performance-related and other reference information.

At some point during the final selection process, and certainly before the employee reports to work, organizations that work with children conduct

1. *Choose a method.* Reference checks can be made by letter or by phone with phone checks more detailed, more honest, and less subject to applicant pressure.

2. *Choose a time.* Many employers in the human services require letters of reference from the final group of candidates only as a means of streamlining the screening process and avoiding undue applicant burden. *If calling references, many times it is better to do so after the interview as a means* of confirming certain qualifications or clarifying questions or inconsistencies in the application and/or interview (e.g., writing ability and performance under stressful conditions).

3. *Obtain at least three references.* Obtain multiple references with phone numbers and addresses so that you can weigh the comments of at least three people.

4. *Be business-like and job-focused when calling references.* Use non-directive, open-ended questions that elicit detailed answers, and do not sound too eager to hire the person. Former employers may be reluctant to disappoint you with negative information.

5. *Ask a preplanned series of questions such as:*
   a. What were Mary's dates of employment with you?
   b. Describe briefly the job the individual has applied for.
   c. What were her duties or responsibilities?
   d. How long did she work for you? In what capacities?
   e. How would you describe the level of her performance?
   f. She tells me she earned $2,800 per month with you.
   g. How was her attendance records? Punctuality?
   h. How did she get along with fellow workers? Clients? With you?
   i. Would you rehire Mary?

6. *Be sure to ask the rehire question.* This may be the most important question you ask, as it checks the honesty of the preceding questions and provides a "bottom line" assessment of that employer's opinion of the applicant.

7. *Do not reveal reference information to candidates.* This information was provided in confidence to you and should not be disclosed unless you are required to document and defend your hiring decision. Above all, do not tell the non-chosen applicants that they were not hired because of poor references. Instead, rely on the fact that the person selected had better qualifications for the position.

Figure 5.6   Strategies for checking applicant references

Sources: Brody, R. (2004) and Jensen, J. (1981).

criminal background checks for all new employees. Therefore, it is important for each organization to be aware of their procedures and to incorporate that need into the recruitment and selection timeline.

SELECTING THE PERSON AND
NOTIFYING THE OTHER APPLICANTS

After contacting references of the highly rated candidates, the selection committee chooses one person by assessing the information collected about his or her job-related qualifications, and the degree to which the candidate's career goals, practice skills, and philosophy of work fit the agency and the position. The person selected is usually offered the position over the phone and, if he or she accepts, is sent a written letter of confirmation, or asked to stop by the agency to confirm acceptance of the offer. Once the acceptance has been received, other applicants should be promptly notified and thanked for their interest in the position and the agency.

Committee members should be encouraged to take their time to weigh carefully all of the information gathered to determine the most qualified and committed applicant. They also should ensure that the agency has a firm commitment from the primary candidate before notifying the other applicants. Finally, the letter notifying the other applicants should be reviewed carefully, ensuring that it is tactfully worded so as to ease their disappointment and to thank them for their interest in the position. (See Figure 5.7.)

«Inside Address»

Dear «Salutation»:

Thank you for your interest in the Social Worker position. We received a large response from a number of qualified people to our advertisement, which made the review and selection process difficult. If time and other resources had permitted, we would have been pleased to invite many more candidates to our agency for interviews; so, as a result, we made some very difficult decisions based primarily on the paper presentation of credentials.

Although your background and experience are impressive, there were other applicants whose qualifications seemed to more closely fit our particular needs; consequently, we are not able to pursue your application further at this time.

Thank you for taking the time to apply for this position. We appreciate your interest in Hobart Child and Family Services.

Sincerely,

Terry S. Johnson, M.S.W,
Director of Clinical Services

Figure 5.7   Sample response letter to job applicants who were not selected for an advertised position

Summary

This chapter has presented an overview of the screening and selection process of staff in nonprofit organizations. The chapter outlined strategies for screening new employees. Sound recruitment and screening practices help ensure that effective staff is hired, and that a minimum number of people are released during the probationary period. Although this process requires organizational, analytical, and interpersonal skills, it is critical for obtaining high-quality personnel. The next chapter discusses the characteristics of an effective work team and what distinguishes a workgroup from a team. Team development strategies are also described.

References

Age Discrimination in Employment Act, P.L. 101-433 (1967).

American Psychological Association. (1996). *Statement on the disclosure of test data.* Berkeley, CA: Author. Retrieved April 12, 2006, from http://www.apa.org/science/disclosu.html

Americans with Disabilities Act, 42 U.S.C. §12010–12213 (1990).

Association of Social Work Boards. (2005). *Social work laws and regulations online comparison guide.* Retrieved June 16, 2005, from http://www.aswbdata.powerlynxhosting.net/

Brody, R. (2004). *Effectively managing human service organizations* (3rd ed.). Thousand Oaks, CA: Sage.

Casey Family Programs. (1997, Sept). *Competencies, recruitment, and selection committee executive summary.* Seattle: Author.

Christina, S., & Latham, G. P. (2004). The situational interview as a predictor of academic and team performance: A study of the mediating effects of cognitive ability and emotional intelligence. *International Journal of Selection and Assessment, 12,* 312.

Cohen, D. (2001). *The talent edge: A behavioral approach to hiring, developing and keeping top performers.* New York: Wiley.

Equal Employment Opportunity Act, P.L. 92-261 (1972).

Evers, A., Anderson, N., & Voskuijl, O. (2005). *The Blackwell handbook of personnel selection.* Malden, MA: Blackwell.

Goodale, J. G. (1989). Effective employment interviewing. In R. W. Eder & G. R. Ferris (Eds.), *The employment interview: Theory, research and practice* (pp. 307–324). Newbury Park, CA: Sage.

Harvard Business School. (2002). *Hiring and keeping the best people.* Boston, MA: Harvard Business School Press.

Holly, T. M. (2003, July). *A hire standard: Improving employee selection can help keep you fully staffed and out of court—Legal trends.* Retrieved February 14, 2006, from http://www.findarticles.com/p/articles/mi_m3495/is_7_48/ai_105438764/print

Jensen, J. (1981). How to hire the right person for the job. *The Grantsmanship Center News, 9*(3), 30–31.

Keller, S. (2004). Employee screening: A real-world cost/benefit analysis. *Risk Management, 51*(11), 28–30.

Kirkwood, W. G., & Ralston, S. M. (1999). Inviting meaningful applicant performances in employment interviews. *The Journal of Business Communication, 36*(1), 55–77.

Klehe, U. C., & Latham, G. P. (2005). The predictive and incremental validity of the situational and patterned behavior description. *International Journal of Selection and Assessment, 13*, 108–115.

Koen, C. M. (2004). A supervisor's guide to effective employment interviewing. *SuperVision, 65*(11), 3–6.

Latham, G. P. (1989). The reliability, validity, and practicality of the situational interview. In R. W. Eder & G. R. Ferris (Eds.), *The employment interview—Theory, research and practice* (pp. 169–182). Newbury Park, CA: Sage.

Lavigna, B. (2005, April). *Winning the war for talent: Part II—Some solutions.* Retrieved October 21, 2005, from http://proquest.umi.com/pqdweb?index=154&sid=4&srch mode =1&vinst=PROD&fmt=3

Mathis, R. L., & Jackson, J. H. (2006). *Human resource management* (11th ed.). Mason, OH: Thomson Southwestern.

O'Leary, T. (2002). *Using your team for recruiting—A retention strategy for the human resources professional.* Retrieved June 20, 2007, from http://humanresources.about .com/library/weekly/aa022402a.htm

Strauss, S. G., Miles, J. A., & Levesque, L. L. (2001). The effects of video conference, telephone, and face-to-face media on interviewer and applicant judgments in employment interviews. *Journal of Management, 27*, 363–381.

Tvrdik, B. (2007). Hiring good employees. Retrieved July 17, 2007, from http://www.agmrc .org/agmrc/business/operationalbusiness/hiringgoodemployees/htm

Tyler, K. (2005, May). *Train for smarter hiring: train hiring managers to communicate their needs to HR as well as to ask candidates probing questions.* Retrieved February 14, 2006, from http://www.findarticles.com/p/articles/mi_m3495/is_5_50/ai_n13721392/print

Vocational Rehabilitation Act and Rehabilitation Act, 29 U.S.C. §794d (1974).

Web-Based References

American Psychological Association. (1996). *Statement on the disclosure of test data.* Berkeley, CA: Author. Retrieved April 12, 2006, from http://www.apa.org/ science/disclosu.html

Bristow, N. (1999). *Using your HR systems to build organizational success.* Orem, UT: Targeted Learning. Retrieved March 20, 2007, from www.targetedlearning.com

Suggested Readings

Anderson, N. (2003). Applicant and recruiter reactions to new technology selection. *International Journal of Selection and Assessment, 2*, 121–136.

Arthur, D. (2004). *The employee recruitment and retention handbook.* New York: Amacom Books.

Bristow, N. (1999). *Using your HR systems to build organizational success.* Orem, UT: Targeted Learning. Retrieved May 15, 2007, from www.targetedlearning.com

Harvard Business School. (2006). *Hiring smart for competitive advantage.* Cambridge, MA: Harvard Business School Press.

Thompson, C. B. (2002). *Interviewing techniques for managers.* New York: McGraw Hill.

6

Facilitating Groups and Teams

Jean Kruzich and Nancy Timms

Introduction

This chapter begins by distinguishing between workgroups and teams. Choosing the type of group format to use is an important organizational decision with long-term ramifications. Next, criteria are presented for evaluating a workgroup's effectiveness. The remaining elements of the chapter describe developmental stages for both groups and teams, along with practice tools and exercises to help supervisors facilitate movement through and success with each stage.

The current emphasis on workgroups reflects a growing awareness that the complexity of work across a wide variety of settings, including human services organizations, increasingly requires collaboration. Over two decades ago, Peter Senge (1990) noted that groups are the fundamental learning unit in an organization. Group learning is a process in which groups take action, obtain and reflect on feedback, and make changes to adapt or improve (Edmondson, 2003). Supervisors are in a unique position to support their staff members' development as effective workgroup members and leaders.

ARE WE A GROUP OR A TEAM?

Two factors that distinguish groups from teams are the level of interdependency and the degree of commonality (Williams, 1996). Interdependence means that team members cannot achieve their goals single-handedly but must rely on each other to reach shared objectives. Workgroup members may share the same office space and successfully meet their work outcomes with low interdependence when the nature of their work activities does not require members to work effectively as a team. The other distinguishing factor is the degree to which the goals of the team override the goals of individual members. Teams exist to achieve a shared goal, and they produce outcomes for which members have collective responsibility.

Working groups are widespread and effective in agency settings where individual accountability is most important (Katzenbach & Smith, 1993). Consisting of people who share information, perspectives, and decision making, working groups focus on individual goals and accountabilities (Thompson, 2004). Teams differ fundamentally from working groups because they require both individual and mutual accountability; rewards are based on both individual performance and the individual's contribution to the team's overall performance (Thompson, 2004). Only when the degree of commonality is high does it make sense to think of the group as a team and to treat it accordingly.

Because of their higher levels of interdependency and commonality, teams need to meet different requirements than other working groups in the following four areas (Williams, 1996) and supervisors need to understand the distinction between teams and other forms of working groups in order to support a group format that best meets the group's performance challenge.

1. *Expectations:* In terms of the nature of relationships among group members, a team requires high levels of commitment, involvement, cooperation, and support. In other types of groups, the requirement can be to coexist comfortably with each other even with minimal levels of support and cooperation.

2. *Communications:* All groups develop a communication structure that includes many dimensions of communication—level of formality, forum, frequency, function, and parameters. All effective workgroups need to define clearly the appropriate structure within the group. Teams are likely to require more sophisticated communication structures because the need for exchanging information, group decision making, developing openness, and building relationships is higher than in other types of workgroups.

3. *Process:* Team members need to work well together because of greater dependency on each member in order to accomplish their goals effectively. Teams are more likely to take the time to decide on procedural processes, including agenda setting, length, time, and frequency of meetings, who leads meetings as well as group processes for facing and resolving conflict and how leadership responsibility is shared. Although all groups work better if they are managed well, problems in this area are less likely to lead to a crisis within a working group than they are within a team.

4. *Intimacy:* How well people need to get to know each other and therefore how open they need to be with each other varies with the type of workgroup. The level of intimacy between group members should be dictated by the degree and nature of the interdependency. Because intimacy involves disclosure and risk, you want to generate it only if needed for the team's effectiveness.

There is less need to focus on team-building exercises if it is a workgroup and not a team.

Case Example: An example of a group would be a juvenile justice advisory committee meeting quarterly. Members represent agencies throughout the county that work with at-risk youth. The purpose of the meeting is to hear from each agency about continued and/or new services being offered and to meet the funding requirements for the juvenile detention facility. Although the agencies all serve youth, they vary greatly from homeless shelters to tall ship adventures to probation officers. Therefore, despite some commonality, the goals of the individual agency are not secondary to the goals of the juvenile justice committee.

An example of a team would be the multidisciplinary hospice team made up of doctors, nurses, chaplains, social workers, physical therapists, bath aids, and volunteers. Although each discipline has its focus, in this team, the individual goals are determined by the team goal of providing the best care for the dying patient and his/her family and what each member of the team does affects achievement of the common goal.

How supervisors conceptualize a workgroup is important. Although team structures are sometimes perceived as being more effective or preferable to working groups, their effectiveness depends on the values of the organization and nature of the work. Because of the complexity of human services work, it may seem as though the only type of group that can be used is a team, but as evidenced by the case example above, there are many situations where a workgroup rather than a team is needed.

Group work, whether workgroups or teams, requires skilled supervisor facilitation to increase the effectiveness of services provided. A supervisor's knowledge of group development and his/her skills in creating supportive learning environments influence his/her ability to increase the effectiveness of the staff she/he supervise as well as service outcomes. For example, recent studies of hospital intensive care units found a link between group work and patient mortality rates (Wheelan, Burchill, & Tilin, 2003). More specifically, staff members on intensive care units with lower mortality rates perceived their staff groups as less engaged in conflict with authority figures, more organized, and more trusting of each other than did members of units with higher mortality rates. Additionally, patients have also been found to have significantly better outcomes across multiple dimensions when served by professional teams with higher levels of mutual respect (Wells, Jinnett, Alexander, Lichtenstein, Liu, & Zazzali, 2006).

Having acknowledged that not all groups are not teams, the term "workgroup" or "task group" would be used interchangeably when referring to all types of groups with "team" reserved for instances where it specifically applies.

Characteristics of Effective Workgroups and Teams

SIZE

Research studies indicate that size does influence group functioning with larger groups having lower member satisfaction, less cohesion, and reduced productivity (Wheelan & Mckeage, 1993). The increased participation made possible in smaller groups increases the attraction of the group members. Although the optimum size is related to the task, a survey of 500 managers identified five or six as the optimum size: large enough to include members with differing skills but small enough that those reticent members are still willing to contribute (Thompson, 2007). As group size grows beyond seven or eight, contributions may be stifled; more assertive or aggressive individuals may dominate and become the central spokespersons for the group, whereas the other members assume passive roles (Patton & Downs, 2003). In addition, with increasing size, responsibility is more diffuse; individuals are more likely to view their contribution as less important and group members' concern about getting credit for their work increases, which can lead to individuals slacking off (Thompson, 2007).

GOAL CLARITY

For a group to function effectively, members need to have a shared commitment to achieving group goals. Group members identify with each other when the group goal is important to them. The supervisor has primary responsibility for defining the task in a way that all members know exactly what they are to accomplish and to frame the task in ways that link performance to compelling organizational goals. The group supervisor needs to understand the expectations clearly, the needs and goals of the stakeholders, and be able to translate how and what may be delivered, including inherent barriers and challenges to the group.

SHARED LEADERSHIP

This chapter adopts a shared leadership perspective. Leadership should be executed by the members of the group and not solely by the group supervisor. In this alternative framework, leadership is not primarily determined by a position of authority but by an individual's capacity to influence peers and by the leadership needs of the group at a given stage of development (Pearce & Conger, 2003). Leadership is perceived as a shared process, of enhancing the collective and individual capacity of people to accomplish their work roles effectively. It does not require an individual who can perform all of the essential leadership functions, only a set of people who collectively perform them. Although there may be little initial opportunity for shared leadership in a newly formed group, the leader's design decisions and, later, the expectations that the leader sets for group interaction and performance will contribute to the ultimate development of shared leadership (Pearce, 2004).

Earlier leadership theories viewed group leadership, power, and authority as vested in a single, appointed, vertical leader who served as the primary source of influence, wisdom, and guidance to the group. In contrast, distributed leadership recognizes that some leadership functions (e.g., making important decisions) may be shared by several members of a group, some leadership functions may be allocated to individual members, and that a particular leadership function may be performed by different people at different times in the group's life.

Although some of the vertical leader's traditional roles are undertaken and shared by group members, important roles remain for the vertical leadership in the shared leadership process. Working to develop leadership skills in group members, filling the skill areas where group members' skills are lacking or still developing, and nurturing group members' confidence and desire to share leadership are key roles for the designated leader (Houghton, Nick, & Manz, 2003).

EMOTIONAL INTELLIGENCE

Although the ability to perceive and express emotions, understand, manage, and use emotions is perceived as an individual characteristic (Mayer & Salovey, 1997), emotional intelligence is crucial for workgroups. Studies have found that a group's ability to manage emotions enhances their information-processing capability in a way that enables greater ability to motivate, plan, and achieve (Druskat & Wolff, 2001). A group's Emotional Intelligence climate includes group empathic concern, emotion management and norms, as well as acceptable standards of behavior within a group that are shared by the group's members. Although norms usually develop gradually and informally as group members learn what behaviors are necessary for the group to function more effectively, it also is possible for the norm development process to be addressed explicitly early in the groups' life (Feldman, 1984). Postmes, Spears, and Cihangir (2001) demonstrated that when norms were established for critical thinking as opposed to norms for consensus decision making, groups achieved an improvement in the quality of their decisions.

Supervisors need to know how to minimize destructive reactions to emotional events (e.g., conflict) to facilitate increased group performance. These results point to a major role for the supervisor in helping to ensure their group has sufficiently well-developed norms. In the case of conflict, the supervisor can initiate a discussion that involves the group jointly developing positive group norms for members interacting constructively with each other before, during, and after conflicts. The supervisor may consider a range of options, including developing preventive norms that prescribe positive interaction behaviors or proscribe negative interaction behaviors before they occur.

WORK GROUP PSYCHOLOGICAL SAFETY

Psychological safety refers to a shared belief by group members that the group is a safe place for interpersonal risk taking. Lencioni (2005) notes that, for a group to establish trust, the members, beginning with the leader, need to be willing to take risks without a guarantee of success. Learning behaviors—such as seeking feedback, sharing information, asking for help, and talking about errors and experimenting—involve taking risks. The sense of perceived threat invoked in discussing problems or acknowledging difficulties limits individuals' willingness to engage in these behaviors, even when it would benefit the group or organization. Psychological safety reflects a sense of confidence that the group will not embarrass, reject, or punish someone for speaking up; this confidence stems from mutual respect and trust. Psychological safety extends beyond interpersonal trust to encompass an interpersonal climate characterized by trust, respect for each other's competence, and caring about each other as people. The next section describes the stages of group development. Recognizing the predictable stages of group development is a crucial skill for a supervisor to be able to facilitate a workgroup effectively.

The Five Stages of Group Development

OVERVIEW

The stages of group development may be difficult to recognize at times because member behaviors are not exclusively confined to their designated stages. Although groups move through stages that can be identified and described, group development does not proceed on a precise schedule so that even groups of similar ages may be dealing with different developmental issues (Buzaglo & Wheelan, 1999). While one may observe behaviors from all five stages in a single meeting, the majority of member behaviors and dominant themes will usually reflect the current stage of the group. Table 6.1 includes a model of group development that provides a framework within which a workgroup can be viewed and compared (Wheelan, 2005). After the discussion of each stage of group development is a menu of exercises and tools supervisors can use to help strengthen groups operating at each stage. These tools are designed to assist in the process of becoming a mature, high-performing task group. Note how many of these facilitative behaviors relate to a task, process, or relationship focus. The next sections highlight each of the five stages.

Table 6.1   Group Development: Stages, Behaviors, Tasks, and Skills

Stages	Members' behavior	Leader's tasks	Leader's skills
1. Dependence and inclusion *(Forming):* People are recruited or assigned to work together on a common task.	• Questioning the leader about the group's purpose, appropriate behaviors of members, and leader's role • Attributing in-group status to members on the basis of outside-of-group information • Following and cooperating with the leader may be inconsistent • Discussion patterns are jerky, with long periods of silence	• Provide structure regarding boundaries of the group (such as the frequency and place of meetings, the organization's reason for forming the group, timelines for achieving the group's task) • Offer guidance in setting directions for the accomplishment of the task • Solicit each member's opinions and ideas • Encourage dialogue	• Awareness of a personal leadership style • Effective communication • Thorough knowledge of the fit between the group's task and the organizational goals
2. Counter-dependency and fight *(Storming):* Individual and subgroup differences of opinions, values, skills, and interests start to surface.	• Expressing opinions and disagreements • Exploring the degrees of individual power and challenging the leader's role and style • Attending to and/or avoiding the group's task • Emergence of cliques and bonds	• Discuss the group's decision-making process • Model appropriate awareness of self and others • Provide the group with the resources necessary to accomplish the task • Help the group to establish procedures and norms for the resolution of conflict	• Management of different values, behaviors, and skills • Awareness of her own and others' personal strengths and limitations

(Continued)

Table 6.1 (Continued)

Stages	Members' behavior	Leader's tasks	Leader's skills
3. Trust and structure *(Norming):* The group focuses on the need for order and guidelines for how to work together.	• Stabilizing the group's purpose, authority relationships, individual levels, and types of participation • Exhibiting in-group humor • Emergence of informal leadership • Establishing procedures for the resolution of conflict and the accomplishment of the task	• Adhere to the group's established structure and procedures • Ensure that the group's actions are in accordance with what the group *really* wants to do • Infuse the group with enthusiasm and energy • Reward individual and group efforts • Acknowledge and reinforce informal leadership • Protect the group from outside interferences	• Mentoring • Management of agreements • Balancing work with play • Buffering the group from some of the needlessly stressful aspects of ongoing program operations
4. Work *(Performing):* The group delivers the completed task.	• Producing results: alignment of members' energies and interests with the group's task	• Attend to the group's need for fine tuning its skills and attitudes • Develop mechanisms for the continued monitoring of the group	• Visioning • Listening with a "third ear" (i.e., using intuition and empathy skills) • Evaluation
5. Termination and ending *(Adjourning):* The original need for the group no longer exists.	• Assessing process and product • Dissolving the group	• Publicly acknowledge the group's accomplishments	• Positive regard of self and others

Source: From "Developmental sequence in small groups," by B. Tuckman, 1965, *Psychological Bulletin, 63,* pp. 384–399. Copyright 1965 by American Psychological Association. Reprinted with permission. From "Stages of small group development revisited," by B. Tuckman & M. Jensen, 1977, *Group and Organizational Studies, 2,* pp. 419–427. Beverly Hills, CA: Sage. Copyright 1977 by Sage. Reprinted with permission.

STAGE 1: FORMING

In the first stage, there is uncertainty about both the task itself and the group members. Although the major focus of workgroups is increasing the quality of services to clients, groups must also provide a place where staff can meet their interpersonal needs. Schutz (1966) identified three types of interpersonal needs that individuals bring to any group: inclusion, control, and affection. Together the dynamics generated by these needs create a group dynamics level that is separate from the "task" level of the group but can interact with this task level. Members often try to ignore this "interpersonal underworld," and in short-term projects or workgroups organized primarily for information sharing, this may be possible without interfering significantly with group performance. Recognizing how the importance of interpersonal needs varies with the stage of the group's development helps the leader identify ways to help satisfy them within the group. The leader's responsibility in the forming stage includes helping group members establish a sense of safety, get to know one another, and develop a shared understanding of the group's purpose, tasks, and management expectations. Because of the lack of familiarity, this is a time when members are on their best behavior. Members are getting to know each other and discovering how they fit into the group system. Politeness, cooperation, minimal conflict, and limited participation are the rule rather than the exception. This is a time in the group process to discuss group norms, values, goals, and mission. A group may be stuck at Stage 1 if the members do not need to work interdependently to achieve their goals, the supervisor does not provide sufficient structure, or the leader provides little opportunity for members to participate.

Case Example: A statewide child protection agency failed a federal review/audit. Program improvement projects were required. One of the projects dealt with revamping the entire computer data base system. A task force was formed made up of social workers and information technology workers. The group was to meet monthly. The first several meetings were disorganized and confusing as members did not know each other, did not know how to proceed, and did not know who had what roles. It took several months to get to know each other before the real work could begin. It is now 2 years later and the group has been so productive that they also made recommendations about future technology that would benefit the field.

STAGE 2: STORMING

The second stage begins when members begin to feel safe within the group structure. The group's goal at Stage 2 is to develop a group culture, a unified set of shared perceptions about values, norms, and goals. To reach its goal, some degree of conflict with the leader and among group members is inevitable (Wheelan, 2005). As in any relationship, after the preliminary "get acquainted period," members begin to reveal more of their personalities. It becomes easier to exhibit idiosyncrasies; demand privilege; disagree with the group goals, members, and leadership style and standing; allow real feelings to be known; and be more vocal. Members test and find their own boundaries, the boundaries of the other members, and the group.

Dealing With Conflict. There is a tendency for supervisors to perceive conflict as counterproductive and as a judgment of their ability or inability to lead. It is important to remember that some conflict at this stage is productive, normal, and necessary if the group is to move successfully to the next stage of development. When supervisors think conflict is an indictment of their leadership skills, they begin to focus on personal perceived failings rather than on the group process. Consequently, this stage of development can be painful and quite uncomfortable for supervisors. If the supervisor can step back and look at the big picture of the process and use basic conflict resolution skills (listening, validating, finding commonalities, and focusing on issues not personalities), this stage will be less painful to the supervisor and the group members will develop confidence in their ability to handle differences.

The supervisor also needs to remember that a major task of Stage 2 leadership is to help group members' deal with their differences with each other and with the leader. With a systemic view of this group dynamic, the supervisor can observe the jockeying for positions, manage conflict, and help the group through the stage. The ability of group members to disagree and resolve their differences helps the group develop a sense of trust. A group may be stuck at Stage 2 if a supervisor avoids conflict. In this case, the group never has the opportunity to work through differences in members' perceptions and values concerning their work.

Case Example: A government entity colocated economic services, labor and industries, and child protection into a new building last year. The safety committee was created to meet Occupational Safety and Health Administration requirements. Members of the committee did not interact with each other except at the safety committee meetings. There had never been much dissension as they politely scheduled fire drills and talked about what to do in case of tornados or hurricanes. On this occasion, the committee met for an emergency meeting when the building manager learned that a client had threatened to shoot up everyone in the building. It was well known that this client had a history of violence as well as mental illness. This was considered a serious threat, and the police were notified. Committee members were no longer sitting back politely as their fear and concerns for their safety emerged. The discussion became contentious and lively as the committee members talked about their feelings of vulnerability and why this was not dealt with before it became an emergency, as well as what could and could not be done.

STAGE 3: NORMING

The third stage of development is one of the group developing internal respect and a group-like structure. The Stage 3 leadership tasks are to demonstrate sufficient trust in members so that they are comfortable to challenge the leader's decisions when they disagree. Common goals need to be developed along with an action plan through dialogue with the group. More members of the group take leadership responsibilities, becoming intragroup specialists. Leaders who take on too much of the responsibility run the risk of becoming so involved in the work that they overlook opportunities to help the group develop into an increasingly competent unit. The supervisor takes on a consulting rather than a directing role.

This stage of the group is characterized by more mature negotiations about goals, roles, and procedures (Buzaglo & Wheelan, 1999). There is less conflict and greater attention to developing positive relationships with one another. Collaboration increases as task completion and the goals of the group become the focus. There is a sense that the group can accomplish tasks that would not otherwise be completed by the individual. Additionally, there is a sense of identification and satisfaction with being part of the group.

Task and Process Roles Become Especially Important at Stage 3

All groups operate simultaneously on two levels—a task level that is concerned with the accomplishment of concrete goals and the process dimension concerned with the social–emotional needs of group members. Task roles are behaviors members perform that help the group achieve its goal or complete its task. Maintenance process roles are behaviors that enhance the group climate and help build cohesiveness. To be successful, both task and social–emotional roles have to be performed and ideally distributed among group members. Distinct from group roles are individual roles—behaviors performed to satisfy an individual's personal goals—often at the expense of the group's well-being. Some of the individual roles such as the blocker and dominator are disruptive to the group. Others, like the digresser and withdrawer, deprive the group of the energy and input the member might have contributed if he or she were engaged in group-oriented roles. Table 6.2 lists the roles included in each of the three categories.

Norms Are a Crucial Component of Group Process

Individuals who come together in groups tend to develop standards that prescribe acceptable behavior in a group or agency. Norms are the "ought to's"

Table 6.2   Group Roles

Task roles (behaviors that help accomplish the group task)	Maintenance/process roles (behaviors that keep the group harmonious)	Individual roles (self-oriented behaviors)
• initiating • clarifying • seeking information and opinions • giving information and opinions • summarizing • evaluating • consensus taking	• encouraging • harmonizing • gate-keeping • standard setting • observing • tension relieving • following	• blocking • dominating • digressing • withdrawing • attacking

Source: From "Functional roles of group members," by K. D. Benne & P. Sheats, 1948, *Journal of Social Issues, 4*, pp. 41–49. Copyright 1948 by Wiley-Blackwell. Reprinted with permission.

of behavior. They are what are considered acceptable behavior as prescribed by groups. Although often not written down or even discussed, norms can regulate the way people interact with each other even more than official agency policy. The power of group-level norms is highlighted by research indicating that group-level differences in norms for reporting medication errors in hospitals had the potential to limit organizational learning about preventing similar errors in the future (Edmondson, 2003) (See Table 6.3 for the "What Is Normal Around Here?" worksheet.) An example is an official agency policy that the workday starts at 8:30 a.m., but the norm is that no one will take exception to staff arriving at 9 a.m.

Norms usually develop gradually and informally as group members get to know each other and determine what behaviors are necessary for the group to function. Most norms develop in one of the following four ways as a result of (a) explicit statements made by supervisors or coworkers; these may include a group leader dictating norms or ground rules about being late, making personal phone calls, or forbidding the consumption of alcohol at lunchtime; (b) a critical event in a group's history, for example, a supervisor having a car accident after a staff lunch where alcohol was served may lead to no longer going as a staff to a restaurant for lunch; (c) primacy, how things were done the first time the group met, can influence norms such as where people sit in subsequent meetings; or (d) as a result of behaviors carried over from past situations such as meetings being scheduled on Wednesday mornings (Feldman, 1984).

Table 6.3   What Is Normal Around Here?

Start or continue		Do less of
Do more of		**Stop doing**
Reinforce		**Extinguish**

Case Example: Aaron is 12 years old. He has been in the care of his grandparents for 2 years. His mother is a heroin addict, and his father uses methamphetamines. Neither has the ability to offer Aaron a stable home. Aaron is a challenging child, as he has been diagnosed with attention-deficit hyperactivity disorder (otherwise known as ADHD) and frequently acts out in school. His grandparents wonder whether they can keep him as he heads into his teen years. About a year ago, a group of child welfare social workers, teachers, home support specialists, therapists, psychiatrists, probation officers, police officers, school counselors, and the grandparents met to try to stabilize the placement. The group members now know each other and have processed the different perspectives that each member brings to the table. In the last 6 months, they have developed a plan that everyone in this child's life can follow. He has a consistent response from everyone in his life. Even though Aaron's behaviors escalated when the plan was first enacted, the response from the community and the group was consistent. In the past couple of months, his behaviors have improved. This group feels, and is, productive.

STAGE 4: PERFORMING

An effective and productive workgroup is one that has successfully navigated the earlier stages of development and has emerged as a mature, high-performing unit capable of achieving its goals (Wheelan, 2005). This is the time when the group is the most effective and productive. Less time is needed for interpersonal issues. Members feel secure enough to express positive and negative emotions in the group, although communication is usually positive with members supporting and acknowledging each other's contributions. The group is committed to working on the task. Roles are defined, and members assume leadership roles for delegated tasks. There is a good flow of information, feedback, and communication. Unfortunately, many individuals have never been members of a Stage 4 group.

At this stage of group development, the "group" has taken on a life of its own. The group has become a "learning group" where data are collected on individual and group performance and are used to revise their ways of working. Members know and accept their roles. This stage does not need much direction from the supervisor. The task, how the task will be completed, and the confidence that the group will be successful is high. How does the supervisor keep the group in this productive "work" stage? As is true in any long-term relationship, the supervisor should provide opportunities for feedback on the group process and goal clarity. This reexamination will refresh the group and will reenergize their commitment. This effort will also reduce any tendency to get off track from the agreed upon goals or to become stagnant. Supervisors can use the "What Is Normal Around Here?" exercise in Table 6.3 to assess group performance.

A second way to provide support during the work stage is to encourage creativity, humor, and fun. Levity and laughter promote enjoyment of the process, as well as commitment to being part of the group. Included in this fun might be acknowledging birthdays, anniversaries, and other attainments or even "mis-steps" to help maintain group cohesion. Another supervisory task during this stage is to acknowledge publicly the strengths, efforts, and successes of individuals and the group as a whole. A little positive reinforcement goes a long way in keeping workers interested in and motivated to do the task.

Case Example: The probation officers at juvenile detention have been together a long time. The senior officer has worked in the agency for 30 years, and the newest officer has been there for 10 years. The 10 officers have weathered autocratic agency directors, budget cutbacks, floods, and the death of colleagues and children on their caseloads. They are attuned to each other from years of working side by side. When one officer is out because of illness, another will pick up the slack and the production continues without missing a beat. The group works like a well-oiled machine.

STAGE 5: ADJOURNING

Workgroups with a single task and a specified deadline have a clear ending. For other workgroups, their ending point is less obvious because of multiple tasks and performing the same task multiple times. In the latter case of continuously operating, groups' beginnings and endings are created by organizational processes based on timelines, including quarterly financial reporting periods, annual audits, and yearly staff retreats. Hackman and Wageman (2005) suggest there is a human need for temporal markers; hence, if they do not exist, we create them and use them to pace our activities. For the supervisor, it is important to recognize that the end of a performance period or completion of a major task is a time particularly suited to educational coaching interventions. In other words, group members are less anxious than they were in the performing stage. The group supervisor's role is to support members in taking the time to reflect on their performance and help generate collective learning from their experience that will strengthen the group's capabilities as a task-performing unit (Hackman & Wageman, 2005).

A case example of a group ending with the completion of a task would be Aaron's group who, after being together for 2 years, has seen Aaron stabilize and have stopped meeting. Aaron has not had acted out in school and has completed his probation, and his grandparents finally feel that they will be able to raise this child and have filed for nonparental custody.

Another type of ending is represented by the transitions when someone leaves or enters the group. Supervisory groups are often ongoing, and there is no clear termination stage. Yet, because long-term members and group leaders may leave a group, the leader and group need to recognize that the composition of the group has changed and attention should be paid to acknowledging the changes, and their impact on the member and on the remaining members. The mature group tends to evaluate their work together, give feedback, and express feelings about each other and the group. Processing what is valuable to individual members can significantly enhance their ability to work effectively in the future. Acknowledgment of the transition can take place through dialogue, ritual, or protocol.

Case Example: A group of hospital medical social workers has been together for the last 2 years. Samantha gives notice that she will be leaving next month to return to the university to pursue a PhD. At a staff meeting, the group discusses its appreciation of what Samantha has brought to the group, the loss to the group, and how the group will go about selecting a new member and re-building.

Special Aspects of Group Supervision

ARE HUMAN SERVICES GROUPS UNIQUE
IN TERMS OF THE SKILL SET SUPERVISORS NEED?

Unlike manufacturing or many service industries, human services professionals intervene with unique individuals, not standardized objects. Professional decisions often involve complex ethical and legal dilemmas. Although professionals carry out much of their activities in private, the sensitivity of the work requires clear and careful oversight (Hasenfeld & Abbott, 1992). Because of these factors, supervisor-led groups are more prevalent in human services than in other types of organizations where self-governing or self-managing teams are more pervasive. Members of teams in manufacturing or business organizations where the "raw material" is nonhuman, responds predictably, and is inanimate, are likely to have far more authority. Human services groups must contend with pressurized, complex, publicly scrutinized decisions that have major impacts on clients served, their families, and the larger community and as a result have direct oversight.

To develop a high performance work unit, a supervisor needs to possess knowledge, skills, and an orientation that is different from what the supervisor needs when interacting individually with staff. To be effective at improving work-group performance, supervisors must be prepared to adjust their leadership style to meet the developmental stages of the group as presented earlier. A group leader's style requires an interpersonal orientation as opposed to an intrapersonal one (Burns, 1994). An intrapersonal style that focuses on individual group members impedes group process, whereas an interpersonal style that focuses on facilitation of the group members' interactions and the quality of those interactions improves processes. By understanding critical aspects of group functioning and being familiar with tools that can support group development, the supervisor assumes the knowledge-building role that is an important component of creating a learning organization. By adopting such an approach, the supervisor enhances her practice as well as the competency of those with whom she works.

HOW DO WE MEASURE GROUP EFFECTIVENESS?

The criteria used to judge a group's effectiveness is an important factor that guides the design of the group structure, its decision-making processes, and the attention given to task and process dimensions. Hackman and Wageman's (2005) criteria for group effectiveness includes (a) the group's product or service meets its stakeholders' standards for quantity, quality, and timeliness; (b) the social processes used to carry out the work enhance members' capability of working together interdependently in the future; and (c) the experience contributes positively to the learning and personal well-being of individual group members. Although the first criterion alone may be sufficient to judge a group that will disband after it completes a short-term project, ongoing workgroups need to be able to learn from their experience so their competence increases over time. Furthermore, the second and third criteria will only be met if group members increase their capability to work together. These later criteria are what group learning is all about.

To build a learning group, supervisors must understand group process and develop skills in using successful group interventions (Buzaglo & Wheelan, 1999). They include the following strategies:

1. Perform accurate assessment of the group's current developmental level.

2. Maintain focus on the group as a system and on how it is functioning—not on individuals, personalities, or emotional issues.

3. Provide training for members about groups' developmental stages so they can take more active, informed actions to improve functioning.

4. Devise strategies that allow group members to be involved in deciding what to change and how to make changes in their group's functioning.

Group Facilitation Tools

The effectiveness of a group intervention is dependent not only on the supervisor's awareness of available tools and ability to use a tool or exercise but also on the group's readiness for the intervention. Recent literature suggests that a group's readiness for coaching interventions varies systematically across its' life cycle (Hackman & Wageman, 2005). Groups that are functioning at higher stages of development are more productive and more effective in accomplishing their goals than groups at lower stages (Wheelan, 2005). Recognizing the crucial relationship between group readiness and timing in introducing interventions, we have organized these tools by the stage of group development presented above where they are most likely to help strengthen groups and assist in the process of developing a mature, high-performing group.

STAGE 1 TOOLS

Assessment Inventories

A learning group requires members who are aware of how they and those they work with learn. One way to enhance self and group awareness of this is with assessments. To be effective in helping individuals learn, the leader needs to know how a staff person takes in information. One key to effective skill development is the ability to identify and understand the different ways staff process information and acquire skills. If group members are to share the teaching role and learn effectively, they need to know how they and their group members process information. In a group of six or seven members, different learning styles will most likely be present. Lacking knowledge of individual learning styles, we tend to assume that others take in information the way we do, which is an untenable assumption.

Another major benefit of assessment tools identified by Lencioni (2005) is their use in helping to improve trust by giving group members an opportunity to demonstrate vulnerability in a low-risk way and help group members understand one another's strengths, limitations, and preferences so they can avoid making false attributions about behaviors and intentions.

The three assessment tools described below vary in their focus, breadth (number of dimensions addressed), and purpose. The Myers-Briggs Type Indicator (MBTI) (http://www.myersbriggs.org/my-mbti-personality-type/mbti-basics/) is probably the most frequently used assessment tool in work settings. It aims to help individuals identify their preferences for taking in information, organizing their work, communicating, and making decisions. The original measure is copyrighted and must be purchased and administered by a qualified person.

The Keirsey Temperament Sorter is an alternative choice. It measures the same areas and can be completed online and scored for free: http://www.keirsey.com/. In addition, the measure and scoring instructions are included in David Keirsey's (1998) book, *Please understand me II: Temperament, character, intelligence.*

The VARK (Visual, Aural, Read/write, and Kinesthetic) is a set of 13 multiple-choice questions designed to reveal an individual's preferred modes of receiving and working with information and the ways in which they prefer to deliver their own communication (Fleming & Bonwell, 2009). The VARK inventory identifies five possible learning preferences: visual, aural, reading/writing, kinesthetic, and multimodal. The VARK is a copyrighted measure and can be accessed at http://www.vark-learn.com/english/index.asp. A downloadable print version with scoring instructions for the instrument is available at http://www.vark-learn.com/english/page.asp?p=advice. The Web site gives permission to complete the measure without charge to teachers and students, not professionals or trainers. The VARK Web site also provides help sheets for individuals to develop additional, effective strategies as well as to increase understanding of other's learning preferences as well as ideas about how to best communicate information with individuals with different styles.

Studies demonstrate that individuals learn more easily and remember better, when they are taught through their preferred learning style. There are multiple benefits for a supervisor and supervisees to complete this brief inventory. Discussion of results alerts members to the variety of ways individuals learn. If two or three members of the group prefer kinesthetic learning, their learning will be greatly strengthened by role-playing, whereas members whose predominant style is aural will learn best by listening to information and discussing it with others. For the new supervisor, identifying the kinds of learning experiences that will best support group members' skill development is helpful.

Another option is The Index of Learning Styles (ILS), a psychometrically supported measure designed to assess preferences on four dimensions: sensing–intuitive, visual–verbal, active–reflective, and sequential–global (Felder & Spurlin, 2005). The ILS can be completed and scored at no cost by individuals who wish to assess their own preferences at http://www.engr.ncsu.edu/learn ingstyles/ilsweb.html.

In addition to increasing the effectiveness of learning strategies used both in individual and in group supervision, this information helps the supervisor identify strategies he or she can use to maximize staff learning. If we are to follow the common adage, "Start where the individual is," we need to recognize different learning styles and be attentive to clues that tell us how a particular staff member processes information. The aim of assessment tool results is to provide information that can be used to enhance individual worker's job performance; assessment results should never be used as a rationale for poor performance.

Contracting

One of the major reasons for group ineffectiveness is that individuals come with different expectations, wants, and needs, and yet these differences are not discussed or resolved. If unaddressed, these concerns are likely to go "underground" and become a source of hidden agendas that detract from the group's stated tasks. The Hopes and Concerns exercise, adapted from Herman and Korenich's work (1977), is a contracting exercise that performs several important functions. First, it allows individuals to begin to know what is important to different members of the group. Second, it allows for the sharing of concerns. Although it is not unusual for group members to share hopes for their future work together, sharing concerns is equally important and happens much less frequently. The value of sharing concerns is that it begins to develop a norm that the group is a place where members can acknowledge difficult issues. Third, group member responses provide a basis for contracting and the beginnings of joint development of group norms. The Hopes and Concerns exercise may be helpful in this regard (see Figure 6.1.)

STAGE 2 TOOLS

Ladder of Inference

The Ladder of Inference, presented in the opening chapter of this workbook, is an important tool for supervisors to help groups and individuals create and sustain awareness. Senge (1994) notes that:

The steps include the following:

1. The supervisor introduces the activity by acknowledging that when entering a new group or a group with new members, we bring hopes for how we would like the group experience to be and concerns about what might detract from the group's effectiveness. The supervisor then briefly summarizes the steps in the exercise.

2. Group members are asked (and the supervisor joins them) to spend a few minutes writing down their hopes and concerns for the group's work together. Even if the group has been together for some time and a new supervisor has joined them, the exercise remains a useful way for the supervisor and group members to understand better what is important to each group member. Hearing their hopes and concerns provides a fuller understanding of the members' needs.

3. Everyone in the group is asked to review their written lists and to identify their top two hopes and top two concerns. Each person takes turns sharing their most important hopes while a member of the group writes down responses on newsprint or white board. Items listed under the "Hopes" and "Concerns" headings are numbered for easy reference. In some cases, individuals will share the same hope or concerns; in which case, the number of people endorsing each item can be recorded.

4. When the top two hopes and concerns of each member have been recorded, the supervisor facilitates a discussion of actions the supervisor and group members will take to help ensure that their hopes are met and their concerns are minimized. A group member types up the lists of hopes, concerns, and agreements and distributes them to group members. As a group, members can agree to evaluate periodically their success in meeting hopes and minimizing concerns, and identify whether they need revising or whether adding to their initial agreements would be helpful to the group's functioning.

Figure 6.1   Hopes and concerns: A contracting exercise

Source: Schaubhut, N. A. (2007).

We live in a world of self-generating beliefs that remain largely untested. We adopt these beliefs because they are based on conclusions, which are inferred from what we observe, plus our experiences. Our ability to achieve the results we truly desire is eroded by our feelings that (a) our beliefs are the truth, (b) the truth is obvious, (c) our beliefs are based on real data, and (d) the data we select are the real data (p. 242).

Misguided beliefs often occur somewhere in the "ladder of inference."

Thomas-Kilmann Conflict Orientations

Difficulty with resolving conflict is a major issue for many groups and deserves added attention. Although the traditional view advocated suppression of conflict as necessary to organizational functioning, Thomas and Kilmann (1974, 2002) characterized conflict as a phenomenon that can have constructive or destructive effects, depending on its management. The Thomas-Kilmann Conflict Mode Instrument (TKI) includes two dimensions:

1. Assertive to Unassertive—representing the degree to which one assertively pursues one's own interests.

2. Cooperative to Uncooperative—representing the degree to which one attempts to satisfy the other's concerns.

As illustrated in Figure 6.2, these dimensions result in five distinct strategies or behavioral approaches: competing, compromising, avoiding, accommodating, and collaborating. Unlike earlier writers on conflict, Thomas and Kilmann (2004) did not see one way of handling conflict as superior to the others. Rather, the most appropriate approach was dependent on a variety of factors, including the importance of the issue and time available. Below is a definition of each orientation and situations when a certain orientation may be the preferred choice.

- Competing is an aggressive, uncompromising approach to conflict that is power-driven. The individual pursues his or her own personal goals without regard to others.
- Compromising is intermediate in both assertiveness and cooperativeness. Its approach focuses on quick, mutually agreeable decisions that partially satisfy both parties.
- Avoiding is simply not addressing the conflict; it is an unassertive and uncooperative response. For example, this approach is appropriate when the other party is more powerful, the cost of addressing the conflict is higher than the benefit of resolution, there is no chance of goal attainment, or time is needed to gain composure or gather information. Avoidance results in prolonging the resolution rather than in resolving the issue. For example, the worker delays visiting parents with history of violence until law enforcement is able to join her.
- Accommodating is characterized by cooperative, but unassertive, behavior. For example, the accommodating individual exhibits a self-sacrificing behavior by neglecting his or her own concerns to satisfy the concerns of the other person. Accommodation promotes harmony and gains credits that can be used later. The supervisor supports staff's request for a flexible work schedule.
- Collaboration is both assertive and cooperative. For example, it involves an attempt to work with the other person to find a solution that fully satisfies the concerns of both parties. This approach leads to mutually satisfying decision

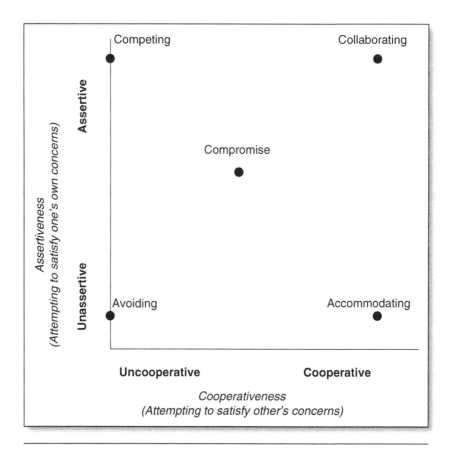

Figure 6.2   Two-dimensional taxonomy of strategic intentions

Source: Schaubhut, N. A. (2007).

making. The worker collaborates with family and service providers to develop case plans.

For more than 30 years, the TKI has helped individuals in a variety of settings understand how different conflict styles affect personal and group dynamics. Familiarity with these five ways of dealing with conflict can help individual group members better understand the options available to them for dealing with disagreements, as well as the costs and benefits of the various choices. Another option is for group members to identify what their collective conflict handling orientation is in relation to various areas of disagreement and determine whether a change in conflict orientation would be more productive.

STAGE 3 TOOLS

Group Roles Observation Chart—Meeting Key Role Requirements

To be effective, group supervisors need to recognize what is going on in the group. Sharpening our observation skills by expanding the variety of areas we observe and making our observations more systematic is an excellent way of increasing group effectiveness. Guidelines to help ensure the observer role is manageable and that the information will be helpful to the group include the following:

1. Choose one aspect of group functioning for your observations. Decide ahead of time whether you are going to observe interaction patterns among group members, the roles being played, problem-solving processes used, nonverbal communication, leadership styles, or some other area that allows you to choose the observation tool most helpful for your aims.

2. Your observation data will be most helpful if you separate your descriptions of the group's behavior from your interpretation or judgments based on your data. A useful approach is to share your observation data with group members, offer a possible explanation, and invite members to share their perspective.

3. Do not comment on everything you observe. Focus on a few main points that you see as most helpful to the groups' learning.

4. Provide a balance of positive and negative feedback. Groups need feedback that affirms what is going well and helps keep them committed and motivated, as well as constructive, critical feedback that provides direction for their improvement efforts.

5. Avoid focusing on one or two members. There can be a tendency to watch one or two key members and miss what less active members are doing or communicating through their body language or other nonverbal behavior.

6. The demands of observing a group remove the observer from participating. One option is to act as participant-observer, observing a 5-minute sample out of every 15 or 20 minutes and participating during the remaining time (see Table 6.4). Although the group leader may initially assume the role of observer, group members also ought to develop the knowledge and observational skills that allow them to engage actively in strengthening their group's functioning

The Group Roles Observation Chart is one of the most popular and versatile group observational tools. The focus of this tool is not on the content of a verbal or nonverbal message but on the behavior it represents. Each statement made by group members can be categorized by using the 18 roles listed in Table 6.4. Before using the tool, the observer should familiarize themselves with the three types of roles, and identify how a variety of comments would be

Table 6.4 Group Roles Observation Chart

Task roles	Group member's initials						
Initiator outlines purpose of group, defines the task, suggests method or process for accomplishing the task							
Clarifier gives examples, defines terms, offers rationales for suggestions							
Information/Opinion seeker asks for more facts, seeks individual opinions, ideas, and suggestions							
Information/Opinion giver offers facts, states beliefs and opinions							
Evaluator assesses validity of assumptions, quality of information, reasonableness of recommendations							
Summarizer pulls together related ideas, restates suggestions after the group has discussed them							
Consensus tester checks with group to see how much agreement has been reached, asks if group is nearing decision							
Maintenance/process roles							
Encourager demonstrates warmth, supports others' suggestions							
Harmonizer attempts to reconcile disagreements, reduces tensions, helps members explore differences							

	Group member's initials						
Gatekeeper facilitates others participation, asks individuals for their opinion or for information							
Standard setter helps group define its ground rules, reminds group of shared standards and norms							
Observer comments on the mood, tensions in the group, acknowledges own feelings about group functioning							
Tension reliever uses humor to increase group fun							
Follower expresses agreement, accepts other ideas							
Individual roles							
Blocker is unreasonable, refuses to concede point, sees own view as only one worthwhile							
Dominator interrupts and has long monologues, is authoritarian, monopolizes others' time							
Digresser gets off subject, leads discussion in "personally oriented" direction, monopolizes others time							
Withdrawer daydreams, engages in irrelevant side conversations, leaves room							
Attacker belittles others, creates hostile or intimidating environment, criticizes the group or its values, is often sarcastic							

Source: From "Functional roles of group members," by K. D. Benne & P. Sheats, 1948, *Journal of Social Issues, 4*, pp. 41–49. Copyright 1948 by Wiley-Blackwell. Reprinted with permission. From *How to observe your group* (4th ed., pp. 80–81), by H. G. Dimock & K. Raye, 2007, Concord, Ontario, Canada: Captus Press. Copyright 2007 by Captus Press. Reprinted with permission.

categorized. If the goal is to describe the group as a whole, the observer could simply check a role for each statement made by group members during a 5- or 10-minute time sample. The result would be listing the number of times each function was performed. The group members could review the results and discuss what roles were not played, overplayed, or underplayed and whether they want to consciously change the role distribution in their group.

If the group leaders' interest is in helping members increase their awareness of the roles they assume, a member's initials are included at the top of each column, and a checkmark is then placed across from each role that each individual took on each time he or she spoke.

Identifying Group Norms

Although attention to developing norms is a useful activity at the beginning of a group, the reality is that besides the norms that a group has consciously decided to adopt, there are "ways of doing things" that have likely developed that may hinder the group's development. The norming stage of the group's development is a time when Alexander's (1977) description of 10 categories of norms can be helpful to a group as they assess their group norms. Group members can read the description of each category and list what positive and negative norms currently exist within their group in relationship to that category:

1. Organizational pride. Norms in this category are associated with and influence the feeling of identification and pride the individual has with his or her organization. Norms of a positive nature lead the person to perceive the organization as his or her organization. Negative norms are reflected in a "we/they" attitude toward the organization and its goals.

2. Performance excellence. This category of norms is associated with behavior that strives toward either quality and productivity or acceptance of mediocrity. Negative norms are reflected in an acceptance of "good enough," whereas positive norms promote improvement over past performance.

3. Group work and communications. These norms are reflected in cooperation and in individuals working together. Negative norms foster individuality, secrecy, and the belief that success is achieved by an attitude of "every person for themselves." Positive norms promote sharing of information and working together for common goals.

4. Supervision/leadership. Norms of leadership promote or detract from the effectiveness of supervision. Positive norms result in supervisors assuming the role of helpers, coaches, and developers of subordinates. Negative norms lead to supervisors assuming the role of police and checking on subordinates.

5. Stewardship/cost effectiveness. This group of norms determines people's behavior with respect to profit and cost consciousness. Positive norms encourage people to save money and reduce costs; negative norms foster a lack of concern for bottom-line performance.

6. Colleague relations. Norms in this category determine the quality of relationships between people. Positive norms lead to strong interpersonal relationships. Negative norms lead to individualistic behavior and a nonsupportive climate.

7. Client relations. Norms in this cluster result in individual's behavior that affects the manner in which a client is served. Positive norms are directed toward maximizing client satisfaction. Negative norms lead to viewing the client as an obstacle to be avoided.

8. Innovation and change. This cluster of norms determines to a large degree whether original and creative behavior is supported and encouraged. Positive norms lead to the stimulation of new ideas and to change. Negative norms support the status quo and discourage experimentation.

9. Training and development. Positive norms in this cluster encourage training and view development as an essential part of the ongoing operation of the agency. Negative norms treat development as a nonessential, nice-to-do, but not as a critical aspect of providing services.

10. Candor and openness. This cluster of norms determines the degree of freedom in which communication can take place both vertically and horizontally. Positive norms indicate a high degree of trust and lead to open communication. Negative norms result in a closed and guarded attitude in interpersonal communication.

Assessing Group Norms

As mentioned, another tool to enhance group norms is an exercise called "What Is Normal Around Here?" (Porter & Mohr, 1984). The four quadrants represent four different responses a group can make in relation to any norm they have identified. Table 6.3 (see p. 117) illustrates a range of options available to a group about current group norms and enables the group to discuss alternative behaviors that might produce greater openness, clearly establish such behavior as desirable, and then monitor it with respect to what happens subsequently.

STAGE 4 TOOLS

All leaders when making a decision need to decide what the ideal level of staff participation is in a given decision. Although it is not practical to include group members in all decisions, where does the leader draw the line, particularly if she or he is working with a high-performing group? After all, the group is functioning very effectively; why not involve them in most decisions?

Vroom and Jago (1988) developed a decision methods analyses model that enables a supervisor to determine what leadership style represents the best fit with a given situation. As shown in Table 6.5, their model identifies five styles along a continuum ranging from autocratic, where the leader makes the decision with little or no involvement from other group members, to total delegation of decision making, where the group makes the decision without the leader. The leader, by asking a series of sequenced questions about the nature of the problem, decision, and consequences, can determine how much involvement others should have in the decision. A major benefit of the model is that it prompts leaders to be more deliberate in their decision-making process. Results of multiple studies comparing the effects of decisions according to the model's prescriptions, and decisions made without the model, support the use of the model as a tool for improving decision-making effectiveness (Thompson, 2007). The detailed decision tree analysis protocol can be found online at http://faculty.css.edu/dswenson/web/LEAD/vroom-yetton.html.

Table 6.5   Possible Decision Methods Analysis Model

Decision-making approach	Description	Involved
Autocratic I	Leader solves the problem by using information that is readily available to him/her.	Leader only makes the decision.
Autocratic II	Leader obtains additional information from some group members and then makes decision alone. Group members may or may not be informed.	Some group members involved in information exchange only.
Consultative I	Leader shares problem with group members individually, and asks for information and evaluation. Group members do not meet collectively, and leader makes decision alone.	All group members provide input.
Consultative II	Leader shares problem with group members collectively but makes decision alone.	All group members provide input.
Group II	Leader meets with group to discuss situation. Leader focuses and directs discussion but does not impose will. Group makes final decision.	All involved in decision.

Source: From *Leadership and decision-making,* by V. H. Vroom & P. W. Yetton, 1973, Pittsburgh, PA: University of Pittsburgh Press. Copyright 1973 by University of Pittsburgh Press. Reprinted with permission. From *The new leadership: Managing participation in organizations* (p. 13), by A. Jago, 1988, Englewood Cliffs, NJ: Prentice Hall, p. 13.

STAGE 5 TOOLS

The termination of tasks, members, and/or the group itself can be a difficult time for participants. Change disrupts the equilibrium and group process. However, group rituals can moderate the tendency for groups to regress to earlier stages of development during times of stress. These rituals provide members with the ability to fall back on activities that have been meaningful and beneficial in the past to the group.

Ending Rituals

It is the supervisor's responsibility to help the group establish rituals well before the termination stage. Why would this be important? First, checking in rituals might help group members describe their concerns and fears. Second, celebratory rituals (such as those used for birthdays, anniversaries, and benchmarks) used for termination, transition, or change can act as a symbolic, retrospective, and thought-provoking rite of passage. Members might be asked to bring one thing from their workspace that symbolizes how they feel about this event. Perhaps the eraser on a pencil will symbolize the ending, erasing what was and clearing a space for beginning anew. The objects and their meanings will provide a rich foundation for discussion.

Critical Incident Ritual and Protocol

One ritual that is critical for the group is a protocol for debriefing critical events such as the death of clients or colleagues. For example, in child protection, the death of a child on a caseload can have cataclysmic repercussions for the assigned worker and other staff. The grief of the loss, the sense of guilt, the fear of blame by the agency and media, and the worry that this may be a career-ending event is devastating. The event affects not only the worker involved but also everyone around him or her. Other members of the group think, "If it could happen to her, it could happen to me." There is no longer a feeling of safety within the group. The trauma is unavoidable. However, a pre-established protocol can mediate the damage.

To create a protocol, it is important that the supervisor ask the group to develop a crisis plan early in group development, most likely in the dependency and inclusion stage. The questions to be answered by the group include:

- If an event occurs, what will the group do?
- How has each member historically reacted during a time of extreme stress?
- What does each member need from the group? Some workers will want to talk. Others will want to be left alone. Someone else may say, "I will cry and scream. This is what I need from you to get through it. . . ."

- What process should the group use to debrief the incident?
- Should an outside facilitator be brought in?
- Who will do what, when, and where?

Although dealing with a critical incident is never easy, having a protocol will help the group get through the trauma and will aid in the healing process. It may be valuable to practice the protocol on events that are less than critical (e.g., a colleague on medical leave) so that when an incident does occur, there will be familiarity with the process.

Summary

This chapter has described a frequent situation encountered by supervisors—leading and coaching a group—where there are fewer practical materials readily available in the supervisory management literature. Yet, there are practical conceptual frameworks for gauging the groups' stage of group functioning and ways of helping the group be productive—no matter their stage. Therefore, gauging group roles and norms can be helpful, as well as how analyzing what group member assumptions and strategic assumptions may be operating. The next chapters provide strategies for closely related supervisory skills: designing and conducting worker performance appraisals.

References

Alexander, M. (1977). Organizational norms. In J. E. Jones & W. Pfeiffer (Eds.), *The 1977 annual handbook of group facilitators* (pp.123–125). La Jolla, CA: University Associates Inc.

Burns, C. (1994). Innovative team building: Synergistic human resource development. *Administration and Policy in Mental Health, 22*(1), 39–48.

Buzaglo, G., & Wheelan S. A. (1999). Facilitating work team effectiveness—Case studies from Central America. *Small Group Research, 30*(1), 108–129.

Druskat, V. U., & Wolff, S. B. (2001). Building the emotional intelligence of groups. *Harvard Business Review, 79*(3), 81–90.

Edmondson, A. C. (2003). The local and variegated nature of learning in organizations: A group-level perspective. *Organization Science, 13*, 128–146.

Felder, R. M., & Spurlin, J. E. (2005). Applications, reliability, and validity of the Index of Learning Styles. *International Journal of Engineering Education, 21*(1), 103–112.

Feldman, D. C. (1984). The development and enforcement of group norms. *The Academy of Management Review, 9*(1), 47–53.

Fleming, N. D., & Bonwell, C. C. (2008). *VARK—A guide to learning styles.* Retrieved July 5, 2008, from http://www.vark-learn.com/english/index.asp

Hackman, J. R., & Wageman, R. (2005). A theory of team coaching. *Academy of Management Review, 30,* 269–287.

Hasenfeld, Y., & Abbott, A. D. (1992). *Human services as complex organizations.* Newbury Park, CA: Sage.

Herman, S. M., & Korenich, M. (1977). *Authentic management: A gestalt orientation to organizations and their development.* Reading, MA: Addison-Wesley.

Houghton, J. D., Nick, C. P., & Manz, C. C. (2003). Self-leadership and super leadership: The heart and art of creating shared leadership in teams. In C. L. Pearce & J. A. Conger (Eds.), *Shared leadership: Reframing the how's and whys of leadership* (pp. 123–140). Thousand Oaks, CA, Sage.

Katzenbach, J. R., & Smith, D. K. (1993). The discipline of teams. *Harvard Business Review, 71,* 111–120.

Keirsey, D. (1998). *Please understand me II: Temperament, character, intelligence.* Del Mar, CA: Prometheus Nemesis.

Lencioni, P. (2005). *Overcoming the five dysfunctions of a team: A field guide for leaders, managers and facilitators.* San Francisco: Jossey-Bass.

Mayer, J., & Salovey, P. (1997). What is emotional intelligence? In P. Salovey & D. Sluyter (Eds.), *Emotional development and emotional intelligence: Implications for educators* (pp. 3–31). New York: Basic Books.

Patton, B. R., & Downs, T. M. (2003). *Decision-making group interaction: Achieving quality* (4th ed.). Boston: Allyn & Bacon.

Pearce, C. L. (2004). The future of leadership: Combining vertical and shared leadership to transform knowledge work. *Academy of Management Executive, 18*(1), 47–57.

Pearce, C. L., & Conger, J. A. (2003). All those years ago: The historical underpinnings of shared leadership. In C. L. Pearce & J. A. Conger (Eds.), *Shared leadership: Reframing the how's and whys of leadership* (pp. 1–20). Thousand Oaks, CA: Sage.

Porter, L., & Mohr, B. (1984). *Reading book for human relations training* (7th ed.). Arlington, VA: NTL Institute for Applied Behavioral Science.

Postmes, T., Spears, R., and Cihangir, S. (2001). Quality of decision-making and group norms. *Journal of Personality and Social Psychology, 80,* 918–930.

Schaubhut, N. A. (2007). *Technical brief for the Thomas-KIlmann Conflict Mode Instrument: Description of the updated normative sample and implications for use.* Mountain View, CA: CPP Inc.

Schutz, W. (1966). *The interpersonal underworld.* Palo Alto, CA: Science & Behavior Books.

Senge, P. M. (1990). *The fifth discipline: The art and practice of the learning organization.* New York: Doubleday.

Senge, P. M. (1994). *The fifth discipline field book: Strategies and tools for building a learning organization.* New York: Doubleday.

Thomas, K. W., & Kilmann, R. H. (1974). *Thomas-Kilmann conflict mode instrument.* Tuxedo, NY: Xicom Publishing. Retrieved March 10, 2009, from http://www.kilmann.com/conflict.html

Thompson, L. L. (2004). *Making the team: A guide for managers* (2nd ed.). Upper Saddle River, NJ: Prentice Hall.

Vroom, V. H., & Jago, A. G. (1988). *The new leadership: Managing participation in organizations.* Englewood Cliffs, NJ: Prentice Hall.

Wells, R., Jinnett, K., Alexander, J., Lichtenstein, R., Liu, D., & Zazzali, J. L. (2006). Team leadership and patient outcomes in US psychiatric treatment settings. *Social Science & Medicine, 62,* 1840–1852.

Wheelan, S. A., & Mckeage, R. L. (1993). Developmental patterns in small and large groups. *Small Group Research, 24*(1), 60–83.

Wheelan, S. A. (2005). *Creating effective teams: A guide for members and leaders.* Thousand Oaks, CA: Sage.

Wheelan, S. A., Burchill, C. N., & Tilin, F. (2003).The link between teamwork and patients' outcomes in intensive care units. *American Journal of Critical Care, 12,* 527–534.

Williams, H. (1996). *The essence of managing groups and teams.* London: Prentice Hall.

Web-Based Resources

The Keirsey Temperament Sorter (Alternative to the MBTI, free with online scoring). Retrieved March 11, 2009, from http://www.advisorteam.com/temperament_sorter/register.asp?partid=1

The Meyers-Briggs Type Indicator Test (MBTI) (Personality test based on the work of Carl Jung). Retrieved March 15, 2009, from http://www.myersbriggs.org/my-mbti-personality-type/mbti-basics/

The VARK (Visual, Aural, Read/write, and Kinesthetic). (Thirteen point multiple choice questionnaire that identifies learning preferences). Retrieved March 9, 2009, from http://www.vark-learn.com/english/index.asp

Suggested Readings

Ayoko, O. B., Callan, V., & Hartel, C. (2008). The influence of team emotional intelligence climate on conflict and team members' reactions to conflict. *Small Group Research, 39,* 121–149.

Edmondson, A. C. (1999). Psychological safety and learning behavior in work teams. *Administrative Science Quarterly, 44,* 350–384.

Ephross, P. H., & Vassil, T. V. (2005). *Groups that work: Structure and process* (2nd ed.). New York: Columbia University Press.

Hackman, J. R. (2002). *Leading teams: Setting the stage for great performances.* Boston: Harvard Business School.

Hollingshead, A. B. (1996). The rank order effect in group decision making. *Organizational Behavior and Human Decision Processes, 68,* 181–193.

Johnson. D. W., & Johnson, F. P. (2006). *Joining together: Group theory and group skills* (9th ed.). Boston: Allyn & Bacon.

Jordan, P., & Ashkanasy, N. M. (2006). Emotional intelligence, emotional self-awareness, and team effectiveness In V. Druskat, F. Sala, & G. Mount (Eds.), *Linking emotional intelligence and performance at work: Current research evidence with individuals and groups* (pp.145–164). Mahwah, NJ: Lawrence Erlbaum.

Levi, D. (2007). *Group dynamics for teams.* Thousand Oaks, CA: Sage.

Mossbrucker, J. (1988). Developing a productivity team: Making groups at work. In W. B. Reddy & K. Jamison (Eds.), *Team building: Blueprints for productivity and satisfaction* (pp. 88–97). San Diego, CA: NTL Institute for Applied Behavioral Science and University Associates.

Sala, F., Druskat, V., & Mount, G. (2006). *Linking emotional intelligence and performance at work: Current research evidence with individuals and groups.* Mahwah, NJ: Lawrence Erlbaum.

Seers, A., Keller, T., & Wilkerson, J. M. (2003). Can team members share leadership? Foundations in research and theory. In C. L. Pearce & J. A. Conger (Eds.), *Shared leadership: Reframing the hows and whys of leadership* (pp. 77–102). Thousand Oaks, CA: Sage.

Thomas, K. W., & Thomas, G. F. (2004). *Introduction to conflict and teams: Enhancing team performance using the TKI.* Mountain View, CA: CPP, Inc.

Toseland, R. W., & Rivas, R. F. (2004). *An introduction to group work practice* (5th ed.). Boston: Allyn & Bacon.

Wageman, R., Hackman, J. R., & Lehman, E. V. (2004). *Development of the team diagnostic survey.* Working paper, Tuck School, Dartmouth College, Hanover, NH.

West, M. A. (2004). *Effective teamwork: Practical lessons from organizational research.* Malden, MA: BPS Blackwell.

Wolff, S. B., Druskat, V., Koman, E., & Messer, T. E. (2006). The link between group emotional competence and group effectiveness. In V. Druskat, F. Sala, & G. Mount, (Eds.), *Linking emotional intelligence and performance at work: Current research evidence with individuals and groups* (pp. 223–244). Mahwah, NJ: Lawrence Erlbaum.

Yukl, G. (1999). An evaluation of conceptual weaknesses in transformational and charismatic leadership theories. *The Leadership Quarterly, 10,* 285–305.

7

Designing and Conducting Worker Performance Appraisals

Introduction

This chapter focuses on an important aspect of supervision—the provision of feedback to agency personnel. Feedback to employees through a formal appraisal system is a primary method for supervisors to engage with personnel in the ongoing operations of the group and in mentoring employees with regard to their own career and skills development. The material presented in this chapter is designed to provide supervisors with a full view of a useful and sound set of performance appraisal practices.

CONTEXT FOR PERFORMANCE APPRAISAL

Every organization should have a *performance management system*—a process used to identify, measure, communicate, develop, and reward employee performance (Mathis & Jackson, 2006). In contrast, *worker performance appraisals* are used for the systematic assessment of how well agency staff members are performing their jobs over a specified period of time. Performance evaluations are designed to measure the extent to which the worker is achieving the requirements of his or her position and his or her fit within the group. Evaluations should be based on clearly specified, realistic, and achievable criteria reflecting agency standards (Arvey & Murphy, 1998; DelPo, 2007; Kadushin & Harkness, 2002). But it should be acknowledged that the value of an employee to the organization he or she works for is often more than "just" his or her work performance. An individual may be valued by an organization because he or she possesses particular personal characteristics such as valuing diversity, sense of humor, and the ability to encourage colleagues in times of crisis (Arvey & Murphy, 1998).

Superior performance appraisal methods encourage supervisors and workers to set realistic and measurable goals for job performance. Measurable evaluation criteria also help to motivate, direct, and integrate worker learning while providing staff with examples of how they can evaluate their own performance.

The process actually begins with orienting new staff to their position. This is a key aspect because it helps a new employee learn about the specific job requirements, strategies for success, organizational and work unit norms, how the group functions, the supervisor's leadership style, and how to best work with the supervisor. Some of the job requirements may stem from federal, state, county, or city laws and regulations. One of the most crucial supervisor responsibilities then is to help staff develop skills and grow.

We recognize that in most organizations the supervisor will not have the opportunity to select or customize a performance appraisal method. But understanding the underlying concepts of appraisal and the particular strengths and limitations of your agency's system can help you apply the system more effectively.

SETTING A GOOD FOUNDATION

The performance appraisal process is fundamentally about providing constructive and affirming feedback to employees (Billikopf, 2003):

> Supervisors who tend to look for worker's positive behaviors—and do so in a sincere, non-manipulative way—will have less difficulty giving constructive feedback or suggestions. Furthermore, in the negotiated approach, the burden for performance analysis does not fall on the supervisor alone, but requires introspection on the part of the individual being evaluated. (pp. 60–61)

A respectful appraisal process is especially important because many social services organizations are becoming flatter in terms of organizational layers of management, becoming more decentralized, and are increasingly relying on more team approaches to work (Cascio, 1995). The inability of staff members to meet certain performance standards may be from dysfunctional or unclear agency policies, a shortage of critical resources, inadequate supervisory feedback, or other administrative-related shortcomings. Sound performance evaluations help supervisors and managers distinguish agency-related problems that should be corrected through some form of organizational change from worker-related performance difficulties that may be addressed by supervisory coaching, staff training, or other strategies.

Evaluating staff with less formal feedback sessions 3–4 times per year is important for determining pay raises, likelihood for promotion, future assignments, and the need for coaching or corrective action plans. Sound performance appraisal systems assist agencies in meeting the requirements of Equal Employment Opportunity laws in the areas of promotion or discipline (DelPo, 2007). Finally, given the amount of autonomy and discretion of most social services agency staff, consumers have a right to expect a minimum amount of staff supervision and monitoring as part of agency quality control. Despite the multiple advantages of performance evaluation, human services organizations continue to struggle with two primary challenges. First is the challenge of specifying the basis on which a worker's job performance is judged (i.e., what performance standards or criteria should be used?). Second is the challenge that the criteria have been identified, but to what extent can they be measured?

A worksheet for addressing these questions that was partially completed by a supervisor in a recent workshop is included in Table 7.1. The supervisor listed one of the major job tasks performed by a subordinate (provide counseling to birth parents in order to reunite family). That task was written in the space provided in Table 7.1, following the guidelines described in Chapter 4 (e.g., is the task statement specific? Does it describe who will do what? Does it have an "in order to" outcome clause?).

After writing the task statement, the supervisor thought about how she knew when the task was done in an "acceptable" manner (i.e., how she would distinguish between ineffective performance and acceptable performance of that task). She described these standards in Column 2 (e.g., parent–child visitation occurs once a week).

Finally, the supervisor considered how she would know whether someone had in fact done the task with an acceptable level of performance; she developed some methods for measuring whether and how well the task was performed (e.g., by means of a worker contacts log). That information was written in Column 3. In reviewing all three columns, you should see a logical flow of ideas from tasks to performance standards to measurement methods. Although listing this information does not result in a complete performance appraisal method, the information described in Table 7.1 constitutes the core of the most effective appraisal methods available today.

A wide variety of process or outcome criteria is being used by human services agencies in order to evaluate worker performance. Research suggests that performance consists of both task-oriented and contextually oriented facets, and there seems to be attributes that lead some applicants to excel in specific aspects of performance (e.g., performing individual job tasks)—different from those that lead some applicants to excel in other aspects of job performance (e.g., working well with others) (Arvey & Murphy, 1998; Borman, Hanson, & Hedge, 1997; Pearce, 2006).

Table 7.1   A Worksheet for Developing Performance Criteria and Measures

Task statements (job responsibilities)	Performance standards (What constitutes acceptable job performance?)	Measurement (How will performance be measured?)
(1) Provide counseling services to parents experiencing severe difficulties in their marital relationship.	(1a) Meet with parents at least twice a month. (1b) Case plan and services focus on the parent–child relationship strengths and deficits. (1d) Both parents report substantial improvement in 40% of cases.	(1a) Case progress notes. (1b) Case plan and review summaries. (1c) Customer feedback surveys.
Your position:		

Performance criteria could be clustered into the following general categories:

1. Results achieved

2. Responsiveness to client needs

3. Output quality (client assessments completed is an output, the end product of a work process and quality here refers to the usefulness of the assessment to other workers)

4. Output quantity (quantity here refers to the volume of work done against set requirements of the job)

5. Work habits and attitudes

6. Accident rates

7. Learning ability

8. Judgment or problem-solving ability

But supervisors also should evaluate staff in relation to adherence to treatment fidelity standards (the protocol for an intervention, how a service is required or expected to be delivered, and how close it is actually delivered is considered fidelity), innovation and learning, and financial performance criteria related to good stewardship of agency resources and efficiency (a combination of how much time and resources it takes to accomplish the work) (Kaplan &

Norton, 2005). Some worker performance criteria are more directly framed by agency performance parameters, such as when social services agencies adopt a "Balanced Scorecard" approach (Kaplan & Norton, 2005).[1]

Many performance appraisals, historically, concentrated too much on subjective personality traits or on the peripheral aspects of the worker's performance (e.g., general attitude and punctuality) and not enough time examining the degree of attainment of specific job-related outcomes. For example, see Table 7.2 for an example of a graphic rating scale that focuses on a set of important performance factors, but the rating scale is insufficient because it does not enable ratings of key job outcomes.

Table 7.2   Graphic Rating Scale Appraisal Method

Name:		Appraisal date:	
Areas of consideration	Does not exhibit competency	Exhibits competency	Exhibits competency in exemplary ways
1. *Adaptability:* Flexibility. Acceptance of changed procedures. Ability to cope with the unexpected. Ease in shifting from one assignment to another.			
2. *Analytical skills:* Ability to think through the dynamics and dimensions of a situation.			
3. *Attitude:* Enthusiasm, optimism and loyalty toward associates, job and agency, and its objectives.			
4. *Communication skills:* Ability to provide and receive information in oral or written form.			
5. *Cost consciousness:* Awareness of costs to agency. Efficiency within organization.			
6. *Creativity:* Developing novel and unusual approaches to situations.			

Name:		Appraisal date:	
Areas of consideration	Does not exhibit competency	Exhibits competency	Exhibits competency in exemplary ways
7. *Customer service:* Orientation toward meeting customer needs in a diplomatic and effective way.			
8. *Dependability:* Follow-through, ability of others to count on this person to perform.			
9. *Drive:* Has the ambition and energy applied to the job to get things done. Self-starting ability.			
10. *Expression:* Ability to state point of view clearly in written and oral presentations.			
11. *Flexibility:* Able to change approach as needed; nimble; open to new ideas.			
12. *Foresight:* Vision. Forward thinking and planning. Consideration of the broad aspects of management decisions.			
13. *Initiative/Motivation:* Does not wait to be told everything that might need to be done to help the program achieve its goals; anticipates what is needed and helps begin the work processes without excessive prompting.			
14. *Knowledge of work:* Knowledge of functional skills for job and agency practices.			
15. *Leadership:* Able to help a group of staff work together effectively to accomplish goals.			

(Continued)

Table 7.2 (Continued)

Name:			Appraisal date:
Areas of consideration	Does not exhibit competency	Exhibits competency	Exhibits competency in exemplary ways
16. *Obtaining results:* Application of time and facilities. Amount and quality of work produced.			
17. *Outcomes-oriented/Results-oriented:* Focuses not only on high-quality processes but on achieving the program goals and outcomes.			
18. *Planning and organizing:* Development of work plans and schedules. Organizing others to get an effective job done.			
19. *Problem-solving:* Ability to identify the causes of performance and other difficulties and to develop and implement solutions.			
20. *Reasoning and judgment:* Mental alertness. Critical observation. Logic. Soundness of decisions.			
21. *Relations with others:* Ability to get people to work together. Consideration. Interest to people.			
22. *Resourcefulness:* Ability to improvise, to find ways to get things done with specific instructions. Ability to overcome obstacles.			
23. *Self-confidence:* Self-assurance. Self-reliance in meeting new situations and developments.			

Name:		Appraisal date:	
Areas of consideration	Does not exhibit competency	Exhibits competency	Exhibits competency in exemplary ways
24. *Self-control:* Self-restraint. Control of emotions. Evenness of temper.			
25. *Sense of responsibility:* Dependability. Assuming and discharging duties. Training and developing subordinates. Considering effect of actions and decisions on company.			
26. *Groupwork-oriented:* Values having a group of staff work together to achieve.			
27. *Willingness to delegate:* Sharing work load with his people. Entrusting responsibility to others.			
Appraiser's signature and date:			

Sources: Adapted from DelPo, A. (2007), Hunt, S. (1996), and Odiorne, G. S. (1970).

Another criticism of some performance appraisal methods stems from those who focus on applying total quality management (TQM) using Deming's principles. In fact, Deming ranks the traditional evaluation of performance, merit rating, or annual review third in his list of the Seven Deadly Diseases of the Western style of management.[2] Deming advocates argue that many of the faulty management practices in performance appraisal originate from a failure to understand variation among workers and a failure to distinguish between the "common causes," those problems caused by a failure of process to be designed properly, not worker error and the "special causes" of variation, which may in fact be worker-related errors. Deming (1982) emphasized quality control charts as a proper tool for distinguishing between types of causes. These kinds of charts are useful then in monitoring the stability of a system and for detecting who among the workers is performing within the system, out of the system on the good side, or out of the system on the poor side (Bakir, 2005).

Thus, various TQM tools, service fidelity assessments, and outcome data are beginning to be used as ways of providing more objective data for worker performance appraisals. For example, several mental health and family social services agencies are beginning to implement evidence-based treatment (EBT) models of intervention. Virtually all of the better EBTs require that a certain amount of fidelity assessment be conducted to help ensure that the EBT is being implemented as it has been designed (Bruns, Rast, Peterson, Walker, & Bosworth, 2006; Jensen, Weersing, Hoagwood, & Goldman, 2005). Consumers receiving the service are often asked about what was provided to them and how to monitor service fidelity and quality.

In addition to reliance on personality traits, supervisors must resist the appraisal traps posed by the halo or horns effects. The "halo" effect is the tendency to give a subordinate excessively high ratings because of such factors as the worker's past performance, pleasant personality, non-job-related attributes (e.g., impressive appearance and same college program), or the absence of bad feedback. The "horns" effect is the use of arbitrarily low ratings because the performance appraisal is based on such factors as the recent performance difficulty, or guilt by association. This issue is serious: Ganzach (1995) found that in terms of a worker's overall performance rating, more weight is given to negative attributes of their job performance than to positive attributes.[3]

The use of incomplete appraisal systems such as the one in Table 7.2 and the tendency of supervisors to be affected by various biases pose serious challenges to social services agencies, especially in light of court decisions in business and industry stressing that performance appraisal systems should be formal, standardized, and objective (DelPo, 2007). In addition, the system should be job related, administered by supervisors who have been trained in how to interpret performance criteria and the meaning of various rating scores and who have frequent contact with the employee.

Methods of Performance Appraisal

OVERVIEW OF TYPES

Most organizations in the United States use "pay-for-performance" systems (Mathis & Jackson, 2006), and most U.S. workers say they want to be paid on the basis of performance (LeBlanc & Mulvey, 1998). Meta-analytic reviews of groups of research studies have found that increasing the connection between pay and performance can be very effective for improving performance, along with using appraisals to provide feedback (Rynes, Gerhart, & Parks, 2005).

Performance appraisal methods can generally be categorized into relative or absolute rating systems. With a relative rating system, the supervisor compares an employee's performance with another employee (e.g., simple ranking, paired comparisons, and forced distributions). With absolute rating systems, raters judge employee performance with performance standards, independent of between-individual comparisons (e.g., management by objective-based approaches, critical incidents, behavior checklists, graphic rating scales, and behaviorally anchored rating scales—BARS) (Wong & Kwong, 2005). The more objective methods generally focus on examination of concrete outputs (e.g., payment error rates, foster homes recruited, and children reunified with parents) or some form of economic analysis.

With these distinctions in mind, the following questions can be used to assess your agency's system for analyzing job performance:

1. Does the method concentrate on evaluating what the employee *is* or *does?* To what extent does the method rely on subjective rather than objective measures? Are qualitative aspects of effective work behavior ignored because of an overemphasis on quantifiable standards?

2. To what extent can the method be used throughout a program unit or agency (i.e., is it "tailored" to a particular program area or a more "standard" agencywide approach)?

3. Is the appraisal system used primarily for performance appraisals or for multiple purposes (e.g., salary determination, promotions, layoffs, reassignments, and disciplinary action)?

4. Does the method take into account and promote worker commitment to both organization and professional work goals?

5. Is the method reliable (i.e., would workers or supervisors be rated consistently if the rating process was repeated a few days later)? Is the method valid (i.e., does it actually measure job performance)? Does the method use mutually agreed upon performance goals or standards?

6. How difficult is it to use the method in terms of technical expertise, time, and commitment? (Arvey & Murphy, 1998; Morrisey, 1983a; Rynes et al., 2005)

Although there are many appraisal methods, there seem to be 16 major approaches. A brief description of each of these is included in Figure 7.1. These approaches can be categorized into five major groups with some overlap between the first two groups:

1. *Personality-based systems:* Lists of personality traits that are assumed to be significant to the job are rated (essay/narrative, graphic rating scales, ranking, forced choice).

2. *Generalized descriptive systems:* Although similar to the personality-based systems, terms descriptive of good worker performance are used, such as organizes, communicates, assesses, motivates, but often without sufficient definition (essay/narrative, graphic rating, ranking, forced choice).

3. *Results-centered systems:* These systems are especially job related as supervisors and subordinates mutually define work objectives and measures (360-degree ratings, management by objectives and results—MBO/MOR, work standards).

4. *Behavioral descriptive systems:* Using detailed job analysis or job descriptions, work behaviors required for success are identified (behaviorally anchored rating scales, weighted checklist, critical incidents models, and assessment centers).

5. *Miscellaneous:* Systems less frequently used that are relatively unique or combine various components of the other methods (forced distribution, field observations of worker actions and results achieved [adapted from Mathis & Jackson, 2006, pp. 343–350; Odiorne, 1984, pp. 258–259]).

---

1. ***Ability Requirements Scales (ARS):*** The Ability Requirements Scales method developed by Fleishman and Mumford (1991) is useful for identifying ability requirements for different occupational specialties.

2. ***Assessment Center:*** Employees engage in actual or simulated job tasks where their work behaviors can be measured to assess current job performance or, more typically, to predict their potential for managerial positions.

3. ***Behaviorally Anchored Rating Scales (BARS):*** Behaviors necessary to achieve program objectives are identified and then used as scale anchors to rate employee performance.

4. ***Critical Incident:*** Positive and negative work behaviors or incidents are recorded in relation to mutually agreed upon performance objectives or job tasks.

5. ***Essay/Narrative Summary Description Method:*** Supervisors develop narrative evaluations of the employee's work behavior or job-related personality traits. In this approach, individual tasks or behaviors are not rated.

6. ***Field Review:*** Worker appraisal ratings or rankings are reviewed by a small group of supervisors to reassess the appraisal and to develop uniform standards for performance appraisal.

7. ***Forced Distribution:*** Raters are forced to place staff on a bell curve where only a certain percentage of staff can receive superior, average, and poor ratings.

8. ***Forced-Choice Rating:*** Key traits or behaviors identified through a form of job analysis are inserted into multiple-choice questions that require supervisors to choose the trait or behavior that best fits the worker.

9. ***Graphic (Trait) Rating Scales:*** Workers are rated on a 5–7-point scale in relation to a series of personality traits, abilities, and other performance factors.

10. ***Management by Objectives Results (MBO/MOR):*** Workers and their supervisors establish individual performance objectives to be accomplished in a specific time period along with action plans for attainment and with methods for monitoring progress.

Figure 7.1 *(Continued)*

11. **Management Position Description Questionnaire (MPDQ):** The MPDQ is a standardized instrument, with about 250 questions, that describes managerial activities to help develop job descriptions, performance appraisals, and job evaluation criteria. Because it is standardized, results can be compared across incumbents and managerial jobs.

12. **Multisource 360-Degree Systems:** The most comprehensive and costly type of appraisal. It includes self-ratings, peer reviews, and upward assessments by subordinates of the person being rated. Sometimes customer reviews are also included.

13. **Position Analysis Questionnaire (PAQ):** The PAQ is a structured job analysis questionnaire that measures job characteristics and relates them to human characteristics. The information can then be used to identify performance criteria.

14. **Ranking Techniques:** Workers are rank ordered in relation to certain traits and each other using straight, alternative, or paired comparison methods of ranking.

15. **Weighted Checklist:** Work behaviors are assigned weights according to their importance, and supervisors indicate which behaviors are demonstrated by the worker using a checklist where the weights are omitted.

16. **Work Standards:** Uniform, measurable performance standards are developed to evaluate worker behaviors.

Figure 7.1   Major approaches to performance appraisal

Sources: Adapted from Arvey, R.D. & Murphy, K.R. (1998); Brannick, M.T., Levine. E.L., & Morgeson, F.P. (2007).; Cummings, L. L., & Schwab, D. P. (1973); Driskill, W. E., Weismuller, J.J., Hageman, D. C. & Barrett, L. E. (1989); Fleishman, E.A. & Mumford, M.D. (1991); Haynes, M. G. (1978); Klingner, D. E., & Nalbandian J. (1985); Organizational and Staff Development Unit. (2007); PAQ Services (2007); and Rynes, S.L., Gerhart, B. & Parks, L. (2005).

The personality-based and generalized description systems, although widely used in human services agencies, have some serious limitations. Subjective behavior-oriented measures offer several potential advantages relative to results-based measures (Rynes et al., 2005). First, they can be used for any type of job. Second, they permit the rater to factor in variables that are not under the employee's control but nevertheless influence performance. Third, they permit a focus on whether results are achieved using acceptable means and behaviors. Fourth, they generally carry less risk on measurement deficiency, or the possibility that employees will focus only on explicitly measured tasks or results at the expense of broader prosocial behaviors, organizational "citizenship," or contextual performance (see Arvey & Murphy, 1998; Wright et al., 1993). Despite these potential advantages, the subjectivity of behavior-oriented measures limits their ability to differentiate employees (Rynes et al., 2005):

[E]vidence finds a mean interrater reliability of only 0.52 for performance ratings (Viswesvaren et al. 1996), making it difficult for organizations to justify differentiating employees based on such error-laden performance measures (360-degree appraisals may be helpful in this regard). The subjectivity in these PE measures has led the PE literature to focus on identifying cognitive biases in evaluation (in hopes of reducing them) and examining how various features of PE measures (and PE-related processes) influence employee's perceptions of fairness (in hopes of improving PE's legitimacy and effectiveness). (p. 583)

Thus, research indicates that the results-centered (e.g., management by objectives or MBO) and behavioral description systems (e.g., behaviorally anchored rating scales or BARS) provide more job-related and valid measures of performance and withstand litigation well (Rynes et al., 2005). Each method, however, has various strengths and limitations. For example, the Multisource 360-degree feedback method is the most comprehensive and costly type of appraisal because it includes self-ratings, peer reviews, and upward assessments with feedback sought from everyone (Organizational and Staff Development Unit, 2007; Rynes et al., 2005). Although it may not be realistic for many organizations, the foundation concepts are powerful (Toolpack Consulting, 2007):

It gives people a chance to know how they are seen by others; to see their skills and style; and may improve communications between people. 360 degree feedback helps by bringing out every aspect of an employee's life. Cooperation with people outside their department, helpfulness towards customers and vendors, etc. may not be rewarded by other types of appraisal. This system also helps those who have conflicts with their manager. 360 degree feedback generally has high employee involvement and credibility; may have the strongest impact on behavior and performance; and may greatly increase communication and shared goals. (p. 1)

Another example is the MBO system, which seems to work best for jobs where workers have a large amount of autonomy and use various technical strategies to achieve performance goals. In contrast, the BARS method seems to be very sound for jobs where the work requirements are known, specific, and repetitive. In the next section of this chapter, we focus on one method that seems to be the most cost-effective for human services agencies; namely, management by objectives and results.

Management by Objectives and Results (MBO/MOR)

With this technique, individual performance objectives and their standards are mutually developed by workers and their supervisors within the overall agency performance context. As stressed in Chapter 4, workers and supervisors need to have a clear idea of what specific job tasks must be accomplished. Furthermore, workers also should be able to help set specific individual performance goals or objectives as each job requires a unique contribution by the employee to achieve the overall objectives of the organization.

The MBO approach to performance appraisal involves the following steps:

1. Identify the key results areas of the job and the corresponding skills and actions.

2. Set objectives for key results areas consistent with the above assessment, including developing acceptable performance standards for each area stated in terms of measurable outcome criteria where possible.

3. Develop action plans for objective attainment.

4. Modify or reprioritize performance objectives throughout the year, as needed through supervisory consultation.

5. Monitor worker performance and provide periodic feedback.

6. Conduct a year-end performance review.

Once an objective is agreed, the employee is expected to self-audit, that is, to identify the skills needed to achieve the objective. Typically they do not rely on others to locate and specify their strengths and weaknesses. Employees are expected to monitor their own development and progress (Archer North & Associates, 2006).

A refinement of the MBO approach (the MOR or management by objectives and results) can be a cost-effective performance appraisal method. The MOR approach differs slightly from the MBO method in that it emphasizes key results areas, performance indicators, and standards. An abbreviated example of an MOR appraisal plan for a foster care worker is presented in Figure 7.2; note the specification of key responsibility areas, indicators of achievement, and use of measurable performance standards.[4]

Among the many advantages to the MOR approach is its flexibility and ability to incorporate performance targets for both job output and personal development. One variation of MOR recognizes that professional development should therefore be represented in the key results area (important worker tasks) and in the corresponding objectives. A second variation of the appraisal format recognizes that many human services agencies have established performance standards for certain program areas and tasks. These performance standards can be incorporated into the performance appraisal plan.

Developing an MBO/MOR Performance Appraisal Plan

Variations of the MBO/MOR system have been applied in both the public and the private sectors in varied ways (Casey Family Programs, 2007; Morrisey, 1983a, 1983b). The process is composed of the following six steps.

Step 1: Defining roles and missions. Both workers and supervisors need to have a common "vision" and understanding of the central purposes, goals, functions, and philosophy of the organization. This understanding forms the

Name: Position:

Work Unit: Review Period:

Rating Definitions

- **Does Not Meet Expectations:** Completely or mostly fails to fully achieve the requirements of the position, goal(s) set by supervisor, or goal(s) identified in the Performance & Development Plan (PDP), or meets goal(s) only with inordinate supervision or assistance. Many gaps in performance or achievement of goals noted.
- **Partially Meets Expectations:** Partially achieves the requirements of the position, goal(s) set by supervisor, or goal(s) identified in the Performance & Development Plan (PDP), or meets goal(s) only with inordinate supervision or assistance. Gaps in performance or achievement of goals noted.
- **Meets Expectations:** Fully achieves requirements of the position, goal(s) set by supervisor, or goal(s) identified in PDP without supervision or assistance, or with appropriate supervision and assistance from others. No material gaps in performance.
- **Exceeds Expectations:** Fully achieves requirements of the position, goal(s) set by supervisor, or goal(s) identified in PDP and goes beyond them. Assists others in the accomplishment of their goals. Performance is distinguished by its consistent excellence.
- **Significantly Exceeds Expectations:** Fully achieves requirements of the position, goal(s) set by supervisor, or goal(s) identified in PDP and goes significantly beyond. Assists others in the accomplishment of their goals. In addition to consistently excellent work, is responsible for the achievement of broader organization results through initiative, dedication, and extra work.

I. Performance Goals

Goal 1—Assessing and counseling families. (functioning level of parents and of children, assessment records)

Performance Objectives/Standards: (1A) To meet with birth parents at least twice a month to assist them in improving family conditions. (1B) Provide parent–child in-home therapy at least once a week. (1C) At least 75% of the children on the caseload will remain with their family.

Employee Self-Assessment Rating:

Does Not Meet Performance Expectations	Partially Meets Performance Expectations	Meets Performance Expectations	Exceeds Performance Expectations	Significantly Exceeds Performance Expectations

Employee Self-Assessment Comments

Figure 7.2 *(Continued)*

Supervisor Assessment Rating:

▣ Does Not Meet Performance Expectations	▣ Partially Meets Performance Expectations	▣ Meets Performance Expectations	▣ Exceeds Performance Expectations	▣ Significantly Exceeds Performance Expectations

Supervisor Assessment Comments

Other goals would follow . . .

II. Professional Development

Development Area No. 1—Increase interviewing skills for working with Latino families.

Employee Self-Assessment Rating:

▣ Does Not Meet Performance Expectations	▣ Partially Meets Performance Expectations	▣ Meets Performance Expectations	▣ Exceeds Performance Expectations	▣ Significantly Exceeds Performance Expectations

Employee Self-Assessment Comments

Supervisor Assessment Rating:

▣ Does Not Meet Performance Expectations	▣ Partially Meets Performance Expectations	▣ Meets Performance Expectations	▣ Exceeds Performance Expectations	▣ Significantly Exceeds Performance Expectations

Supervisor Assessment Comments

Other development goals would follow . . .

III. Values

(This section could be used to rate and comment if the employee performed his or her job responsibilities in a manner consistent with or in furtherance of the organization's key values such as social justice, building positive relationships with the local community, and stewardship of financial and other resources.)

Figure 7.2 *(Continued)*

Figure 7.2 (Continued)

Employee Self-Assessment Rating:

Does Not Meet Performance Expectations	Partially Meets Performance Expectations	Meets Performance Expectations	Exceeds Performance Expectations	Significantly Exceeds Performance Expectations

Employee Self-Assessment Comments

Supervisor Assessment Rating:

Does Not Meet Performance Expectations	Partially Meets Performance Expectations	Meets Performance Expectations	Exceeds Performance Expectations	Significantly Exceeds Performance Expectations

Supervisor Assessment Comments

IV. Overall Evaluation Summary

[This section evaluates employee's total contributions to the organization for the reporting period, relating to performance, development, and values. Choose only **one** overall rating.]

Employee Self-Assessment Rating:

Does Not Meet Performance Expectations	Partially Meets Performance Expectations	Meets Performance Expectations	Exceeds Performance Expectations	Significantly Exceeds Performance Expectations

Employee Self-Assessment Comments

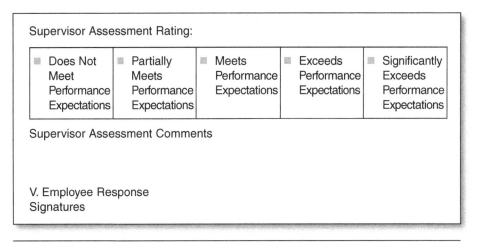

Figure 7.2   A partial example of a results-oriented performance appraisal plan for a home-based services therapist

foundation for both worker commitment and clarity of job tasks to be performed. For example, many juvenile justice welfare programs are rethinking their purpose and goals as they shift to an emphasis on strengthening families and providing crisis intervention services rather than primarily placing children in secure detention.

Step 2: Selecting key results areas. The most important job tasks or major activities are selected for the appraisal plan. These activities represent the 5 to 10 areas of greatest importance in terms of the worker's time, energy, and talent. For example, in looking at a foster care worker's job, some key result areas might include "working with birth families to address the family conditions necessitating child placement," "goal planning," "monitoring of ancillary services," and "arranging parent–child visits." The use of task-based job descriptions (see Chapter 4) will facilitate this process greatly. In determining key results areas, supervisors identify all major areas within which the accountable individual will be expected to invest time, energy, talent, and other resources during the projected time period of commitment (usually 6 months to 1 year).

Supervisors should include "soft" or difficult-to-measure areas, such as staff communications and working relationships, as well as "hard" tangible areas that are easier to measure, such as number of cases served and cost of a unit of service. These areas will not necessarily cover the entire job, but they will identify the "critical few" areas in which priority effort should be directed. They will be limited, generally, to one, two, or three words and will not represent activities as such but areas within which activities and, more important, where results will occur. Each area will not be measurable as stated, but it will contain elements that are capable of being measured.

Step 3: Identifying performance standards and indicators (measurement and documentation methods). How do we know whether key results areas are being performed effectively? Indicators are those measurement criteria that we can use to assess worker job performance. For example, in child welfare, it might be the number of intake investigations completed or the proportion of children in the worker' caseload who are provided some form of adoptive or more permanent placement within a year of foster care placement. For a mental health worker with a caseload of primarily depressed clients, it might be the percentage of his or her clients whose symptoms of depression that do not result in emergency unplanned hospitalizations are alleviated.

It is important that these indicators be reasonable, as well as mutually chosen by supervisors and subordinates, as they are not absolute measurements and many can be manipulated by staff if the system is not respected by all involved (Rynes et al., 2005). Indicators in the human services arena include work output, deadlines met, client progress, children returned home, error rates, number of client complaints, meeting attendance, plans developed, and client or collateral contacts made. More specifically, in the home-based services therapist example in Figure 7.2, we used "parents and children seen at least once a week," "timely preparation of comprehensive court reports," and "child placement avoided in 75% of the cases." These examples illustrate that indicators "identify only what will be measured, not how much or in what direction. They serve as an intermediate step, prior to setting objectives (or performance standards) designed to increase the probability that we are directing our resources to where they will get the best payoff" (Morrisey, 1983a, p. 27).

When considering performance standards and indicators, consider any special responsibilities or challenges that a staff person may have. For example, staff members from communities of color are often called on to provide support to those communities or consultation to other staff. Both activities take time away from other duties but often enhance the workgroup's effectiveness. Those factors must be considered in some work situations.

Step 4: Developing performance objectives. The supervisor and worker need to collaborate in developing statements of the measurable results to be achieved for each key results area. For example, in the area of intake related to child protective services, a performance objective could be "to complete investigations of physical abuse within 2 weeks from referral date at a cost not to exceed an average of 20 work-hours per investigation." This approach uses an action verb (to complete), an outcome (investigation), a time frame (2 weeks), and an estimated cost in time (20 hours.)

In designing clear program or performance objectives, use specific measurable outcome objectives that are mutually agreed upon by workers and supervisors. Performance objectives should:

1. Start with the word "to," followed by an accomplishment verb (e.g., "To complete," "To implement," or "To reach agreement").

2. Specify a single measurable key result to be accomplished as well as a target date or a time span for its accomplishment. Be as specific and quantitative (and, hence, measurable and verifiable) as possible. (The indicator step is especially useful here.) Specify only the "what" and "when"; it avoids venturing into the "why" and "how."

3. Be readily understandable by those who will be contributing to its attainment. Be consistent with the resources available or anticipated.

Avoid or minimize dual accountability for achievement when joint effort is required. They should be realistic and attainable but still represent a significant challenge, providing maximum payoff on the required investment in time and resources, as compared with other objectives being considered.

1. Objectives need to be consistent with basic organizational policies and practices. They should be willingly agreed to by both supervisor and employee, without undue pressure or coercion, and they should be recorded in writing, with a copy kept and periodically referred to by both supervisor and employee.

2. Finally, the objectives should be communicated in writing and in face-to-face discussions between the accountable person and those individuals who will be contributing to its attainment (Morrisey, 1983a, p. 337).

Step 5: Listing action plans. Action plans include the specific worker behaviors that must be carried out to achieve the objective. In many organizations, these action plans are found in the employee's performance development plan—a document developed annually by the employee and his or her supervisor that specifies the key job parts and expected outcomes for the year, along with professional development objectives (e.g., Casey Family Programs, 2007). The level of detail may vary from general statements listing what major steps must be taken to detailed plans listing who will do what, when, how, and at what cost. The critical function of action plans is mapping out what needs to happen to achieve the objective in sufficient detail in order to establish accountability for completing each of the substeps and to establish a basis for supervisory monitoring.

An example of this is the development of detailed and measurable practice protocols for social work services in hospital settings. For example, a protocol for serving cancer patients included steps for assessment (e.g., reviewing the chart, interviewing the patient, contacting the family, and so on), the information that must be recorded (demographic, type of cancer, premorbid level of functioning, patient's statement of how much they want to be told, and the like), and what aspects of the casework plan should be recorded. These protocols provide specific guidelines for worker practice behavior along with indicators for measuring levels of worker compliance and performance. Protocols for child protective services intake represent a similar approach to developing specific worker steps and guidelines for major areas of job responsibility (e.g., National Resource Center for Child Protective Services, 2007).

Step 6: Establishment of controls. Controls are methods for keeping the supervisor informed of the progress made in relationship to the objectives. A supervisor might use bar charts to plot the caseload numbers and placement outcomes of his or her permanency planning workers in order to measure worker progress on the foster care appraisal plan illustrated in Figure 7.2. A mental health agency supervisor might summarize the key tasks and a timeline for writing a major grant proposal in a Gantt chart to monitor a subordinate's progress.

Communication between supervisors and their subordinates is also essential for successful implementation. A process that meaningfully involves workers by setting clear performance objectives followed by timely check-ins and proactive feedback increases worker commitment. This is important because human services supervisors tend to rely on supervisee self-reports of performance. Few spend the time observing staff in the field or even in the office. But a supervisor can obtain objective information about worker performance via some opportunities for direct observation, coleading groups and programs, and via audio and video tapes of sessions with parents, youth, or entire families (G. Shaffer, personal communication, January 23, 2008).

Planning and Conducting Performance Appraisal Conferences

The appraisal conference must be carefully planned, requiring adequate time, clear definitions of worker and supervisor roles, and a conducive environment free from unnecessary distractions. Falcone and Sachs (2007) believe that the most important part of performance appraisal is the process itself:

> By working together to analyze and evaluate the employees' performance as well as their place within the department and the organization as a whole, and by setting goals . . . , you and your employee

can strengthen your relationship and become a team of two . . . working towards a common agreed-upon goal. (p. 7)

Social services organizations are concerned about maximizing the consistency of performance appraisal ratings. For example, some organizations provide "frame-of-reference training" to increase rating accuracy by calibrating raters so the scores on a rating scale being used by the organization have similar meanings for all raters (Duncan, Jackson, Atkins, Fletcher, & Stillman, 2005; Murphy & Cleveland, 1995, p. 201).

There are a few general principles for conducting performance appraisals that, if followed, result in a much more effective and comfortable process for the worker and supervisor (see DelPo, 2007; Kadushin & Harkness, 2002). For example, staff should be involved in choosing an appraisal system and in establishing the evaluation criteria that are used. This participation increases commitment to the evaluation process and clarifies expectations regarding evaluation. The primary, if not the exclusive, focus of the evaluation should be on the work performance of the supervisee rather than on any evaluation of the worker as a person. In addition, the appraisal method and criteria should be formulated with some consistency across both workers and supervisors as well as from one evaluation period to the next.[6]

Evaluation should be a continuous process rather than a one-time or occasional event with time to prepare for the assessment prior to the formal evaluation built into the supervision process. As such, evaluation needs to occur within the context of a positive working relationship. Evaluations should be conducted with some recognition and consideration of the total range of factors (worker controlled or not) that may be determining the worker's performance. Both worker strengths and areas for improvement should be reviewed in a way that is fair and balanced (see Table 7.3).

THE VALUE OF WORKER SELF-APPRAISAL INFORMATION

You can make the performance evaluation task easier and more effective by extensively involving staff in the process. Ask the employee being appraised to bring three lists to the performance appraisal interview: (a) areas where the employee contributed positively to the operations of the program or organization, (b) areas where the worker has shown recent improvement, and (c) areas that the worker feels need improvement or thinks his or her supervisor would like to see improvement. Employees need time to think through these lists, and so enable employees to take a few weeks to complete the assignment.

This approach is effective for several reasons. First, because you as the supervisor will also fill out the three lists, employees are more likely to bring candid responses to the table. This process will enable you to discuss the performance

Table 7.3 Providing Effective Feedback

Principle	Ineffective	Effective
1. Focus discussion on behavior rather than on the person.	"You don't seem too motivated lately."	"In the last 2 weeks, you've arrived at 8:30 and left early on 2 days. Anything I can help with?"
	"Your attitude and concern make you one of our best employees."	"The extra hours you worked last week made it possible for me to finish that Schedule X. I appreciate your dedication to this program; it will help us obtain another position."
2. Focus discussion on observation rather than on opinions. (Avoid GLOP: Generalized Labeling of People.)	"The distribution of the last set of food baskets was done poorly."	"The last set of food baskets was delivered late in the evening with six baskets delivered to the wrong address. How can we prevent that from happening again?"
3. Focus discussion on what was done, exploring in a diplomatic manner why it was done.	"I think you have a problem with anger control with the children. You don't like working with the toddlers?"	"I noticed last week that you raised your voice a few times when Susan and Michael wandered away from the painting area."
4. Focus discussions initially on sharing of ideas and information, not dictating ideas.	"You should revise the intake worksheet by adding items requesting the names, addresses, and phone numbers of friends in the area as well as relatives."	"What questions do you think might be useful to add to the intake worksheet to help us locate our loan recipients in case they move?"

Sources: Adapted from Austin, M.J. (1981); DelPo, A. (2007); Jensen, J. (1980); Kadushin, A. & Harkness, D. (2002); and Shulman, L. (1993).

areas you value in their work as well as areas for improvement. This latter point is particularly critical from a psychological perspective (Billikopf, 2003):

> It is human nature not to want to bring up our faults; but it is also human nature to prefer to point out our own shortcomings rather than having someone else do it. This process allows the subordinate

to think in terms of both his own performance expectations and perceived supervisor expectations. (p. 63)

There is a fourth list, which is just as vital as the first three. The fourth list is the employee's response to the question: *What can I do differently, as your supervisor, so you can be more effective in your job?* If a supervisor is not truly willing to listen to what the employee may have to say here, the negotiated performance appraisal will not work as it should, and a more traditional performance appraisal would work better. It is important to include this question as an assignment ahead of time so the employee has time to think about it and will come to the appraisal conference prepared (Billikopf, 2003). In summary, an effective negotiated performance appraisal helps the employee take additional ownership for both continuing effective performance and improving weak areas.

PLANNING THE APPRAISAL CONFERENCE

As mentioned, the appraisal conference must be carefully planned, requiring adequate time, clear definitions of worker and supervisor roles, and a conducive environment free from unnecessary distractions. To provide this environment, the supervisor must move out from behind the desk, postpone visitors and phone calls, and generally show the worker that the appraisal is high priority. The evaluation procedure should be a mutual, shared process with worker participation encouraged but with both taking some responsibility for reviewing the evaluation form and preparing a preliminary assessment. In preparing draft revisions of the performance appraisal, the supervisor and worker should provide some documentation of his or her views. To facilitate this process, there should be assurances regarding the confidentiality of what is being said and written. In conducting performance evaluations, supervisors should not merely list excellent and poor work behaviors but should analyze why certain behaviors are desirable or not desirable as well as set goals for future performance. Evaluations should be viewed as part of a continuous assessment process whereby worker job performance is continuously changing and open to improvement.

Finally, in providing staff with feedback, it is important to follow some of the principles described by Lehner (undated as cited in Austin, 1981). Some of these principles include focusing feedback on behavior rather than on the person—using observational data rather than inferences. It is helpful to focus feedback on description rather than on judgment, using descriptions of behavior as part of a range of possible behaviors (e.g., more or less) rather than simple qualitative distinctions (e.g., good or bad). In addition, behavior related to a specific situation should be highlighted (e.g., preferably the "here and now" rather than the "there and then").

Feedback is most effective when it is based on sharing of ideas and information rather than on giving advice. Exploration of alternatives should be the focus rather than exclusively on producing answers or solutions. Feedback should be focused on the value it may have to the recipient, not on the value or release that it provides to the person giving the feedback. Concentrate on the amount of information that the person receiving it can use rather than on the amount that the supervisor might like to give. In addition, choose a time and place that is unhurried and comfortable so that personal data can be shared at appropriate times.

During those difficult interviewing moments, focus feedback on what is said rather than on why it is said. Although not a negotiating process, some of the principles for providing staff with feedback are reflected in some of the literature on negotiating. For example, Fisher and Ury (1983) identify four major strategies for "Principled Negotiation":

(1) **People:** Separate "people issues" (e.g., personality, emotions, relationships, or ego) from the problem or issue at hand.

(2) **Interests:** Focus on the underlying interests at stake and not on a person's current "position" on the issue.

(3) **Options:** Generate a variety of possibilities (all with mutual gains for you and them) before deciding on a course of action.

(4) **Criteria:** Whenever possible use objective criteria, standards, laws, or other policies to decide or settle some differences rather than resorting to a contest of wills or stubbornness. (Also see Fisher & Shapiro, 2005; Ury, 1991; http://www.pon.harvard.edu.)

Thus, conducting performance appraisal conferences requires a valid method, careful documentation, preparation for the interview, and communication skills for conducting the appraisal. (See Figure 7.3 for practical guidelines.) To apply the principles discussed above successfully, supervisors may need to role-play performance appraisal interviews to practice providing feedback in constructive ways and handling various employee responses.

EVALUATING GROUP PERFORMANCE

Increasingly, the performance of an organization is the result of good teamwork or results when a group of people work effectively together. Assessing group performance is made much easier when performance criteria are specific and the role of each group member is clear and measurable. Watch for these aspects. For example, Mankins and Steele (2005 as cited in Silverstein, 2007) found that groups were not effective in 37% of the performance areas. The top three reasons for this were as follows, in order of importance: (a) inadequate or unavailable resources, (b) poorly communicated strategy, and (c) failure to define actions required to execute the strategy.

Irrespective of the particular evaluation method used, the appraisal process should take into account the following guidelines:

1. Staff should be involved in establishing or modifying evaluation criteria to ensure that more relevant criteria are used, to intensify commitment to the evaluation process, and to clarify expectations regarding evaluation.

2. Evaluation should be a continuous process rather than a one-time or occasional event with periods of assessment prior to the formal evaluation built into the supervision process.

3. The supervisor should discuss the evaluation procedure in advance with the supervisee.

4. The evaluation should be communicated in the context of a positive working relationship.

5. Evaluations should be made with some recognition and consideration of the total range of factors (worker controlled or not) that may be determining the worker's performance.

6. The primary, if not the exclusive, focus of the evaluation should be the work performance of the supervisee rather than any evaluation of the worker as a person.

7. The evaluation should review both strengths and weaknesses, growth and stagnation, and should be fair and balanced.

8. Evaluations should be framed as tentative assessments of worker job performance that are continuously changing or modifiable.

9. Evaluations should be formulated with some consistency both across workers and supervisors, as well as from one evaluation period to the next.

10. The appraisal interview must be carefully planned, requiring adequate time and a conductive environment free from unnecessary distractions.

11. Supervisors should be willing to accept evaluation of their own job performance from the supervisee.

12. The evaluation procedures should be a mutual, shared process with worker participation encouraged, but with both taking some responsibility for reviewing the evaluation form and preparing a preliminary assessment.

Figure 7.3 *(Continued)*

Figure 7.3   (Continued)

13. There should be assurance regarding the confidentiality of what is being said and recorded.

14. In preparing draft revisions of the performance appraisal, the supervisor and worker should provide some documentation of their views.

Figure 7.3   Guidelines for conducting performance appraisals

When teams are formed, a diversity of worker skills, personalities, and work styles are brought together to function cohesively and effectively. Yet sometimes organizations do plan in a good strategic way, and two workgroups or teams clash in terms of their culture. Or the organization discounts innovations developed by the team if they are not from headquarters. All of these factors hinder team performance. Thus, in evaluating workgroup performance, it is crucial to help the group establish a common purpose and set of general strategies to achieve that purpose. The workgroup can then more easily set milestones for success as benchmarks and hold regular meetings to gauge progress (Silverstein, 2007).

SELECTING A PERFORMANCE APPRAISAL METHOD

Many organizations will not have the time to implement fully all components of the MOR approach. The key concepts and principles, however, can be incorporated easily into more streamlined MBO approaches. One example is shown in Figure 7.2. A performance appraisal form similar to this (but with job tasks tailored for each position) was implemented across an entire organization involving social work, finance, administrative support, and information services personnel. It focused on the evaluation of up to five key job parts and their related performance goals. And it included the evaluation of how well the employee has achieved his or her professional development plan for the year. This last section, and the career goals/aspirations section, is an aspect of appraisal that is often short changed. And yet, planning for the future can be a major motivation for the employee: "Career objectives can become attainable goals" (Falcone & Sachs, 2007, p. 33).

As mentioned, with the exception of certain graphic rating scales, no universal appraisal forms are in existence today. Most agencies customize a method or form to meet their individual needs. The critical questions we reviewed at the beginning of this chapter should provide guidance for choosing the best method for an agency. In choosing a method and in customizing the form, remember to include space on the form to include worker or supervisor comments, as well as to record accomplishments, worker strengths, areas for improvement, and an overall rating of performance.

Whatever variation of performance appraisal you choose, the actual *form* developed should incorporate space on the form itself or in the backup documentation for addressing five elements:

1. Performance expectations

2. Entering modifications based on changing circumstances

3. Recording accomplishments

4. Recording performance strengths and areas for improvement

5. Supervisor summary comments and employee final comments

One major strength of the MBO approach to performance appraisal is that it focuses attention on major work responsibilities where performance is assessed using specific performance goals, clear indicators, and measurable performance criteria. A classic review of goal planning research concluded that goal planning led to more focused work activity and improved job performance (Latham & Locke, 2007; Locke, Shaw, Saari, & Latham, 1981; Mind Tools, 2008). In addition, to the extent that the appraisal approach can support job enrichment and establish a clear connection to compensation, worker productivity can be improved (Locke, Feren, McCaleb, Shaw, & Denny, 1980; Rynes et al., 2005).

Summary

Worker performance appraisals are used for the systematic assessment of how well agency staff members are performing their jobs over a specified period of time. But we acknowledged here that an individual may be valued by an organization because he or she possesses particular personal characteristics such as valuing diversity, sense of humor, and the ability to encourage colleagues in times of crisis. Nevertheless, performance evaluations are generally designed to measure the extent to which the worker is achieving the requirements of his or her position and fitting within the group. Evaluations should be based on clearly specified, realistic, and achievable criteria reflecting agency standards. Measurable evaluation criteria also help to motivate, direct, and integrate worker learning while providing staff members with examples of how they can evaluate their own performance. And the performance appraisal process is fundamentally about providing feedback to employees. The next chapter discusses how task-based job descriptions and objective performance appraisals are essential for addressing employee performance problems. It also provides some general guidelines regarding employee discipline and outplacement.

Endnotes

1. The balanced scorecard is a *management system* (not only a measurement system) that enables organizations to clarify their vision and strategy and translate them into action. It provides feedback around both the internal business processes and the external outcomes to improve strategic performance and results. When fully deployed, the balanced scorecard transforms strategic planning from an academic exercise into the nerve center of an enterprise (Arveson, 1998, p.1; Balanced Scorecard Institute, 2007).

2. See The W. Edwards Deming Institute (TM), http://www.deming.org, or the Kaizen Institute, http://www.kaizen-institute.com/

3. Yet the research data are mixed—in another study, the supposed biasing effect of a supervisor disliking a supervisee was actually found to be due mostly to poor job performance (Varma, DeNisi, & Peters, 1996). Finally, Sackett and DuBois (1991) using data from 36,000 individuals in 174 jobs found that raters do *not* generally give more favorable ratings to members of their own race. But relatively few studies have been conducted on this topic. (Also see DuBois, Sackett, Zedeck, & Fogli, 1993.)

4. For practical guidelines for applying the MBO or MOR approach, see Archer North & Associates (2006) and Morrisey (1983a, 1983b).

5. Adapted from Casey Family Programs (2007).

6. See Arvey and Murphy (1998) and Rynes et al. (2005) for empirically based principles for conducting performance appraisal conferences.

References

Archer North & Associates. (2006). *Results method: Management by objectives (MBO)*. Retrieved June 2, 2007, from http://www.performance-appraisal.com/results.htm

Arveson, P. (1998). *What is the balanced scorecard?* Retrieved June 2, 2007, from http://www.balancedscorecard.org/images/BSC

Arvey, R. D., & Murphy, K. R. (1998). Performance evaluation in work settings. *Annual Review of Psychology, 49*, 141–168.

Austin, M. J. (1981). *Supervisory management for the human services.* Englewood Cliffs, NJ: Prentice Hall.

Bakir, S. T. (2005). A quality control chart for work performance appraisal. *Quality Engineering, 17*, 429.

Balanced Scorecard Institute. (2007). *What is the balanced scorecard?* Cary, NC: Author. Retrieved July 28, 2008, from http://www.balancedscorecard.org/BSCResources/AbouttheBalancedScorecard/tabid/55/Default.aspx

Billikopf, G. E. (2003). *Labor management in agriculture: Cultivating personnel productivity* (2nd ed.). Berkeley: University of California at Berkeley. Retrieved May 16, 2009, from http://www.cnr.berkeley.edu/ucce50/ag-labor/7labor/001.htm

Borman, W. C., Hanson, M., & Hedge, J. (1997). Personnel selection. *Annual Review of Psychology, 48*, 299–337.

Brannick, M. T., Levine, E. L., & Morgeson, F. P. (2007). *Job and work analysis: Methods, research, and applications for human resource management* (2nd ed.). Thousand Oaks, CA: Sage.

Bruns, E. J., Rast, J., Peterson, C., Walker, J., & Bosworth, J. (2006). Spreadsheets, service providers, and the statehouse: Using data and the Wraparound process to reform systems for children and families. *American Journal of Community Psychology, 38*, 201–212.

Cascio. W. F. (1995). Whither industrial and organizational psychology in a changing world of work? *American Psychologist, 50*, 928–939.

Casey Family Programs. (2007). *Performance development plan.* Seattle: Author.

Cummings, L. L., & Schwab, D. P. (1973). *Performance in organizations: Determinants and appraisal.* Glenview, IL: Scott Foresman.

DelPo, A. (2007). *The performance appraisal handbook.* Berkley, CA: Nolo.

Deming W. E. (1982). Out of the crisis: Quality, productivity and competitive position. Cambridge, MA: Cambridge University.

Driskill, W. E., Weismuller, J. J., Hageman, D. C., & Barrett, L. E. (1989). *Identification and evaluation of methods to determine ability requirements for Air Force occupational specialties.* San Antonio: Metrica Inc. Retrieved June 3, 2007, from http://stinet.dtic .mil/oai/oai?&verb=getRecord&metadataPrefix=html&identifier=ADA212772.

DuBois, C. L. Z., Sackett, P. R., Zedeck, S., & Fogli, L. (1993). Further exploration of typical and maximum performance criteria: Definitional issues, prediction, and White–Black differences. *Journal of Applied Psychology, 78*, 205–211.

Duncan, J. R., Jackson, S. G., Atkins, R. B., Fletcher, J. A., & Stillman, J. A. (2005, March). Frame of reference training for assessment centers: Effects on interrater reliability when rating behaviors and ability traits. *Public Personnel Management*, pp. E1–E10. Retrieved July 28, 2008, from http://www.allbusiness.com/human-resources/ 847225–1.html

Falcone, P., & Sachs, R. (2007). *Productive performance appraisals* (2nd ed.). New York: American Management Association.

Fisher, R., & Ury, W. (1983). *Getting to yes: Negotiating agreement without giving in.* New York: Penguin.

Fisher, R., & Shapiro, D. (2005). *Beyond reason using emotions as you negotiate.* Boston: Harvard Negotiation Project. Retrieved March 21, 2008, from http://www.pon .harvard.edu

Fleishman, E. A., & Mumford, M. D. (1991). Evaluating classifications of job behavior: A construct validation of the ability requirement scales. *Personnel Psychology, 44*, 523–575.

Ganzach, Y. (1995). Negativity (and positivity) in performance evaluation: Three field studies. *Journal of Applied Psychology, 80*, 491–499.

Haynes, M. G. (1978). Developing an appraisal program. *The Personnel Journal, 57*(1), 14–19.

Hunt, S. (1996). Generic work behavior: An investigation into the dimensions of entry level, hourly, job performance. *Personnel Psychology, 49*(1), 51–83.

Jensen, J. (1980). *Employee evaluation – It's a dirty job but somebody's got to do it.* The Grantsmanship Center News.

Jensen, P. S., Weersing, R., Hoagwood, K. E., & Goldman, E. (2005). What is the evidence for evidence-based treatments? A hard look at our soft underbelly. *Mental Health Services Research, 7*(1), 53–74.

Kadushin, A., & Harkness, D. (2002). *Supervision in social work* (4th ed.). New York: Columbia University Press.

Kaplan, R. S., & Norton, D. P. (2005, July/August). The balanced scorecard: Measures that drive performance. *Harvard Business Review*, pp. 172–180. (Reprint R0507Q)

Klingner, D. E., & Nalbandian J. (1985). *Public personnel management: Context and strategies.* Englewood Cliffs, NJ: Prentice Hall.

Latham, G. P., & Locke, E. A. (2007). New developments in and directions for goal-setting research. *European Psychologist, 12*, 290–300.

LeBlanc, P. V., & Mulvey, P. W. (1998). How American workers see the rewards of work. *Compensation Benefit Review, 30*(1), 24–28.

Locke, E. A., Feren, D. B., McCaleb, V. M., Shaw, K. N., & Denny, A. T. (1980). The relative effectiveness of four ways of motivating employee performance. In K. D. Duncan, M. M. Gruenberg, & D. Wallis (Eds.), *Changes in working life* (pp. 363–388). New York: Wiley.

Locke, E. A., Shaw, K. N., Saari, L. M., & Latham, G. P. (1981). Goal-setting and task performance: 1969–1980. *Psychological Bulletin, 90*(1), 125–152.

Mankins, M. C., & Steele, R. (2005). Turning strategy into great performance. *Harvard Business Review, 83*, 64–72.

Mathis, R. L., & Jackson, J. H. (2006) *Human resource management* (11th ed.). Mason, OH: Thomson Southwestern.

Mind Tools. (2008). *Locke's goal setting theory: Understanding SMART goal setting.* Retrieved July 28, 2008, from http://www.mindtools.com/pages/article/newHTE_87.htm

Morrisey, G. L. (1983a). *Performance appraisals for business and industry.* Reading, MA: Addison-Wesley.

Morrisey, G. L. (1983b). *Performance appraisals in the public sector: Key to effective supervision.* Reading, MA: Addison-Wesley.

Murphy, K. R., & Cleveland, J. N. (1995). *Understanding performance appraisal: Social, organizational, and goal-based perspectives.* Thousand Oaks, CA: Sage.

National Resource Center for Child Protective Services. (2007). *Safety intervention policy standards and agency self-assessment.* Retrieved June 2, 2007, from http://www.nrccps.org/resources/featured_resources.php

Odiorne, G. S. (1970). *Training by objectives.* New York: Macmillan.

Odiorne, G. S. (1984). *Strategic management of human resources.* San Francisco: Jossey-Bass.

Organizational and Staff Development Unit. (2007). *Guidelines for using 360-degree feedback in the appraisal process.* London: City University of London. Retrieved June 3, 2007, from http://www.city.ac.uk/sd/guidelinesforusing360-degreefeedback intheappraisalprocess.html

PAQ Services. (2007). *The PAQ program.* Bellingham, WA: Author. Retrieved May 3, 2007, from http://www.paq.com/?FuseAction=Main.PAQProgram

Pearce, J. L. (2006). *Organizational behavior real research for real managers: Individuals in organizations.* Irvine, CA: Melvin & Leigh.

Performance-Appraisal-Form.com. (n.d.). *Book of performance appraisal phrases.* Retrieved May 28, 2007, from http://www.performance-appraisal-form.com

Rynes, S. L., Gerhart, B., & Parks, L. (2005). Personnel psychology: Performance evaluation and pay for performance. *Annual Review of Psychology, 56*, 571–600.

Sackett, P. R., & DuBois, C. L. (1991). Rater-ratee race effects on performance evaluation: Challenging meta-analytic conclusions. *Journal of Applied Psychology, 76*, 873–877.

Shulman, L. (1993). *Skills of supervision and staff management.* Itasca, IL: F.E. Peacock.

Silverstein, B. (2007) *Evaluating performance.* New York: Harper Collins.

Toolpack Consulting. (2007). *Alternative performance reviews.* Retrieved June 1, 2007, from http://www.toolpack.com/performance.html

Ury, W. (1991). *Getting past no: Negotiating with difficult people.* New York: Bantam.

Varma, A., DeNisi, A. S., & Peters, L. H. (1996). Interpersonal affect and performance appraisal: A field study. *Personnel Psychology, 49*, 341–360.

Wong, K. F. E., & Kwong, J. Y. Y. (2005). Between individual comparisons in performance evaluation: A perspective from prospect theory. *Journal of Applied Psychology, 90*, 284–294.

Wright, P. M., George, J. M., Farnsworth, F., & McMahan, G. C. (1993). Productivity and extra-role behavior: the effects of goals and incentives on spontaneous helping. *Journal of Applied Psychology, 78*, 374–381.

Web-Based Resources

For articles on human resource management and performance appraisal, see the *Annual Review of Psychology.* http://www.ovid.com/site/catalog/Journal/273 .jsp?top=2&mid=3&bottom=7&subsection=12

For more information about Continuous Quality Improvement, see W. Edwards Deming Institute (TM) http://www.deming.org or the Kaizen Institute http://www .kaizen-institute.com/

Results Method: Management By Objectives (MBO). http://www.performance-appraisal.com

Suggested Readings

Brannick, M. T., Levine. E. L., & Morgeson, F. P. (2007). *Job and work analysis: Methods, research, and applications for human resource management* (2nd ed.). Thousand Oaks, CA: Sage.

DelPo, A. (2007). *The performance appraisal handbook.* Berkley, CA: Nolo.

Falcone, P., & Sachs, R. (2007). *Productive performance appraisals* (2nd ed.). New York: American Management Association.

Rynes, S. L., Gerhart, B., & Parks, L. (2005). Personnel psychology: Performance evaluation and pay for performance. *Annual Review of Psychology, 56,* 571–600.

8

Handling Employee Performance Problems

Introduction

Developing accurate job descriptions, hiring the most qualified personnel, using measurable job-related performance criteria, and conducting effective performance appraisal sessions will provide a solid foundation for dealing with a variety of employee performance problems. Employee performance problems can be minimized and more easily handled if the personnel functions described in the preceding chapters have been adequately addressed. This chapter will focus on general principles for handling performance problems and for being responsive to gender, race, and other diversity issues if they should develop during the process of dealing with performance problems.

Distinguishing Between Worker and Agency Performance Problems When Diagnosing Employee Performance Problems

Differentiating the differences between employee problems and performance problems related to system dynamics can be one of the most challenging tasks supervisors and managers will face. These responsibilities can be handled without causing the agency unwanted legal consequences when supervisors know how to address performance problems, are aware of institutional policies and procedures related to performance problems, and know how to implement a progressive disciplinary process.

Employee performance difficulties are often viewed as evidence of a lack of worker knowledge or skill (training need), poor attitudes (a lack of commitment to the job), need for more supervision, or poor use of time. However, employee performance difficulties may instead be caused by a host of non-worker factors, such as unclear agency policies, resource limitations, vague work priorities or performance standards, poor supervision, caseload demands, and assignment of inappropriate cases. These non-worker-related factors will have an impact on an employee's performance problems. Before any disciplinary action is taken, supervisors must have a clear understanding of the causes of the problems. They have to be able to assess the different types of performance problems and distinguish the need for different types of disciplinary intervention for each employee or efforts to fix systemic problems.

Addressing Employee Performance Problems

OVERVIEW

Supervisors must use caution before they take any action to deal with an employee who is having performance difficulties. Careful and consistent implementation of policies and procedures must be followed for all phases in the disciplinary process. Strict adherence to the process can help the organization avoid adverse legal consequences if supervisory decisions or actions are challenged in court.

To help lessen employee performance problems, the role of a supervisor and his or her manager must be clearly understood by all employees. Employees do best when they perceive their supervisors as being fair; ethical; responsible; able to make decisions; able to perform under pressure; and having the integrity, skills, knowledge, experience, and competency to perform their role (e.g., Kadushin & Harkness, 2002; Lencioni, 2002; Tsui, 2005). Examples of key supervisory actions are listed as follows (Brown, 1984; Kadushin & Harkness, 2002):

1. What do employees expect of a supervisor? Evaluate employees' performance and inform them concerning their progress, giving due credit for good work.

2. Study and develop the abilities of employees.

3. Guide and counsel employees.

4. Deal fairly and impartially (show mutual respect and work equally with all staff members).

5. Maintain adequate supervision records.

6. Encourage employee interest in their job and its relationship to the agency goals.

7. Develop group discipline, confidence, and loyalty: the "feeling of belonging."

8. Set a good example and exercise self-control.

9. Foresee and eliminate possible causes of grievances.

10. Maintain and have adequate knowledge of work and agency policies.

11. Assign the right person to the right job.

12. Organize, plan, and coordinate work.

13. Issue clear, concise, and complete instructions.

14. Cooperate with others in the agency.

15. Recommend changes in employee status as they are needed without delay.

Although this list may repeat some content from previous chapters, these areas are listed above to underscore the value of ensuring that certain supervision fundamentals are implemented well. Supervisors and managers need to take a close look at both worker factors and agency factors that may be contributing to worker performance difficulties before deciding on a course of action. More specifically, in analyzing a "performance problem," it is important to determine whether the performance difficulty relates to one or more factors. Cherrington (1983) as well as DelPo and Guerin (2005) outline several groupings of employee performance problems, some of which are highlighted in the sections that follow:

- Performance or productivity problems
- Interpersonal problems
- Insubordination
- Excessive absenteeism
- Drugs and alcohol
- Theft and dishonesty
- Violence
- Morality issues

Unsatisfactory performance refers to the failure to perform assigned work because a staff member lacks the ability to do so. For example, an employee must take twice the amount of time to complete an assignment because of lack of skills or practice. Some mistakes can be caused by a lack of employee work knowledge, but sometimes inadequate employee motivation can be related to poor agency rewards for performance. Procrastination, intolerant attitudes, being aggressively opinionated, and abrasive competitiveness are all behaviors that can also result in unsatisfactory performance.

First rule violations put colleagues and the organization at risk. These types of violations might include weapons possession, use of alcohol or drugs, abusive or threatening language, insubordination, sleeping on the job, carelessness, smoking in unauthorized places, fighting, gambling, abuse of sick leave, habitual tardiness, and horseplay.

Illegal or dishonest acts include theft, embezzlement, misuse of company facilities, or falsifying records.

Personal problems may result in performance difficulties because of personal or family challenges (e.g., falling in love, getting married, having children, ending a relationship with a life partner, getting a divorce, or a death in the family). These challenges can be temporarily overwhelming for the individual. Alcohol abuse, drug use, and domestic violence/intimate partner abuse can also be causes of performance problems.

Special situations can develop, such as a staff person who feels that his or her position is at a "dead end" or who may be disgruntled as a result of being passed over for a promotion. There also may be "technophobes" on a group who are hesitant to learn how to use certain technological equipment or employees whose skills are no longer matched with the requirements of the job (Brody, 2000). Other performance problems can be attributed to organizational limitations, such as one or more of the following (DelPo & Guerin, 2005; Glisson, 2007; Glisson & Hemmelgarn, 1998):

- Unclear task assignments
- Unclear performance standards
- Mismatch between worker and agency ideology or approach to practice
- Unclear policies
- Lack of resources
- Poor supervision (e.g., little worker feedback, inconsistent monitoring, lack of technical assistance, or poor worker-supervisor relationship)
- Unusually large caseloads
- Assignment of inappropriate cases
- Environmental factors, such as excessive noise, poor lighting, lack of privacy, and depressing decor
- Demeaning or demoralized organizational climate

Each of the above factors is a common cause of worker performance problems. Although chronic underperforming by staff can be exasperating to deal with (Nicholson, 2003), Waldroop and Butler (2000) outlined how even "star performers" in an organization can experience difficulties. Four major root causes seem to be as follows: (a) an inability to understand the world from the perspective of other people, (b) a failure to recognize when and how to use power, (c) a failure to come to terms with authority, and/or (d) a negative self-image that undermines the person's confidence (pp. 90–91). Once these causes have been identified, it is much easier to develop a strategy for addressing them (DelPo & Guerin, 2005).

As a complement to these concepts, "Appreciative Inquiry" can be a helpful approach for proactively exploring issues and identifying potential solutions. Appreciative Inquiry is a way of being and seeing. It is both a worldview and a process for facilitating positive change in human systems, such as organizations, groups, and communities. Appreciative Inquiry is based on a simple assumption: Every human system has something that works right—things that give it life when it is vital, effective, and successful. Appreciative Inquiry begins by identifying this positive core and connecting to it in ways that heighten energy, sharpen vision, and inspire action for change. The basic framework for this approach is "the cooperative search for the best in people, their organizations, and the world around them ... it involves the art and practice of asking questions that strengthen a system's capacity to heighten positive potential" (Cooperrider & Whitney, 1999, p. 10; also see Cooperrider, Whitney, Stavros, & Fry, 2003). In other words, supervisors should have the skills to uncover positive dimensions of the situation, as well as the worker strengths and resources available to help.

GRIEVANCE HANDLING

Employee performance problems are often intertwined with employee grievances. These grievances may be informal complaints or "formal grievances" filed under the agency's grievance procedures. The most common informal and formal grievances relate to wages and salary, where a staff member complains about individual wage adjustments, job classification, or the incentive system (i.e., "I'm not getting what I'm worth" or "My job is worth more"). Supervision is another common issue. This includes complaints about discipline or objections to general methods of supervision (i.e., "My supervisor doesn't like me," "The supervisor plays favorites," or "There are too many rules and regulations").

Other common grievances relate to the assignment of cases, caseload demands, loss of seniority, calculating seniority, performance ratings, layoffs, promotions, disciplinary discharges, and transfers. An effective supervisor attempts to address these issues on an informal basis as they develop. When these grievances become more than informal complaints, the process of handling grievances usually has four major phases: reception, fact finding, settlement, and follow-up (DelPo & Guerin, 2005; Roseman, 1982).

- *Reception* is when the supervisor receives the worker's grievance. At this point, the supervisor should be available or accessible to the employee and should listen attentively. Assuming that the grievance is real, the supervisor needs to demonstrate interest and a willingness to assist. If the grievance concerns the supervisor or if an issue is sensitive to the supervisor, then avoiding defensive or extremely negative reactions is essential. In some situations, it may be necessary to have someone else hear the grievance, as appropriate.
- During the *fact-finding phase,* it is necessary to decide what facts are needed to analyze the situation and to decide on a course of action. In an effort to understand the different viewpoints that are represented by the worker and the target of the grievance, the facts must be differentiated from suppositions or emotions. This process requires taking time to obtain necessary facts without postponing the decision beyond a realistic time limit, because a delay in responding often exacerbates the situation.

- The *settlement* phase requires that priority be given to an early resolution of the issues. The concepts of principled negotiation are useful in arriving at a fair and well-accepted settlement. It is important to strive for mutual agreement so that the parties involved will commit themselves to a definite course of action. This involves seeking mutual gains, making realistic promises, and facing impasses calmly by paying attention to the facts.
- The final phase or follow-up includes the process of *taking prompt action* through memos and/or meetings. During this phase, it is important to keep the lines of communication open so that last-minute adjustments can be made if the situation changes. Avoid taking a punitive or superior stance that can sabotage the settlement. Finally, it is necessary to monitor all actions to ensure that the grievance has been resolved and that the conditions that caused it are no longer present or are reduced (DelPo & Guerin, 2005; Roseman, 1982).

THE IMPORTANCE OF PERSONNEL POLICIES

Handling worker performance problems requires that certain employee regulations and grievance handling procedures have been specified in the agency's personnel policies. Illustrated in Figure 8.1 is a list of discipline procedures for various employee performance problems. Such explicit policies provide guidelines for expected employee behavior and consequences for noncompliance. As such, they form a foundation for addressing performance problems within a "developmental discipline" system. In this system, disciplinary standards and procedures are mutually accepted, are designed to shape behavior and not punish, are performance focused, and are periodically reviewed.

Resignation: Voluntary termination freely made by an employee for any reason he or she chooses. A professional or administrative employee is expected to give a minimum of 1 month's notice. A support staff person should give 2 weeks' notice.

Mutual Agreement: Both the individual and management decide to end the employment relationship for their mutual benefit. Sometimes, the decision to sever a relationship is genuinely arrived at together. Under such circumstances, the record can honestly reflect that there has been a mutual agreement that the individual's skills are not matched to job requirements and that both parties recognize this. Both parties want to part amicably. Under these circumstances, management gives no termination notice; instead, both parties agree on a departure date that allows a reasonable period for the employee to seek other work. Mutual agreement should be recorded as the reason for termination only when the above circumstances exist.

Figure 8.1 *(Continued)*

Figure 8.1 (Continued)

Reduction in Force: Resulting from job elimination caused by reorganization or financial requirement as determined by management. Any employee so affected will be given 1 month's notice plus 1 month's pay, with reasonable time off during the notice period for job interviews.

Individuals who are terminated because of force reduction (layoffs) should be eligible for reemployment (recall) if their same job opens up again within a 6-month period after termination. If another job becomes available in the agency during that same time period, and the terminated employee may be qualified for it, then he or she should be invited to apply and should be given consideration with other candidates. For reduction, terminees remain eligible for reemployment for an indefinite period, but they need not be given special notification after 6 months from the date of their termination.

Unsatisfactory Performance: Failure of an employee to meet performance standards, which includes completing tasks in a timely, competent way or maintaining an adequate attendance record. Prior to termination for unsatisfactory performance, the immediate supervisor must make a reasonable effort to resolve the problem with the employee. He or she must be given written notification that continued employment is in jeopardy and be told what must be done to improve the situation.

With this notice, the person will be placed on 2-month probationary status. If performance has not improved satisfactorily by the end of this period, then he or she may receive advance termination notice. Supervisors may extend this 2-month probationary period if circumstances warrant. Uncooperative behavior or negative attitudes that affect the work or morale of others may result in this 2-month probationary period being shortened. Individuals who are terminated for unsatisfactory performance may receive, at management discretion, 2 weeks' pay at termination in lieu of notice.

Misconduct: Gross misbehavior on the job, refusal to do work reasonably expected, wrongful use of or taking of agency property, or conviction of a felony. Termination for misconduct requires no prior notice or severance pay.

Retirement: At whatever age an employee begins to draw benefits from the retirement plan provided by the agency. There is no mandatory retirement age, although the normal retirement age is 65 years. Continuation beyond age 65 years is subject to meeting the usual performance standards.

Whatever the circumstances of termination, the value of all vacation accrued and not taken is paid to the individual. This payment is made at the time of termination in lieu of extending the termination date and running out of accumulated vacation time in absentia.

Figure 8.1   General guidelines for termination policies

Source: From "Letting go: The difficult art of firing," by J. Jenson, 1981, *The Grantsmanship Center News,* 9, 38–39. Copyright 1981 by The Grantsmanship Center. Reprinted by permission.

When workers are clear about their job assignments and performance standards, it is less likely that such policies will need to be enforced. As the supervisor and worker examine job performance difficulties and possible causes, it is essential as well that the time, place, and nature of the problems have been carefully documented. Effective handling and prevention of performance problems is a characteristic of high-quality supervision. As such, the first line for prevention and remediation is the line supervisor.

Using personnel policies, standard operating procedures, supervision principles, and the job analysis process described earlier, the supervisor can assess the match between worker competencies and the job requisites, seek to clarify performance standards, and remove obstacles to employee success. Supervisors also provide access to training as well as monitor, provide feedback, and reward effective work behaviors (Messmer, 2003). However, supervisors should be sensitive to the possibility that personal factors may be contributing to poor performance. As mentioned, these factors might be a worker's health problems, stress or other emotional difficulties, non-job-related problems (e.g., marital relations or family pressures), and/or poor work habits (e.g., nonauthorized use of company equipment, such as computers, cell-phones, carelessness, and poor time management).

Additional Strategies for Supervisors

Human services organizations have a responsibility to assist workers in addressing performance problems through a referral to medical and mental health programs or, in the case of poor work habits, provision of special on-the-job supervision and coaching. Finally, supervisors should consider whether the employee truly has low performance with no potential for further growth or is just a person whose performance is at a low level but the potential is considered high. Most of the time, the latter situation can be turned around with the appropriate intervention (Messmer, 2003). Depending on a supervisor's management philosophy, he or she may fire the employee with no potential for growth relatively quickly, or he or she may institute a variety of measures to assist the employee who functions at a low level but has considerable potential. Thus, in handling performance problems, most agencies rely on progressive discipline consisting of the following four major phases: (a) discussion of performance issue with employee, followed by counseling and/or training; (b) written reprimands, if the first intervention does not resolve the problem; (c) final warning and a probationary period to allow for changed behavior; and (d) dismissal if poor performance continues despite interventions.

Before supervisors and managers confront an employee's performance problems, they must take into consideration the protection of employees' rights. Many institutions have implemented a process to protect employees' rights called administrative justice.

This practice addresses employees' performance problems and at the same time protects their rights. The use of "due process" and "just cause" are the foundation of administrative justice. Due process protects the employee from arbitrary, capricious, or unfair action by supervisors and management, and it should be articulated in agency policies and procedures. Just cause suggests that any disciplinary action executed by administration is based on objective facts and is performed in a valid and appropriate manner (Cherrington & Dyer, 2003; DelPo & Guerin, 2005).

Many supervisory interventions are available to address employee performance difficulties that do not require immediate employee termination. Those interventions include the following (DelPo & Guerin, 2005):

1. *Analyze the situation accurately.* Performance problems have facts, so focus on the problem and not on the person ("separate people from the problem"). Listen to the kinds of reasons why the problems are happening ("focus on interests and not the positions taken"). Ask for ideas on how to correct the problem ("generate a variety of options").

2. *Handle the issue promptly.* When a supervisor seems to be avoiding a frank discussion with an employee, unnecessary anxieties can be created. Management should welcome the chance to talk about problems. Be prepared. Conduct this conversation in a private meeting. Supervisors should be encouraged to initiate such discussions and not to wait until there is time to investigate all the facts. Get the facts, double-check the facts, and do it quickly. Workers do not like to be kept on hold. An employee may decide to go to a lawyer or an outside agency if a prompt response is not forthcoming from an immediate supervisor.

3. *Be approachable and accessible.* A common problem with internal grievance procedures is how to persuade workers to use them. The contact person should be easily available. Supervisors should encourage complaints and should be held accountable for ensuring that employees make use of the system. When a worker is terminated suddenly for something that has been a chronic problem, the supervisor is at fault for not dealing with the problem promptly.

4. *Address the situation as informally as possible.* Discussions with an employee should be handled in an informal, nonthreatening atmosphere. Face-to-face notification of concern is better than giving an employee a written memo. The grievance system should be simple. Nobody likes to tell his or her story over and over again. No one should only receive a printed form letter in response to a personal problem. Although such a form letter may be perceived as "legal," it may motivate an employee to seek outside help, including perhaps initiating litigation.

5. *Be consistent.* The supervisor should check with the personnel department to be sure that the company position is correct and consistent with past practice. All too frequently, an employee discovers that other workers are being treated differently or learns that there is a difference of opinion among various representatives of management. An executive should never suggest that some other manager made a mistake. Passing the buck is bad psychology. The worker does not care who is at fault, only about what can be done about the problem.

6. *Take corrective actions.* When management was wrong, corrective action should be taken promptly to resolve the problem. Set up an action plan (i.e., "Insist on objective criteria for judging solutions"). Schedule a date for following up on the issue of concern. The grievance procedure should have a payoff for the employee. It can justify itself only if it works. Then, it will be regarded as a respectable part of the organization.

7. *Achieve finality.* The management group should give the employee a final decision, with a full explanation, as soon as the facts are known.

8. *Learn from the situation.* The process should result in change within the organization. Managers should ask: Was the claim justified? Why did this employee misunderstand the situation? Why did the employee feel aggrieved? What can we do to avoid these problems in the future?

Employee Termination

The discharging of staff can be one of the most difficult and unpleasant tasks in managing personnel. Superiors and personnel managers are often given this responsibility with insufficient information and training in conducting employee terminations. A variety of references provides excellent information and guidelines for handling employee terminations (see, for example, California Chamber of Commerce, 2006; University of California Berkeley Laboratory, 2005). This section includes a description of some of the major issues and guidelines for handling the termination process, including the need for explicit policies, common reasons for employee termination, establishing "just cause," conducting termination interviews, and the importance of an exit interview.

Clear job specifications and performance standards are essential to evaluating employee performance. Because employee termination can occur for reasons beyond poor performance or misconduct, explicit policies must be developed that describe the conditions under which an employee can be terminated. Written policies provide the operational guidelines for termination, protect staff from arbitrary actions, and help ensure that termination decisions are legal and fair. A host of legal issues surrounds termination, and nearly all groups of employees have some type of protection under the law that is being enforced by local courts, state human rights agencies, the Equal Employment Opportunity Commission (1980), and in the case of unions, the National Labor Relations Board (Budd, 2004; Cherrington & Dyer, 2003). For example, the "employment at-will" doctrine allowing termination without notice and cause for jobs in nonunion private organizations increasingly is being narrowed by recent court decisions (Cherrington & Dyer, 2003; Schanzenbach, 2003). Recent changes in case law and concerns about arbitrary employee termination provide a powerful incentive for the careful development and execution of termination policies in human services organizations (Budd, 2004; Roehling, 2003).

COMMON REASONS FOR TERMINATING EMPLOYEES

Termination rationales are typically defined in policy statements as resignation, mutual agreement, reduction in force (i.e., job elimination), unsatisfactory performance (i.e., including the inability to establish effective working relationships with coworkers), misconduct on the job, and retirement. Specific items that should be addressed by termination policies are listed in Figure 8.1. Policies should contain provisions for severance pay and termination notice. When terminating long-time employees, it is appropriate to consider a more generous termination payer notice to reward them for their dedication to the organization. The following sections will address establishing just cause, conducting the termination conference, and the importance of exit interviews.

ESTABLISHING JUST CAUSE

Employee termination takes place frequently because of defective job performance, violations of agency rules (e.g., use of drugs or alcohol), challenging supervision (e.g., refusal of a supervisor order), and gross misconduct (e.g., fighting, willful destruction of property, theft, dishonest acts, or immoral conduct on company property). There is a legal, professional, and moral responsibility to establish "just cause"—irrespective of the specific reason for termination (Cherrington & Dyer, 2003; DelPo & Guerin, 2005).

Establishing just cause involves supporting the termination decision with appropriate documentation and an explicit rationale. Several questions and recommendations in the following section will help supervisors make determinations about whether their reasons for termination have been adequately developed (DelPo & Guerin, 2005; Vatave, 2004):

1. *Does any documentation exist that leads to conclusions other than the imminent termination?* Sometimes, positively written performance reviews or letters and memos of commendation contradict the conclusion that someone should be terminated. If so, the supervisor may not be able to act as quickly as necessary. The supervisor must initiate a record showing why the situation has changed for the worse—unless, of course, something drastic has occurred such as misconduct, which immediately overrides any positive record the person may have.

Be sure that the written records of other employees who are not being fired are substantially better than that of the person who is being considered for termination. If others have equally bad records of performance, attendance, attitude, or productivity and are not being terminated, the supervisor may have a difficult time explaining why one person was chosen rather than another. The supervisor should have a very clear answer to the question "why me?" if posed by the person being terminated or someone representing him or her. When a supervisor treats one person differently from another, they must have a solid basis for doing so.

2. *Who, if anyone, will be surprised by this termination?* Certainly, the fired employee should not be surprised by the supervisor's action if he or she has followed a policy for handling unsatisfactory performance as described above. Of course, the person may be shocked that the warning has become reality, but in no case should he or she be able to say that there was no warning. Verbal warnings should definitely be confirmed in writing, because almost all people have marvelous psychological filtering systems when it comes to bad news. Do not expect a verbal message to be heard as intended when the subject is possible termination of employment. If the problem is serious, get the warning on paper to ensure that it is fully understood.

Other employees should not be surprised by the decision either. Peers usually know who is not doing their share of the work before the supervisor does. On the one hand, although that person may be well liked and may even get some sympathy from others, the good sense of most contributing employees will tacitly endorse the termination. That endorsement will probably be silent, not verbal. If, on the other hand, peers are surprised by the action, then their understandable concern is "Am I next?" The savvy supervisor usually knows the informal grapevine well enough to test discretely how others will perceive staff termination.

3. *Was there adequate investigation of alleged misconduct before action was taken?* Never fire someone on the spot or in the heat of anger—no matter what the offense. Chances are that it will be done poorly. Instead, send the person home immediately. Then, in the presence of others or in writing, place him or her on an investigatory leave of 1 to 5 days, with or without pay. Pay status is determined later by the outcome of the investigation. If the result leads to reinstatement, then pay should be given for the investigatory leave period. If not, then pay can cease at the time the employee was put on leave.

The investigation while the accused person is on leave should be focused on confirming facts. Say, for example, that being drunk on the job is the alleged offense. Be sure that others observed what you did regarding the person's behavior, and that the person was not taking prescribed medication with side effects similar to drunkenness. If the offense was on-the-job physical violence, then be sure to find out what provoked it. Circumstances may lead to disciplinary action other than termination, and you need time to investigate those circumstances. The supervisor may even need investigatory leave time to consult with the police or a lawyer if the case involves such matters as illicit drug traffic or larceny. Many organizations write use of investigatory leave into their personnel policies to ensure that misconduct dismissals are handled competently.

4. *Is the person's salary record contrary to that of an unsatisfactory employee?* The supervisor should avoid trapping himself or herself into the inexplicable situation of having recently given the employee to be fired a merit salary increase. As ridiculous as it sounds, this circumstance occurs often enough to justify a cautionary discussion. If the agency has an automatic salary progression based on seniority, it may happen that a termination follows closely after a salary increase. That can be explained because pay is not linked to performance.

There should be no record of salary increases comparable with peers if the agency administers salaries on a merit basis. If there is such a record, then the supervisor may not be able to take dismissal action as quickly as it may be warranted. The supervisor must freeze, skip, or slow down salary increases as a logical first step in dealing with a marginal employee.

5. *Have other employees been treated differently under similar circumstances?* Consistency of treatment is important in all employee relations matters but particularly so in cases of termination. In planning a termination, be sure that there is no similar situation in which another person was not or will not be terminated. In a case of poor attendance, poor attendance should not be ignored if it involves other people but not the intended terminee.

For example, perhaps one employee has poor attendance because of child care problems and the supervisor sympathizes because he or she also is a single parent with similar problems. However, the potential terminee's poor attendance record may be for a reason that is judged to be legitimate. Bias can easily come into play when a case is being built to justify firing a problem employee. Test the decision by discussing it with a trusted member of the management team who can view the matter objectively, and point out possible inconsistencies that may have been overlooked.

Sometimes, the documentation itself can be inconsistent. Sometimes, the record is full of performance observations, and it seems contrived when compared with what exists for other situations or workers. In other words, the personnel record looks like a "paper trail" compared with the usual practice in the organization. The best defense against such an allegation is to be able to demonstrate that the nature of the documentation is not unique, that additional documentation was necessary to determine the performance situation warranted employee termination, and that standard procedures have been followed in this as well as other terminations.

CONDUCTING TERMINATION CONFERENCES

This is generally the most difficult step in the termination process. The process is largely dependent on whether the principles of managing personnel in the preceding chapters have been adhered to and, in particular, how closely the supervisor has worked with the employee in analyzing the situation and in implementing possible solutions.

It is important to acknowledge the large amount of stress that is put on both supervisors and workers during this process. Employees who are terminated tend to experience similar emotional/psychological responses that occur related to loss of an object (i.e., family member and/or friends). They can experience the five phases of a grief and mourning process during and after the termination meetings. The first response is *disbelief* (e.g., "This really is not happening to me"). The second response is *anger*, whereby workers feel rejected, abused, and that they have been dealt with unfairly. The third response is *bargaining*, where the individual tries to convince the supervisor not to proceed with the termination. The fourth response is *depression*. This occurs once the shock has worn off and includes the symptoms of sadness, loss of sleep, inability to make decisions, anxiety, and loss of self-esteem. The fifth response is *acceptance and hope*, whereby the individual accepts the situation and hopes that something good will come out of all this pain.

Employees having experienced the five phases of grief who have worked through the termination process with their manager often enter a phase of *positive activity in new directions*. This depends on how thoroughly each of the preceding responses has been handled. Effectively dealing with the initial and follow-up termination conferences has a direct impact on the reactions of the terminated worker. The supervisor and the employee need to address questions not dealt with or answered during the termination interview, such as how to inform the other agency employees (i.e., by the worker or by the supervisor; verbally or by memo?) and handling references. The supervisor will also need to inform the terminated worker that both positive and negative information will be provided if the worker allows reference information to be divulged.

If the employee remains onsite for a period of time, be aware of the importance of using the follow-up interview, when appropriate, and other contacts to assess how well the employee is handling the termination emotionally. What may be initially calm behavior may quickly change to an angry, depressed, or potentially violent state of emotion. The supervisor or manager should monitor closely employee reactions to determine whether professional counseling is necessary.

In certain situations, however, supervisors may terminate an employee the same day the decision is made with a confirming memo ready to distribute at the meeting. The employee is then instructed to cease working immediately after the meeting. For example, in severe disciplinary situations or where the infraction has been well documented, it is counterproductive to have an employee remain at his or her position and in the work area.

Exit Interviews

The exit interview is a tool that should be used in conjunction with termination and the provision for outplacement services. It can also be used for other terminations, such as resignation, retirement, or transfer. Each time an employee leaves the organization, there is an opportunity to conduct a mini-opinion poll; this is a time when the exiting employee may feel free to say what is on her mind without fear of reprisal. By analyzing the information gained, management can take remedial action to improve working conditions. Management is also made aware of morale and turnover problems (Alberta Human Resources Services, n.d.; Microsoft Office Online, 2006).

The optimum time to interview an employee is a day or two before the employee leaves the organization. The immediate supervisor or manager should not conduct the interview because it may be difficult for him or her to be objective when asking the interview questions. Specifically, the supervisor might be inclined to censor or slant the employee's replies for self-protection. The best person to conduct these interviews is a member of the personnel department. The backbone of the exit interview is the interview form itself, which gathers the worker's opinion about salary, benefits, working conditions, progress within the agency, employee and organizational morale, and any recommendations. Encouraging the worker to be as honest and open as possible will result in more useful information.

When the interview is over and before upper management reviews the exit report, the immediate supervisor should be permitted to read the worker's exit interview and attach a rebuttal memo in which he or she rates the worker's capabilities and attitudes and tells the other side of the story. An exit interview program will not, of course, be a major cure for all problems related to employee relations, but it will support agency efforts to maintain morale, minimize turnover, improve hiring efforts, and correct unsatisfactory work conditions if serious attention is paid to the findings.

OUTPLACEMENT PROGRAMS

Outplacement, termination counseling, or career continuation services are all terms used to describe agency-sponsored assistance to employees to help them cope with the stresses associated with termination and to locate new employment (Pickman, 1994). Largely used to assist corporate executives and mid-managers, some of these services may be useful to human services organizations as well. For example, some agencies provide severance pay to match the approximate amount of time required to locate another job for that type of employee. Other organizations assist the employee in how to share the news with family and friends to minimize family stress and to maintain supportive ties. Organizations employing an outplacement approach also may inform other employers and employment agencies of the availability of individuals facing layoff. Finally, they provide personnel with assistance with preparing resumes, typing letters of application, and interviewing tips. Although many human services agencies may lack the resources to mount an extensive outplacement program, in-house or contracted assistance to the former employee should result in a more comfortable transition, good public relations, and improved employee morale.

RACIAL AND ETHNIC ISSUES IN PERFORMANCE REVIEWS

There has been limited attention in the human resources and management literature for nonprofit and human services organizations on dealing with employee performance when these issues emerge in the context of racial and/or ethnic bias. Although Title VII of the Civil Rights Act, which has been in existence since 1964, prohibits discrimination in recruiting, hiring, and employment termination based on race, color, sex, religion, or national origin, employers continue to violate this legislation. When employers are found in violation of Title VII, it is usually for unlawful discharge and discipline of employees and for refusal to implement a bias-free work atmosphere.

Termination of racial-ethnic minorities can be carried out under different pretexts that mask true racial biases. This practice makes it difficult for employees of color or those from other protected groups (i.e., women, people with physical disabilities, or seniors) to show proof they have been discriminated against by their employer. Additionally, it makes it impossible to account for accurate numbers of employees who have experienced discriminatory practice in the workplace. Because this type of discrimination is masked, the appearance that statutory prohibition against discrimination has not produced an abundance of claims may be an illusion. In fact, a true picture of unlawful employer practices may not be at all evident (DelPo & Guerin, 2005; Thomas & Ely, 1996). Consequently, it is not unusual for people of color to question the motives of supervisors and employers who try to implement disciplinary actions.

A supervisor's discomfort in addressing harassment of any employee, in particularly ethnic minority employees, can have serious adverse consequences for the supervisor and the organization. An employer can be held liable if a supervisor avoids dealing with any type of racial harassment in the workplace. Professional and expert biases are not protected by the law and are in violation of Title VII. For some supervisors, their biases may be attributed to lack of understanding of cultural background differences or to lack of experience in addressing issues of race.

However, the lack of knowledge and understanding, or the inability to recognize and accept employees' cultural differences in the workplace, can promote conflict between workers and/or between individuals and their supervisor. This lack of understanding and acceptance can perpetuate perceptions of job inefficiency or ineffectiveness—resulting in performance problems (Schuler & Jackson, 2007). Under this type of hostile workplace environment, oppression and censorship of employees is likely. These types of employers usually make the workplace so intolerable that the individual terminates prematurely or experiences a punitive termination. These actions by supervisors are in violation of Title VII. This can set the stage for an employee filing a grievance complaint, which could possibly lead to a successful legal action against the organization (Schuler & Jackson, 2007).

Some supervisors develop skills that influence the development of a respectful, acceptable, and safe workplace environment for employees of all racial and ethnic backgrounds. Through the elimination of offensive language and abusive behaviors, and by fostering a collaborative working alliance with employees, higher levels of performance can be achieved by the entire group. At the same time, this approach to diversity in the workplace can ensure equity of job opportunity, nondiscriminatory behaviors by others, reduction in grievances complaints, and potential enhancement of worker productivity (Schuler & Jackson, 2007; Stone, 1997).

Developing knowledge and skills in working with employees from different cultural groups is an ongoing process that supervisors must strive to achieve as an important aspect of their supervisory responsibility. Supervisors' lack of awareness and knowledge about how employees relate to their colleagues who are ethnically and/or racially different from the majority of the staff in an organization can impact job performance and can be costly to the organization. Furthermore, consumers' reaction and interaction with employees of different racial/ethnic groups should be considered sensitively in the individual's performance appraisal. An employee who demonstrates cultural competence in interacting with clients should be recognized in the performance appraisal process. In addition to being aware of staff interactions with clients, as well as with colleagues, both supervisors and managers must be aware of the overall impact of their own behaviors and possible biases when addressing the performance problems of employees who are racially and/or ethnically different from the supervisor.

RACIAL HARASSMENT

Harassment lawsuits can originate from acts of sexual harassment as well as from acts of racial discrimination. Under Title VII of the Civil Rights Act (1964), an employee can sue an employer when the employer makes the workplace environment hostile and uncomfortable for an employee because of his or her race. The employee can also obtain an injunction against the employer to stop the harassment, and if the employee has strong evidence that the employer's actions were blatant or that serious acts of retaliation followed the complaint, then a legal settlement can be negotiated in lieu of a court trial.

Laws regarding suing for racial harassment and the use of the Reconstruction Civil Rights Acts of 1866 and 1867 were passed by Congress to enforce the 14th Amendment and to protect the rights of new citizens of African descent in the late 19th century. A landmark court case (*Patterson v. McLean Credit Union*, 1988) established that individuals can sue for racial harassment under the Reconstruction Civil Rights Act (1866) and be awarded both monetary compensation for damages plus an injunction.

Supervisors have the responsibility to maintain a workplace environment free of racial, sexual, religious, or ethnic harassment if they are to avoid violating Title VII of the Civil Rights Act (1964). For example, an employer who allowed a dummy of a black person with simulated dripping blood to hang for 18 hours at the workplace was held liable by the Seventh Circuit Court of Appeals because the employer failed to investigate the incident and failed to warn employees that racial harassment was prohibited and not tolerated (Jackson, 1993, p. 260). Although that example is blatant and unlikely to occur in a social services setting, racial hostility still exists and incidents may occur. Supervisors can make a difference by investigating incidents of racial harassment and by imposing negative sanctions on employees who exhibit racial and/or ethnic intolerance. Supervisors have the power to influence changes in the workplace by encouraging and supporting professional development and empowerment for workers and, thus, by setting those same standards and expectations for the organization. They can foster the development of more effective and efficient professional skills in communication, professional behavior, and public relations, and they can enhance tolerance for individual differences among workers, which can lead to a safe, trusting, and comfortable work environment (D'Andrea & Daniels, 1997; Schuler & Jackson, 2007).

PROVING DISCRIMINATION BY AN EMPLOYEE

Discriminatory practices against employees are a violation of Title VII of the 1964 Civil Rights Act. Employees do not have the responsibility to validate intent of discriminatory practices against them, but they must only prove that the act was perpetrated against them. When employees can prove the following, they are highly likely to win their case: (a) that they are within a protected class; (b) that they applied for the job; (c) that they were qualified for the job; (d) that they were not hired or they were fired; and (e) that the employer then hired someone of a different race, color, religion, sex, or national origin. Conversely, if the employer can justify his or her actions and have legitimate reasons for terminating the employee, then the employer will be able to defend itself successfully. The employee must demonstrate proof that the employer used a pretext to cover up the unlawful termination based on discriminatory practices (Cherrington & Dyer, 2003).

Up to this point, the kinds of examples provided in this chapter may have conjured up caricatures of White supervisors who are rigorous about policies and procedures, and who are limited in their thinking about people of color. Although these kinds of people may be present in the human services workforce, difficulties can emerge between a supervisor of any racial and/or ethnic background and an employee of any racial and/or ethnic background. In addition, the issues of race can make the difficulty much more complicated. The issues of racial and ethnic discrimination involve power and people's perceptions about "different-ness." Consequently, all social work professionals must be vigilant to recognize their own prejudices in order to keep an open mind about others and to learn from people who are ethnically and racially different from them.

Summary

This chapter has described procedures for handling employee performance problems emphasizing the use of carefully developed policies, thorough documentation, and a systematic process to help ensure satisfactory settlements for both supervisors and line staff. As we outlined in Chapter 1 and have reinforced throughout the book, when essential supervisory functions are handled with skill and a balanced focus on the results is achieved, the supervisory process, employee relationships, and the likelihood of employee performance problems will be minimized.

References

Alberta Human Resources Services. (n.d.). *A guide for support staff: Exit interviewing.* Alberta, Canada: Author. Retrieved June 17, 2006, from http://www.hrs.ualberta .ca/docs/Recruitment/Exit_Interviewing.doc

Brody, R. (2000). *Effectively managing human service organizations* (2nd ed.). Thousand Oaks, CA: Sage.

Brown, J. (1984). *Professional management training manual.* Salt Lake City: University of Utah.

Budd, J. W. (2004). *Employment with a human face: Balancing efficiency, equity, and voice.* Retrieved June 17, 2006, from DigitalCommons@ILR http://digitalcom mons.ilr.cornell.edu/books/3

Cherrington, D. J. (1983). *Personnel management: The management of human resources* (2nd ed.). Boston: Allyn & Bacon.

Cherrington, D. J., & Dyer, W. G. (2003). *Organizational effectiveness* (2nd ed.). Provo, UT: Brigham Young University.

Civil Rights Act, Title VII, 42 U.S.C. §2000e (1964).

Cooperrider, D. L., & Whitney, D. (1999). *Appreciative inquiry.* San Francisco: Berrett-Koehler.

Cooperrider, D. L., Whitney, D., Stavros, J. M., & Fry, R. (2003). *Appreciative inquiry handbook: The first in a series of workbooks for leaders of change.* San Francisco: Berrett-Koehler.

D'Andrea, M., & Daniels, J. (1997). Multicultural counseling supervision: Central issues, theoretical considerations, and practical strategies. In D. B. Pope-Davis & H. L. K. Coleman (Eds.), *Multicultural aspects of counseling series 7* (pp. 290–309). Thousand Oaks, CA: Sage.

DelPo, A., & Guerin, L. (2005). *Dealing with problem employees: A legal guide.* Berkeley, CA: Nolo.

Equal Employment Opportunity Commission. (1980). *Final guidelines on sexual harassment in the workplace.* Washington, DC: U.S. Government Printing Office.

Glisson, C. (2007). Assessing and changing organizational culture and climate for effective services. *Research on Social Work Practice, 17,* 736–747.

Glisson, C., & Hemmelgarn, A. (1998). The effects of organizational climate and interorganizational coordination on the quality and outcomes of children's service systems. *Child Abuse and Neglect, 22,* 401–421.

Jackson, G. E. (1993). *Labor and employment law desk book* (2nd ed.). Upper Saddle River, NJ: Prentice Hall.

Jenson, J. (1981). Letting go: The difficult art of firing. *The Grantsmanship Center News, 9,* 38–39.

Kadushin, A., & Harkness, D. (2002). *Supervision in social work* (4th ed.). New York: Columbia University Press.

Lencioni, P. M. (2002, July). Make your values mean something. *Harvard Business Review,* pp. 113–117. (Reprint No. R0207S)

Messmer, M. (2003, Aug). Managing underperformers. *The National Public Accountant,* p. 25.

Microsoft Office Online. (2006). *Conducting effective exit interviews.* Retrieved June 17, 2006, from http://office.microsoft.com/en-us/FX100621231033.aspx

Nicholson, N. (2003). How to motivate your problem people. *Harvard Business Review, 81*(1), 57–65.

Patterson v. McLean Credit Union, 485 U.S. 617 (1988).

Pickman, A. J. (1994). *The complete guide to outplacement counseling.* Hillsdale, NJ: Lawrence Erlbaum.

Reconstruction Civil Rights Act, 14 Stat. 27–30 (1866).

Reconstruction Civil Rights Act (1867). As cited in Zuczek, R. (2006). *Encyclopedia of the reconstruction era: A-L.* Westport, CT: Greenwood Publishing Group.

Roehling, M. V. (2003). The employment at-will doctrine: Second level ethical issues and analysis. *Journal of Business Ethics, 47,* 115–124.

Roseman, E. (1982). *Managing the problem employee.* New York: AMACOM, A Division of the American Management Association.

Schanzenbach, M. (2003). Exceptions to employment at will: Raising firing costs or enforcing life-cycle contracts? *American Law and Economics Review, 5,* 470–504.

Schuler, R. S., & Jackson, S. (2007). *Strategic human resource management.* Boston: Blackwell.

Stone, G. L. (1997). Multiculturalism as a context for supervision: Perspectives, limitations, and implications. In D. B. Pope-Davis & H. L. K. Coleman (Eds.), *Multicultural aspects of counseling series 7* (pp. 263–289). Thousand Oaks, CA: Sage.

Thomas, D. A., & Ely, R. J. (1996). Making differences matter: A new paradigm for managing diversity. *Harvard Business Review, 74,* 79–90.

Tsui, M. S. (2005). *Social work supervision: Contexts and concepts.* Thousand Oaks, CA: Sage.

University of California Berkeley Laboratory. (2005). *Employee termination process guide.* Berkeley, CA: Ernest Orlando Lawrence Berkeley National Laboratory, Human Resources Department. Retrieved June 17, 2006, from http://www.lbl.gov/LBL-Work/HR/forms/EE_Termination_Process.pdf

Vatave, S. (2004, July). Managing risk. *SuperVision, 65*(7), 6–9.

Waldroop, J., & Butler, T. (2000). Managing away bad habits. *Harvard Business Review, 78*(5), 89–98.

Web-Based Resources

American Management Association (AMA). Retrieved March 25, 2008, from http://www.amanet.org

Industrial Organizational Psychology. Retrieved May 21, 2008, from http://www.socialpsychology.org/io.htm

Suggested Readings

Bundy v. Jackson, 24 EDP 31439 (1981).

California Chamber of Commerce. (2006). *Recruiting, performance & termination.* Retrieved June 17, 2006, from http://www.calchamber.com/Store/Products/RTT

Constantine, M. G. (1997). Facilitating multicultural competency in counseling supervision: Operationalizing a practical framework. In D. B. Pope-Davis & H. L. K. Coleman (Eds.), *Multicultural aspects of counseling series 7* (pp. 310–323). Thousand Oaks, CA: Sage.

DelPo, A., & Guerin, L. (2005). *Dealing with problem employees: A legal guide.* Berkeley, CA: Nolo.

Nicholson, N. (2003). How to motivate your problem people. *Harvard Business Review, 81*(1), 57–65.

Odiorne, G. S. (1984). *Strategic management of human resources.* San Francisco: Jossey-Bass.

Thomas, R. R. (1991). *Beyond race and gender: Unleashing the power of your total workforce by managing diversity* (p. 174). New York: AMACOM, A Division of the American Management Association.

Waldroop, J., & Butler, T. (2000). Managing away bad habits. *Harvard Business Review, 78*(5), 89–98.

Appendix A

Brief History of Social
Work Supervision Concepts

A s the 21st century has begun, the efforts to understand the role of those who provide supervision of staff in social services organizations continue to evolve. Historically, social work supervision has drawn on the practice traditions that emerged from the beginning of the social work profession. And although the current concepts regarding supervision rest on a foundation that was established in the early 20th century (Richmond, 1917; Robinson, 1936), new understanding about supervision shapes new considerations in the social work supervisory role. However, knowing how supervision has developed over time can provide us with perspective as the role changes and grows.

In *Social Diagnosis,* Mary Richmond (1917) offered specific direction regarding providing social services as well as specific direction regarding training and monitoring of staff. In addition to Richmond's foundational work, one of the first periodic and systematic reviews of social work practice issues was the annual social work yearbook. The 1929 annual, the first yearbook produced, was published in 1930. This charter yearbook was the first edition of what was to become the *Encyclopedia of Social Work* (National Association of Social Workers, 1965). Interestingly enough, in this initial edition, although there was mention of the supervisory function in the management of public welfare agencies, there was no other discussion of first-line supervision. The issues of supervision came into and out of sharp focus beginning with *Social Diagnosis* and culminating in 1965, when supervision, as an area of practice, is first mentioned in the 15th edition of the *Encyclopedia of Social Work.* In addition to *Social Diagnosis* and the Annual Social Work Yearbook, *Supervision in Social Casework: A Problem in Professional Education* (Robinson, 1936) was one of the first textbooks specifically about social work supervision.

The following themes regarding social work supervision are threaded through editions of the *Encyclopedia of Social Work* after 1965: (a) *administrative control* (Burns, 1965; Miller, 1971); (b) *training and education* (Burns, 1965; Miller, 1971); (c) *therapeutic support* (Miller, 1971); (d) *professional independence* (Burns, 1965; Miller, 1971; Tsui, 1997a); and (5) *accountability for limited resources* (Miller, 1987; Tsui, 1997a). Although several noted authors elaborated on these themes over time, the following is summary of the initial summaries found in the *Encyclopedia of Social Work*.

The first historical theme of *administrative control* can be viewed from three different perspectives: (a) monitoring worker behavior related to assessing client needs and coordinating services; (b) protecting clients as a responsibility of both the worker and the supervisor; and (c) tutoring the novice worker and student (Miller, 1971, 1977, 1987).

The second historical theme of *training and education* emerged somewhat in tandem with the administrative aspects of supervision (Burns, 1965; Miller, 1971; Tsui, 1997b). Educational supervision gained considerable attention in the late 1920s and early 1930s as theory and skills training became increasingly colocated in both agency and university education programs (Burns, 1965). For example, the following educational concepts began to appear in social work supervision in the 1960s: (a) staff learn in different ways; (b) new information should be shared in relationship to the learner's readiness; (c) new information should build on the understanding of previously shared material; (d) logical thinking is essential for effective practice; (e) a learner's positive identification with the material being shared is an effective factor in facilitating learning; and (f) fostering self-awareness is essential (Burns, 1965). University-based education helped to legitimize the educational function of supervision.

The third historical theme in social work supervision involved the provision of *therapeutic support to workers* (Miller, 1971). Influenced in the 1920s and 1930s by Freudian psychoanalytic theory, the concepts of therapeutic support evolved into the notions of "parallel process" whereby a worker's ability to understand and support the client is similar to the supervisor's ability to understand and support the worker. Other themes related to therapeutic support included the confidentiality in the supervisory session (Tsui, 1997b) and promoting the development of self-awareness in the supervisory session (Miller, 1997). Specifically, the notion was developed that supervision of social work practice should mirror the requirements in practice of maintaining confidentiality as exhibited in therapeutic counseling sessions. Self-awareness and self-understanding were perceived as important as preconditions for understanding and helping others, particularly in relation to supervisor–worker and worker–client conflicts (Miller, 1977). In addition, the supervisor's role in facilitating a worker's ability to handle stressful work situations was introduced by reducing barriers to achieving goals, poor work conditions, incompatible demands, and ambiguous expectations caused, in part, by a lack of effective work habits (Munson, 1993).

The fourth historical theme in social work supervision emerged in the 1950s as a reaction, in part, to the psychoanalytic aspects of supervision, which could violate the individual rights of supervisees (Tsui, 1997b). There was a new call for *professional independence* in response to the perceived increase in worker dependency and the inappropriate "caseworking of the caseworker" by the supervisor (Tsui, 1997b). Experienced practitioners began to question the need for ongoing supervision that seemed to restrict their professional independence and inhibit their professional growth, development, or creativity (Burns, 1965; Miller, 1971, 1977, 1987). Autonomous practice was perceived as the hallmark of professional practice after a specified number of years under supervision (Tsui, 1997b).

The fifth theme emerged in the period of 1970 to 1990 in the form of increased *demand for accountability* for limited financial resources (Miller, 1987; Tsui, 1997b). This requirement has led to increased monitoring of staff using quantitative measures of service delivery in both public and in private social services agencies. It is in this era of accountability (1970s–1990s) that many textbooks regarding supervision in social and human services agencies began to be published. Currently, the expectations regarding accountability have not changed, but the expectations have continued to evolve so that supervisors currently are expected to manage administrative and clinical productivity using computerized information systems.

Current themes in social work supervision, however, place expectations on supervisors to create environments that are centered on knowledge exchanges, continuous quality improvement, and continuous staff refinement of skills as more evidence-based intervention methods are developed. The working environments of today involve the exchange of information within and between workgroups, and in learning action environments. These processes have to be understood and guided by supervisors. Recent supervisorial material represented in Austin and Hopkins (2004) discussed the supervisor's theoretical role as conduit and facilitator for learning processes. Where information and knowledge are perceived as work products and the sharing of information is perceived as a vital method to deliver services for consumers.

As a way of laying a broad conceptual foundation for understanding social work supervision, Tsui (2005) believes this aspect of management has a critical set of components:

A. Philosophy and Principles
- Interpersonal transactions
- Use of authority, exchange of information, and expression of feelings
- A reflection of personal and professional values
- Administrative functions such as monitoring job performance; educational functions such as imparting knowledge and skills, providing emotional support, and dealing with power issues
- Helping the organization achieve long-term and short-term objectives

B. Supervisor Relationships, Which Means Involvement of Four Parties:

- Agency, supervisor, staff, and the client in a certain context

C. Supervisory Process, Which Involves the Interactions Among All the Parties Listed Above and Dyads of Subsets of Each of Them

D. Culture as a Context for Supervision

Tsui builds on some of the authors cited earlier, who in large handbooks have explored these supervisory functions and specific specialty topics. Such topics have included designing and sustaining organizational teams, effective group decision making, and employee dismissal procedures (Edwards & Yankey, 2006; Edwards, Yankey, & Altpeter, 1998). In addition, critical emerging issues include managing for service outcomes, motivating work performance, assessing social psychological perspectives regarding workforce diversity and supervision, and training for staff and volunteers (Patti, 2008).

References

Burns, N. E. (1965). Supervision in social work (pp. 785–791). In H. L. Lurie (Ed.), *Encyclopedia of social work* (15th ed.). New York: National Association of Social Workers.

Edwards, R. L., & Yankey, J. A. (Eds.). (2006). *Effectively managing nonprofit organizations*. Washington, DC: National Association of Social Workers.

Edwards, R. L., Yankey, J. A., & Altpeter, M. A. (Eds.). (1998). *Skills for effective management of nonprofit organizations*. Washington, DC: National Association of Social Workers.

Miller, I. (1971). Supervision in social work. In *Encyclopedia of social work* (Vol. 2, 16th ed., pp. 1544–1551). New York: National Association of Social Workers.

Miller, I. (1977). Supervision in social work. In *Encyclopedia of social work* (Vol. 2, 17th ed., pp. 1494–1501). Washington, DC: National Association of Social Workers.

Miller, I. (1987). Supervision in social work. In *Encyclopedia of social work* (Vol. 2, 18th ed., pp. 748–756). Silver Springs, MD: National Association of Social Workers.

Munson, C. E. (1993). *Clinical social work supervision* (2nd ed.) New York: Haworth Press.

National Association of Social Workers. (1965). *Encyclopedia of social work*. Washington, DC: Author.

Patti, R. J. (2008). *Handbook of human services management* (2nd ed.). Thousand Oaks, CA: Sage.

Richmond, M. (1917). *Social diagnosis*. New York: Sage.

Robinson, V. P. (1936). *Supervision in social case work, a problem in professional education*. Chapel Hill: University of North Carolina Press.

Tsui, M. S. (1997a). Empirical research on social work supervision: The state of the art, 1970–1995. *Journal of Social Services Research, 23*(2), 39–51.

Tsui, M. S. (1997b). The roots of social work supervision: An historical review. *Clinical Supervisor, 15*, 191–198.

Tsui, M. S. (2005). *Social work supervision: Contexts and concepts*. Thousand Oaks, CA: Sage.

Appendix B

Answers to Equal Employment Opportunity Commission Exercise (for Chapter 3)

Note: These answers must be viewed with some caution as Equal Employment Opportunity regulations are periodically revised and local court cases may have implications for employment practices in your agency.

1.T On application forms, this information is separated before the application is screened.

2.T Yes, the Equal Employment Opportunity Commission (EEOC) may broaden its investigation.

3.F The person has to be *convicted* and the crime has to be job related.

4.F This is generally a decision between a woman and her medical doctor except if the woman is ignoring her doctor's orders. In corrections and other fields, if there is a possibility of physical assault, then the employer can require a leave of absence.

5.F Employer could reinstate her in a comparable job.

6.T But the employer is required to make a good faith effort to adjust the employee's schedule before refusing to hire or terminating.

7.T Provided that the employment test is objective, valid, and job related.

8.F Age discrimination is illegal.

9.T The issue is conviction—not merely arrest. And it depends on the job—if the conviction is not job related or if you hired other convicted persons, you may be violating Equal Employment Opportunity policy.

10.F   Generally hair length is not enforceable. But it depends on the job because a hair net may be required, especially in restaurants and institutional food service. In addition, a police department was upheld in a recent Supreme Court case for mandating short hairstyles because of special circumstances such as a safety factor.

11.T   But it applies only in certain cases because it has to be job related (e.g., to work at certain bank jobs, you have to be bonded with the bonding company, which is contingent upon a good credit rating).

12.F   Not owning a car does not mean without transportation—except it may be required possibly in areas without mass transportation where the job requires a personal mode of transportation.

13.F   Because an educational degree is not necessary for the job.

14.T   Possibly, but only if to work in a liquor store or some other position where the age requirement is clearly related.

15.T   But this policy is controversial and varies according to the way it is asked. Use questions such as the following: Are you a citizen (yes or no)? If not, do you have a visa? Do you have a green card? This is a difficult situation as sometimes the personnel department performs a visa/green card check prior to the interview process, but the interviewer does not have this information.

16.T   But how the question is asked is important. One appropriate method: Do you have a physical disability or mental or physical condition that would prevent you from performing this job?

17.F   This is an illegal type of personal question.

Appendix C

Position Description for a
Mental Health Specialist II

Adult Outpatient Services

Definition of Position

Under the agency's policies and professional requirements, this outpatient therapist position provides direct management of assigned clients, is responsible for facilitating teamwork for adult outpatient services, engages in consulting and informational activities for the community and other professional disciplines, participates in program evaluation procedures and professional record keeping, makes referrals to other local and state facilities, coordinates mental health services with other community and state resources, engages in supervision of graduate student interns, and works under the direct supervision of the coordinator of adult outpatient services.

MAJOR RESPONSIBILITIES AND RELATED TASKS

I. Direct Clinical Services (40%)

1. Establishes initial date of a potential client's presenting problems, mental status, treatment history, and medical problems.

2. Provides a diagnostic to determine treatment modalities, assign priorities, provide information, and make appropriate referrals to other treatment resources in the community.

3. Implements crisis or pre-crisis intervention procedures with potentially suicidal, homicidal, or gravely disabled clients in order to prevent destabilization, enhance adaptive functioning, and move clients toward an appropriate treatment program.

4. Gathers treatment-related information with respect to client's presenting problems, mental status, as well as relevant psychiatric, medical, and developmental history, in order to make decisions regarding diagnosis, treatment objectives, and ongoing treatment plans (intake).

5. Evaluates and assesses clients with the SCL 90 and other measures, based on state and DSM III categorizations, in order to provide professional treatment planning, consultation, or referral assistance.

6. Shares information on the mental health center's philosophy, procedures, policies, and treatment modalities in order to help prospective clients, interested citizens, or ongoing clients make treatment decisions, set appropriate goals, or better understand the functions of the mental health center.

7. Interviews collateral contracts, previous and current treatment professionals, and significant others, in order to establish a data base for assessment, treatment, planning, or treatment involvement.

8. Develops therapeutic relationships with ongoing clients (involving hope, trust, empathy, compassion, congruence, teamwork, and so on) to provide an environment whereby clients can make appropriate changes.

9. Constructs a conceptual scheme of the development of client's presenting problems, maintenance of presenting problems, and consequences of presenting problems to strategize for possible therapeutic interventions.

10. Clarifies priority problems, goals for change, and session limits according to agency policy to assist clients in developing appropriate expectations for treatment in relationship to the agency.

11. Uses broad-based insight and cognitive behavioral treatment approaches and interventions in order to change targeted behaviors and stabilize adaptive behaviors with individuals, couples, and families.

12. Manages the termination process and discharge planning to enhance client's ability to retain treatment changes, use community social supports, meet with treatment professionals, and/or continue work on therapeutic change.

II. Client Information System (30%)

1. Establishes appropriate professional files (including initial brief screening assessments, intake evaluations, progress records, treatment objectives and plans, previous treatment records, client's consents for current treatment, confidentiality, release of previous records, exchange of information with other agencies, and health care providers) in order to document work efforts for the agency and state of Washington.

2. Provides necessary client information to other agencies or health care providers (psychiatrists, mental health professionals, mental health agencies, schools, hospitals, and so on), in order to coordinate services to identified clients.

3. Gathers information as available from all potential client information resources to maintain a current and comprehensive fund of client information for treatment purposes.

III. Administrative Activities (20%)

1. Participates in required staff meetings and in-service meetings to keep abreast of agency policy and administrative procedures, meet requirements for continuing education, upgrade professional knowledge, improve adult outpatient teamwork and service coordination, engage in mutual consultation, and share professional support.

2. Uses weekly direct services supervision under the direction of the coordinator of adult outpatient services in order to facilitate professional accountability in the agency.

3. Supervises graduate student interns on a weekly basis to facilitate student development of professional expertise in client relations, therapeutic interventions, teamwork (interfacing with other professionals), constructive participation in agency functions, and client information management.

4. Monitors psychotherapy literature to be abreast of helpful information for delivery of mental health services.

IV. Enhance Adult Outpatient Team Functioning (10%)

1. Provides information to prospective clients or interested citizens in order to promote the program of the agency, increase community interest in mental health, refer client to other appropriate community resources, provide treatment linkages, assess mental health concerns and desires, and facilitate development of appropriate health care planning or connections with appropriate treatment resources.

2. Monitors the adult outpatient waiting list for the satellite office in order to provide for an orderly and fair client intake process in conjunction with the other satellite office.

3. Engages in appropriate teamwork functions (such as mutual support, clarification of office responsibilities and procedures, and mutual assistance) in order to provide a professional working environment and effective service delivery.

4. Develops cooperative relationships with families, physicians, public officials, and all interested agencies or individuals to interpret the mental health center services and provide for the development of mental health services in the community.

V. All Other Responsibilities as Directed by Supervisor or Executive Director

Knowledge and Skills

Activities are governed by a professional code of ethics and rules of confidentiality; thorough knowledge of the techniques and principles of psychological, behavioral, and social disorders; skill in dealing with the public in advocating for mentally and emotionally disturbed, developmental disabled, and drug-dependent persons; ability to develop cooperative relationships with families, physicians, agency personnel and executives, and public officials; ability to interpret mental health services; ability to prepare precise, complete records and to maintain updated client records; ability to participate in social and community planning and to carry out recommendations and directions.

Training and Experience

Must have at least a Master's degree in a mental health-related discipline from an accredited college or university and at least 2 years appropriate experience in the direct treatment of mentally ill clients under the supervision of a mental health professional. The appropriate mental health experience could be acquired in any of a variety of settings, for example, alcohol, drug, mental retardation, physical rehabilitation, and so forth. As such, these requirements meet the state definition of mental health professional, and this staff member can provide clinical supervision to the other staff members.

Appendix D

Sample of Core Competencies for Working in a Human Services Agency

1. *Organization and priority setting.* Prioritizes, organizes, and monitors work to ensure that goals, objectives, and commitments are met.

2. *Flexibility.* Adapts well to changes in direction, priorities, schedule, and responsibilities.

3. *Two-way communication.* Clearly expresses (orally and in writing) thoughts, feelings, concepts, and directions; listens effectively to understand communications from others.

4. *Teamwork.* Works collaboratively and cooperatively in groups for the purpose of achieving shared objectives, consistent with the organization's mission and strategy and individual work goals.

5. *Relationship building.* Builds and maintains productive associations with others who share a mutual interest in and commitment to achieving Casey's strategic objectives.

6. *Valuing diversity.* In the course of accomplishing the job requirements and strategic objectives of the organization, is sensitive to and competent in working with people who are different from one's self.

7. *Developing self and others.* Recognizes and acts on the need for life-long learning and takes personal responsibility for building professional and organizational capability in self and others, which is consistent with the needs of the organization.

8. *Critical thinking and Judgment.* Gathers, organizes, interprets, and processes information for the purpose of making informed decisions in the course of accomplishing work objectives.

9. *Technical expertise.* Demonstrates both technical and organization-specific knowledge required to be proficient in one's profession or job classification (Bristow, 1999).

Reference

Bristow, N. (1999). *Using your HR systems to build organization success.* Orem, UT: Targeted Learning. Retrieved May 15, 2007, from http://ww.targetedlearning.com

Appendix E

Planning, Leading, and
Coaching Professional Meetings

Context

Many social services agencies strive to improve their program effectiveness by increasing leadership capacity. Supervisors are challenged by the need to teach and coach more workers and to collaborate with more community groups with the same or fewer amounts of resources. A fundamental supervisory skill that is often not addressed relates to where agency staff members and supervisors spend substantial amounts of time—*in meetings.*

Effective organizational leadership requires paying attention to and effective management of *relationships, results,* and *processes* (Interaction Associates, 2003, 2005a). In this appendix, we address all three areas of focus within the context of professional meetings, including staff meetings, task group meetings, and problem-solving/crisis management meetings.

Planning and leading meetings effectively takes effort—especially for those supervisors and workgroup leaders who spend the extra time necessary to plan and provide follow-up to further the work of a team or committee. This appendix is directed at those leaders who are supervising a group of staff members, running task-oriented workgroups, leading ongoing committees, or organizing special one-time events where planning and execution of the meeting effectively is important to the outcomes of the organization.

Clarifying the Purpose of the Staff Meeting

Many people approach staff meetings with a sense of dread or boredom. The meetings may be long, boring, tedious, intimidating, conflict-filled, ambiguous, or lack follow-up on the part of a staff member or supervisor. But these dynamics can be avoided with proper planning and execution. First, note that staff meetings have several purposes, including doing the following:

- Establish a workgroup or organizational identity and cohesion, including confirming statuses by clarifying organizational roles of staff members
- Distribute and coordinate work, as well as monitor work progress involved in implementing something
- Provide information and facilitate learning
- Study a problem
- Make decisions (or in some cases confirm or ratify decisions that were made previously)
- Provide a forum for promoting and managing staff change (Interaction Associates, 2005b; Prosen, 2006; Resnick, 1982)

In addition, it may be helpful to approach staff meetings with the following principles in mind: First, an egalitarian and participatory management style is generally most effective. Second, good leaders recognize the needs of staff for autonomy, involvement, and influence. Third, the staff meeting is at the intersection of three organizational systems:

1. The agency *social system* interpersonal and friendship dynamics play important roles.

2. The agency *service system,* the set of programs services and their staff.

3. Agency *administrative* system, people in authority and their roles and functions (Resnick, 1982).

Managing the Pre-Meeting Process

LEADING MEETINGS

One approach to preparing for effective meetings uses a three-phase system developed by Resnick (1982). The phases are as follows: a *preparatory* phase, a *during-meeting* phase, and a *post-meeting* phase. Within each of these phases, some important processes are taking place. Some of these processes include problem solving, norm setting, role clarifying, message sending and receiving, as well as decision making. This model is built on the assumption that each phase of the staff meeting process is as important as any other, and that the success of one phase is linked to the effectiveness of others.

OVERVIEW

The first question to address is strategic: "Why is this meeting necessary?" Are these issues so sensitive or confidential that they would be best handled in a small group or individually? Is there sufficient information to address the topic adequately? Are there important decisions that need to be made by convening this group of people? What outcome will be achieved by raising it before the team? Who is most crucial to involve to accomplish the work without making the meeting size too large (Brody, 1993; Prosen, 2006). Too often meetings are focused on presentations instead of on obtaining a workgroup endorsement to proceed or gain approval for an expenditure of resources. So, would a paper memo, e-mail, or one-on-one supervisory conference be a more effective and efficient way to address a need or issue?

Supervisors may forget that meeting preparation is critical to meeting effectiveness. Proactive planning is essential, such as scheduling the meeting when it is most needed during the work cycle and choosing a time of day that is best for brainstorming or other work that needs to be done. Contentious topics might be handled at a time when staff may be more energized and able to engage in proactive discussion. Supervisors generally avoid Monday mornings and Friday afternoons for meetings because staff are either just becoming engaged again or are in the process of becoming disengaged from the work unit.

AGENDA PLANNING

Leaders often fail to create conditions for the staff to prepare themselves. This leads to the perception that *supervisors own* the meeting, rather than the perception that staff and supervisors *jointly* own and run the staff meetings. Jointly creating the meeting agenda with staff is an important function. Some practice principles for agenda setting are as follows:

A. Solicit items from all levels of the agency so the agenda is a participatory effort.

B. Prioritize the agenda items so that sufficient time can be allotted to important items. Answering the who, what, when, why, where, and how questions may be helpful (Brody, 1993).

C. Place the more important items in the middle of the meeting, rather than toward the end. This is especially important if some people tend to come late and you want to maximize discussion of those items.

The agenda should be viewed as tentative, with agenda items added to or modified during the first 5–10 minutes of the meeting to enhance staff feelings of ownership and to address key issues that have developed or were not thought of when the agenda was first formulated. Sometimes, agenda items can be "clustered" to improve flow and to be more efficient:

- Informational items
- Discussion items
- Brainstorming ideas or options

- Decision-making items
- Future business and agenda-setting items

A tentative agenda should be distributed to staff 2 to 3 days ahead of the meeting. It is also important to anticipate staff reactions to the agenda items so that the facilitator can guide the discussion accordingly. Anticipate criticisms and be ready to listen carefully with an open mind. Note that this is a crucial opportunity to hear a perspective that might not yet have been considered and, if addressed, would strengthen the recommended approach.

Prepare the rationale for an intended direction, although some say the best meeting chair is the person who says the least. A good meeting facilitator also anticipates questions and actions that may be taken so the appropriate resource persons are invited well in advance of the meeting and are present, and the most helpful resource materials are brought to the meeting. Furthermore, most written materials should be prepared and distributed in advance and not handed out at the meeting.

Finally, during the pre-meeting phase, select the room and consider various seating arrangements, food, and resource materials may be needed. In addition, anticipate how staff can be brought to life in the meeting. If there are notes to be kept, a flip chart is often helpful. Consider who might engage in these and other tasks. Notify these people ahead of time that they are needed to facilitate the meeting with you. Cast a wide net of engagement; this makes for less boredom and greater meeting success.

Managing the Meeting Phase

LAUNCHING THE MEETING

The major activities of this phase are as follows: finalizing the agenda in the first few minutes of the meeting, approving the minutes from the last meeting, designating who will take the minutes for today, reviewing the meeting action steps from the last meeting, conducting the meeting, reviewing the meeting action steps, and assigning tasks. Well-organized meetings that begin and end on time are respectful of meeting participants and their workloads.

One of the key aspects of the meeting is to establish some ground rules. Although new ground rules do not need to be established each time there is a meeting, develop a few basic ground rules that can be used to guide meetings. These ground rules cultivate the basic ingredients needed for a successful meeting such as how to make changes to the agenda, decision-making approaches, how new items are introduced, and how to maintain focus as the group moves from agenda item to item (McNamara, 2006).

Note that some organizations require the use of *Robert's Rules of Order Newly Revised* (Robert, 2000). There are a range of tactics to use to be effective in these more unusual situations. One strategy suggested by Sylvester (2006) included using formal motions to advance the work, employing tactics for stopping meeting bullies, and identifying ways to debate more effectively. For example, know when to use a motion to cut off debate that has gone on too long, or call for a "minority report" when the group is having difficulty coming to a reasonable agreement on a committee report. Votes by a small minority of the group can be the key to blocking someone from office, extending the time of the meeting past the scheduled adjournment, and elimination of an agenda item before it is even reached on the agenda (Sylvester, 2006, p. 40).

Purposefully pay attention to *relationships* among team members, as well as be clear about the *results* that are necessary to be achieved, and the *process* that is used to accomplish those results. Prosen (2006) underscores the value of this approach:

> For meetings to be truly effective the focus must be on results rather than people. It's fine to be hard on performance—you should be when results, commitments, and objectives are at risk or go unmet. But, you don't want to be hard on people. Watch your language. Don't make it personal. Instead, focus on removing roadblocks that stand in the way of accomplishing the goal, as opposed to the individual's inability to achieve that goal. (p. 29)

UNDERSTANDING AND COPING WITH GROUP DYNAMICS

To lead meetings effectively, aspects of group process or dynamics must be taken into account, along with the results that need to be achieved (Resnick, 1982; Schuman, 2005). Useful *practice principles* for the facilitator or chairperson of the meeting are phrased as questions below:

1. Are the group's or agency's strategic *objectives understood* by all staff?

2. Is an atmosphere of *mutual trust* being encouraged? What is the *degree of mutual support?* Is it every person for him- or herself, or genuine concern for each other?

3. Are *the abilities, knowledge, and experience* of all staff members as a group being used in the meeting? Workers have different skills that often go unrecognized and unused.

4. Is *communication* guarded and cautious or open and authentic? Is the *organizational environment* one where there is pressure toward conformity, rather than being supportive and respectful of individual differences and initiative? Is the facilitator denying, suppressing, or avoiding *staff conflict,* or gently confronting differences to work them through?

5. Are the acceptable styles of decision making clear so that issues can be purposively moved from a brainstorming or discussion phase to a decision-making phase?

6. Is attention being paid to nonverbal cues, are debriefings held with staff members to gauge their reactions, and does the setting provide a supportive tone for the meeting (Burlson,1990; Doyle & Strauss, 1982; Speer & Zippay, 2005)?

The discussion of each agenda item should be handled separately and should be opened, channeled, and closed. *Opening* involves defining each issue to be discussed and the goals of the discussion (e.g., to provide information, collect information for future decisions, or to make a decision). Make clear requests, offers, and promises to staff (see Healthcare Executive, 2006):

> Good meetings are composed mainly of constructive dialogue—where participants say what is on their mind; address and resolve conflicts; and make tough decisions that result in many requests, offers and promises for action. (p. 60)

Channeling involves making sure everyone talks who has important information to give with rules of discussion flexibly enforced. Minimize extraneous ramblings. Meeting facilitators can often become stuck and need to be able to help the group identify alternative options, establish or re-establish ground rules, remind staff there are multiple paths to achieving something, encourage others to play a "devils advocate" so that alternative ideas are raised and considered, encourage consultation from people outside of the group, think through different scenarios about how others would approach the issue, and finally encourage people to express important worries or reservations about an issue rather than engage in "hallway conversations" (Brody, 1982; Gouran & Hirokawa, 2005; Lencioni, 2005; Wilkinson, 2005).

Closing involves making sure the discussion does not go over the time that the group has allotted. It is often helpful to summarize the conclusions reached or not reached. Clarify what is going to happen next and who will take responsibility for working on the issue or implementing a decision (e.g., John and Mary will follow up on developing a job description for a night crisis worker staff position). Lastly, it is important to evaluate how well the meeting achieved its purpose—either formally through a quick "plus-minus" discussion with the staff at the end of the meeting or more privately through one-on-one supervisor–worker reviews of the meeting process and results. Did the meeting answer staff questions? Did it define or clarify problems efficiently and thoroughly? Did it enable the group to make necessary decisions in a timely way?

MANAGING CONFLICTS IN MEETINGS

Occasionally two or more individuals in a meeting will disagree and clash, resulting in a conflict that may escalate into nonproductive verbal exchanges. But some conflicts should not be avoided (Deutsch, 2003). Conflict that is handled constructively can strengthen the relations among team members and improve productivity. Duncan (1996) developed an overview of the various categories in which conflicts emerge. These categories are depicted in Figure E.1. This diagram shows the sources of conflict, their types, and how they relate to physical/psychological needs and values of employees. A source of conflict could be, for example, a bad relationship between some of the meeting participants. This conflict is psychological and subjective. An example of a subjective and principle-based conflict is when someone's values or beliefs clash with other participants' values or beliefs (Rienks, Nijholt, & Barthelmess, 2006).

RULES HELP

Boundary rules define who is and who is not in the group and can detail the permeability of the group (i.e., whether members can easily enter or exit). These rules determine the extent to which norms developed within the group can be maintained and shared, and the extent to which groups can impose sanctions. More specifically, aggregation rules define how a group reaches a collective decision. Decisions can be by majority, unanimity, or "anyone" rule. The unanimity rule is dangerous because if one person objects it can take a lot of time before an acceptable choice is negotiated. The "anyone" rule means any actor can impose a group choice.

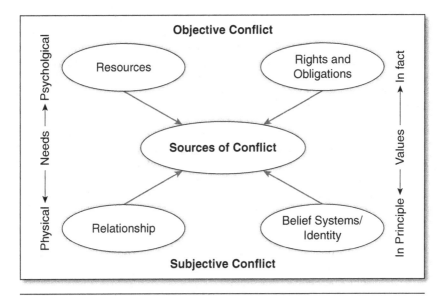

Figure E.1   Sources of conflict

Source: From *Effective meeting facilitation: Sample forms, tools, and checklists,* by M. Duncan, 1996, Washington, DC: National Endowment for the Arts. Copyright 1996 by National Endowment for the Arts. Retrieved May 12, 2008, from http://www.nea.gov/resources/Lessons/DUNCAN2.HTML. Reprinted with permission.

Furthermore, "position rules" define who can act at any point, and thus, they define the authority of the group to a great extent. Some positions have a higher authority than other (lower) positions. In contrast, "information rules" describe how information is shared and what each actor can know, for instance, whether a member can know what other members have done or what they are planning to do (Rienks et al., 2006).

TIPS FOR DEALING WITH HOSTILE QUESTIONS

Supervisors or others leading meetings can be surprised and then react negatively by pointed or "hostile" questions. A few strategies can help:

- *Paraphrase the question.* Sometimes just using active listening skills defuses the hostility. It also gives the facilitator time to compose a response.
- *Remain calm.* Provide answers in a calm, professional manner.
- *Be brief.* Hostile questions often come with a great deal of detail, background information, and emotion. Whether or not that is the case, the response should be brief, pointed, and cool; the contrast will help if the question was overheated, and an overheated response to a cool question will damage individual authority.
- *Offer to meet privately.* After offering one or at most two responses to the question, suggest a meeting with the person at the end of the meeting or at a later time (Parker & Hoffman, 2006, p. 99). Additional strategies for more general kinds of conflict are listed in Figure E.2.

- *Manage the process.* First, be clear about the process and then help the participants follow it. If, for example, in order to be sure of achieving clarity about points of view, be sure that the participants state their positions without jumping to a solution.
- *Do not deny or smooth over differences.* Over time, denying the existence of conflict (i.e., "There is no problem with MP") or minimizing a conflict (i.e., "It's nothing serious") ensures that the issue will remain just below the surface. Unresolved conflict can erupt at inappropriate times (e.g., at the end of a long meeting) or at inappropriate forums (e.g., a project review with senior management). It is the role of the meeting facilitator to help the team members address their differences.
- *Ensure understanding.* Ask everyone to indicate their own position (for example, one staff member might say, "I want to discontinue the brand development project with Market Quest)" Explore the reasons behind the position taken. Use active listening and open-ended questions to get to a thorough understanding. The following are examples of useful open-ended questions:

  "Why is this change necessary?"
  "What can you tell us about your experiences with this issue?"
  "What are your biggest concerns?"
  "So you are saying that Market Quest has not delivered on its promises?"

"In other words, you feel that Market Quest has not been given sufficient time to fulfill its obligations?"

- *Be supportive and encouraging.* Indicate that you have an understanding of why people are concerned about the issue and why they feel so strongly about it, and that it is a legitimate concern. By using this approach, there is no indication of support or opposition to either side of the conflict.
- *Clarify the alternatives.* Help the participants develop a set of possible solutions. Be careful at this stage of the tendency to "split the difference." By agreeing to a middle ground, the problem is not usually solved but leaves both sides feeling dissatisfied. Instead, look here for a list of viable options that are real solutions to the conflict. In many conflict situations, seeking alternatives may require the group to step back and imagine new possibilities rather than accepting one of the initial proposals or jumping to traditional solutions.
- *Avoid jumping to a single solution.* Resist the tendency to get into a discussion that focuses solely on the advantages and disadvantages of just one answer. Most creative solutions result from an examination of a range of possibilities. Sometimes, what begins as a crazy idea can be shaped into an innovative outcome.
- *Consider a pilot program.* If team members cannot reach a consensus on a permanent solution, propose a pilot or trial plan with a limited time frame and specific evaluation criteria. "Let's set up a 3-month trial with Market Quest, at the end of which we will evaluate the extent to which they have signed up the required number of customers."
- *Break the problem into manageable parts.* If a resolution of the total problem is not emerging, consider slicing and dicing the issue into smaller parts. "Since we can't seem to agree on a global solution, let's develop one for the intake team, one for the case records team, and another for the aftercare team."
- *Defuse anger.* If meeting participants become angry and speak to each other in disrespectful ways, immediate action by the team facilitator is required. Some possible responses include the following:

  o Stop the discussion, indicating that this is not appropriate behavior.
  o Take a short break to allow participants to cool off.
  o Review the relevant team norms dealing with such behaviors as respect, being open to new ideas, avoiding personal attacks, and practicing active listening.
  o Remind the participants about the need to present usable ideas rather than just attack the other person's ideas.
  o Revisit the goal of the discussion: to come up with a solution that is best for the team, the project, and the company. The goal is not to win a victory for any specific solution.

Figure E.2   Tips for meeting facilitators for handling conflict

Source: Adapted from *Meeting excellence: 33 tools to lead meetings that get results* (pp. 104–106), by G. Parker & R. Hoffman, 2006, San Francisco: Jossey-Bass.

POST-MEETING PHASE

Some activities of this phase will take place the day of the meeting; others may occur later:

1. Handling short post-meeting meetings of subcommittees to carry out tasks

2. Clarification or discussion with certain staff to describe what really happened at the meeting

3. Contacting staff members who missed the meeting

4. Preparing minutes

5. Beginning the agenda for the next meeting

Some additional principles that may be useful to consider are listed in Figure E.3. Force field analysis is an important analytical tool for group planning in which the factors that are pushing or supporting an issue in one direction are compared with factors that may be counteracting that issue or tendency. "Blocks" in terms of policies or resource restrictions that are less changeable are also identified so that realistic planning can take place (Swinton, 2007). Flow charts are also useful, as well as charts that outline a timeline of what tasks must be done by when and in what order.

- Determine the clarity of the meeting—what is the purpose? What is the work needed to be done? Is it a brainstorming or a decision-making meeting? Is the meeting necessary?
- Select who should be at the meetings, assign roles, and address the need for staff affirmation or recognition.
- Are meetings the *only* way that your staff members receive affirmations and praise for work? If so, then meetings take on too much of a special meeting feeling versus stopping by to see a staff person, using e-mail, and sending notes.
- Make sure each participant understands his or her role.
- Support the meeting chair to really be in charge.
- Who should be there? Could a person's viewpoint be represented in other ways?
- Anticipate questions that might develop regarding the meeting issues:

  A. What materials might need to be available to address those questions?
  B. Can certain issues be discussed in advance with those not in attendance? Whose ideas are crucial to addressing the issue?

- Ensure that the essential people are at the meeting (larger group for brainstorming versus smaller group for decision making). You

Figure E.3 *(Continued)*

are balancing the need for input with the time it takes to get something done.

- Prepare participants beforehand (notify them about the meeting's purpose, what to bring, and how to prepare for the meeting; distribute materials in advance).
- Agenda is prepared, modified at the start of the meeting if necessary, and then followed.
- Group leader should maintain meeting focus.
- If needed, a participant's special role is articulated in advance.
- All staff need basic training and performance expectations around meeting management in the person's job description.
- Keep the level of detail appropriate to the meeting. (Model channeling and the willingness to take feedback well, even mid-stream, in the process.)
- Staff members need to feel comfortable enough to respond to the group leader or another participant.
- Hidden or nonexplicit agenda items need to be raised.
- Sometimes reducing items to writing may facilitate making a decision.
- Finality. There needs to be "closure" at the end of a major planning discussion—what is "material" to whom in relation to project purpose. Review any action plans or goal charts held over from last time for meetings where you are planning a project. Is there an action plan or clear sense that a decision has been made? Project leadership needs to be clear: Who has the responsibility, authority, and resources to accomplish the work? (Use Microsoft Project [Microsoft Corporation, Redmond, Washington] or similar software to create detailed timelines for more complex projects.)

Figure E.3   Additional staff meeting principles suggested by supervision workshop participants

Agenda Design

AGENDA DESIGN VARIATIONS

The next set of figures (Figures E.4–E.6) present different variations of a hypothetical meeting agenda and a recommended structure for committee minutes. Meeting minutes generally result in better follow-through on the part of committee members. Several publications are listed at the end of this appendix that describe the principles for effectively designing and leading meetings. This example begins by reviewing a typical agenda for a meeting (see Figure E.4). Note how the agenda detail may change in relation to the amount of work, the complexity of the work, and the political dimensions that may need to be addressed.

Meeting for the Intake Committee of the Chicago Human Services Association
March 12, 2009
Agenda

1. Introductions
2. Maximizing the responsiveness of the intake unit
3. Making do with less: possible budget cuts and how we might respond.
4. Committee work activities and priorities for the next 6 months

Figure E.4 Typical agenda format used by many leaders

Two other agenda versions that may be more effective are presented in Figures E.5 and E.6 with some concepts from Interaction Associates.

March 12, 2009

1A.	Meeting minutes reviewed (Karen) (2 minutes)
Outcome:	Meeting minutes approved
Item 1.	Maximizing the effectiveness of the intake unit (Karen) (15 minutes)
Outcome:	Ideas for enhancing how the unit operates are identified, clarified, and agreed upon
Item 2.	Preparing for possible budget cuts (Sarah) (15 minutes)
Outcome:	Areas for budget-cutting are identified, clarified, and prioritized, after deciding on the preferred mode of decision making for this topic
Item 3.	Committee work activities and priorities (Mark) (15 minutes)
Outcome:	All participants understand the committee work activities and priorities for the next 6 months
Item 4.	Agenda planning for next meeting (Karen) (5 minutes)
Outcome:	Meeting planned
Item 5.	Meeting debrief (plus/deltas) (John) (5 minutes)
Outcome:	Meeting strengths and areas for refinement identified

Figure E.5 Meeting for the planning committee

March 12, 2009
Operating Agreement

• Listen to Each Other	• Respect Confidentiality	• Speak Without Fear
• Say What You Think/Feel	• Recognize Task/Process Balance	• Recognize Contributions
• Begin and End on Time	• Share Air Time	

Pathways to Action: Problem identification & analysis, visioning, solution development, and implementation

Agenda and Process

	Agenda Item, Leader, and Estimated Time	Process
Item 1A.	Meeting minutes reviewed (Karen) (2 minutes)	• Discuss • Vote
Outcome:	Meeting minutes approved	
Item 1B.	Maximizing the effectiveness of the intake unit (Karen) (15 minutes)	• Brainstorm • List • Clarify • Check for agreement
Outcome:	Ideas for enhancing how the unit operates are identified, clarified, and agreed upon	
Item 2.	Preparing for possible budget cuts (Karen) (15 minutes)	• Brainstorm • List • Clarify • Check for agreement
Outcome:	Areas for budget-cutting are identified, clarified, and prioritized, after deciding on the preferred mode of decision making for this topic	

Figure E.6 *(Continued)*

Figure E.6 (Continued)

	Agenda Item, Leader, and Estimated Time	Process
Item 3.	Committee work activities and priorities: Who will do what by when? (All) (20 minutes)	• List possible areas • Clarify • Develop plan for further discussion
Outcome:	Committee work activities and priorities are identified	
Item 4.	Agenda planning for next meeting (Karen) (5 minutes)	• Brainstorm • List • Clarify • Decide
Outcome:	Meeting planned	
Item 5.	Meeting debrief (plus/deltas) (Peter) (5 minutes)	• List • Decide on action plan
Outcome:	Meeting strengths and areas for refinement identified	

Figure E.6 Meeting of the planning committee

Summary

Managing staff meetings requires specialized skills that are often not addressed in most educational degree or training programs. And yet team meetings offer a powerful and timely venue for addressing staff needs and issues related to the effective leadership of the core concepts that have been emphasized throughout this entire book: *relationships, results,* and *processes.* Supervisors have the greatest success when purposefully paying attention to *relationships* among their team members, as well as being clear about the *results* that are necessary to achieve and the *processes* that are used to accomplish those results (Interaction Associates, 2005a).

References

Brody, R. (1982). *Problem solving*. New York: Human Services Press.

Brody, R. (1993). *Effectively managing human service organizations*. Newbury Park, CA: Sage.

Burlson, C. W. (1990). *Effective meetings: The complete guide*. New York: Wiley.

Deutsch, M. (2003). International handbook of organizational teamwork and cooperative working (pp. 9–44). New York: Wiley.

Doyle, M., & Strauss, D. (1982). *How to make meetings work*. New York: Jove.

Duncan, M. (1996). Effective meeting facilitation: Sample forms, tools, and checklists. Retrieved May 21, 2008, from http://www.nea.gov/resources/Lessons/DUNCAN2 .HTML

Gouran, D. S., & Hirokawa, R. (2005). Facilitating communication in group decision-making discussions (pp. 351–360). In S. Schuman (Ed.), *The IAF handbook of group facilitation*. San Francisco: Jossey-Bass.

Healthcare Executive. (2006, Sept/Oct). Meeting management: Leading independently. *Healthcare Executive*, p. 60.

Interaction Associates. (2003). *Facilitative leadership*. San Francisco: Author. (See http://www.interactionassociates.com)

Interaction Associates. (2005a). Chartering a team using five key attributes. Retrieved June 16, 2005, from http://www.interactionassociates.com/tips_detail.cfm?id=11

Interaction Associates. (2005b). Meeting material resources. Retrieved June 16, 2005, from http://www.interactionassociates.com/tips_detail.cfm?id=8

Lencioni, P. (2005). *Overcoming the five dysfunctions of a team: A field guide for leaders, managers and facilitators*. San Francisco: Jossey-Bass.

McNamara, C. (2006). Basic guide to conducting effective meetings. EMA Learning. Retrieved May 14, 2009, from the Free Management Library at http://www .managementhelp.org

Parker, G., & Hoffman, R. (2006). *Meeting excellence: 33 tools to lead meetings that get results*. San Francisco: Jossey-Bass.

Prosen, B. (2006). How to cure meeting mania. *Municipal World*, December 29–30. http://www.municipalworld.com. Retrieved May 15, 2009, from http://www .kisstheorygoodbye.com/pdf/Municipal%20World-Prosen.pdf

Resnick, H. (1982). Facilitating productive staff meetings (pp. 183–199). In M. J. Austin, & W. E. Hershey (Eds.), *Handbook on mental health administration*. San Francisco: Jossey-Bass.

Rienks, R. J., Nijholt, A., & Barthelmess, P. (2006). *Pro-active meeting assistants: Attention please!* (pp. 213–227). Proceedings of the fifth workshop on Social Intelligence Design, Graduate School of Human Sciences, Osaka, Japan.

Robert I, H. M., Robert, S. C., Robert III, H. M., Evans, W. J., Honemann, D. H., & Balch, T. J. (2000). *Robert's rules of order newly revised* (10th ed.). Cambridge, MA: Perseus.

Schuman, S. (Ed.). (2005). *The IAF handbook of group facilitation*. San Francisco: Jossey-Bass.

Speer, P. W., & Zippay, A. (2005). Participatory decision-making among community coalitions: An analysis of task group meetings. *Administration in Social Work*, 29(3), 61–78.

Swinton, L. (2007). Kurt Lewin's Force Field Analysis: Decision making made easy. Retrieved June 3, 2007, from www.mftrou.com http://www.mftrou.com/Lewins-force-field-analysis.html

Sylvester, N. (2006). *The guerrilla guide to Robert's Rules.* New York: Penguin Books.

Wilkinson, M. (2005). Consensus-building: Strategies for resolving disagreement (pp. 361–380). In S. Schuman (Ed.), *The IAF handbook of group facilitation.* San Francisco: Jossey-Bass.

Web-Based Resources

Designing and facilitating meeting resources. Retrieved December 21, 2008, from http://www.effectivemeetings.com/

Force field analysis summary and diagrams; see Management for the Rest of Us. Retrieved January 4, 2009, from http://www.mftrou.com

Suggested Readings

Kaner, S., Lind, L., Toldi, C., Fisk, C., & Berger, D. (1996). *Facilitator's guide to participatory decision-making.* Philadelphia: New Society Publishers.

Lencioni, P. (2005). *Overcoming the five dysfunctions of a team: A field guide for leaders, managers and facilitators.* San Francisco: Jossey-Bass.

Parker, G., & Hoffman, R. (2006). *Meeting excellence: 33 tools to lead meetings that get results.* San Francisco: Jossey-Bass.

Schuman, S. (Ed.). (2005). *The IAF handbook of group facilitation.* San Francisco: Jossey-Bass.

Timm, P. R. (1997). *How to hold successful meetings: 30 action tips for managing effective meetings* (30-minute solutions series). Franklin Lakes, NJ: Career Press.

Tropman, J. E. (1996). *Effective meetings—Improving group decision-making* (2nd ed.). Thousand Oaks, CA: Sage.

Index

About the Authors

Emily J. Bruce, PhD, LCSW, began her career in social work by receiving a BS in applied behavioral science from the University of California (UC)–Davis in 1981 and then receiving an MSW from the University of Washington in 1983. After working for 10 years in public child welfare, first as a child welfare social worker and then as a child welfare supervisor, she began a PhD program at UC–Berkeley. She completed her PhD in social welfare in 2002.

Professor Bruce began at teaching at San José State University (SJSU), School of Social Work, as a part-time lecturer in 1998, and she became a full-time member of the faculty in 2002. Currently, Professor Bruce is an associate professor at the SJSU. She teaches social welfare policy, child welfare policy, and research. In addition, Professor Bruce continues to design and implement research in the area of child welfare services and child welfare administration.

Finally, she is one of the co-founders of the Connect, Motivate, and Educate (CME) Society, a program at SJSU that functions to provide support for former foster youth enrolled at SJSU. In academic year 2008/2009, Professor Bruce will be working to help implement a research institute at SJSU: The Research Institute for Foster Youth Initiatives (RIFYI). Professor Bruce is married and lives in Stockton, California.

David A. Cherin, PhD, is a professor, department chair, and social work program director at California State University–Fullerton. Prior to returning to work on his MSW and PhD, Professor Cherin was an administrator and corporate vice president for over two decades with a large, multinational health care management company. In this arena, he was a vice president with responsibilities in acute hospital operations as well as mergers and acquisitions. Since entering the field of social work, Professor Cherin has held faculty positions at California State University–Long Beach, California State University–Bakersfield, the University of Southern California (USC), and the University of Washington's School of Social Work. He was the administrator of the Hamovitch Research Center at USC as well as director and chair of the Social Work Program at California State

University–Bakersfield. He currently holds the position of the founding director of the social work program at California State University–Fullerton. He has performed extensive research, evaluation work, and publishing in the areas of health care service delivery, organizations, evaluation, and child welfare. His work in health services focuses on service delivery systems in end-of-life care. He has received the Soros Project Death in America's Social Work Leadership Award for his work on end-of-life issues with AIDS patients.

Peter J. Pecora, MSW, PhD, has a joint appointment as the managing director of research services for Casey Family Programs and as a professor in the School of Social Work, University of Washington, Seattle. Casey Family Programs is the largest operating foundation in the United States dedicated to improving the lives of children in foster care. Professor Pecora was a line worker and later a program coordinator in several child welfare service agencies. He has worked to implement intensive home-based services, child welfare training, and risk assessment systems for child protective services. He also has served as an expert witness for the states of Arizona, Florida, New Mexico, Washington, and Wisconsin. His co-authored books and articles focus on child welfare program design, administration, and research, including:

- *The legacy of family foster care: How are alumni faring as adults?* New York: Oxford University Press (2010).
- *The child welfare challenge.* New Jersey: Transaction de Gruyter, 1992, 2000, 2009.
- *Enhancing the well being of children and families through effective interventions—UK and USA evidence for practice.* London: Jessica Kingsley, 2006.
- *Quality improvement and program evaluation in child welfare agencies: Managing into the next century.* Washington, DC: Child Welfare League of America, 1996.

Currently, Professor Pecora is co-leading a project with the REACH Institute to improve youth access to evidence-based mental health services. He also coordinates a data workgroup as part of a national effort to reduce racial disproportionality in the child welfare system.

Trinidad de Jesus Arguello, RN, LISW, MSW, PhD, born in Santurce, Puerto Rico, has a 32-year history working in mental health. Her professional experience has included work both as a psychiatric nurse and as a psychiatric social worker. She has been able to integrate her direct practice experience with management of clinical teams and supervision of master-level students in social work. Her management work has involved development and directorship of a home health program; supervisor for a mental health team providing services to the mentally challenged; supervisor of a batterer's domestic violence program; children and family program coordinator for Hispanics at Centro de Bienestar, San Jose,

California; and director of Children and Family Out-Patient Services in Taos, New Mexico. Professor Arguello has developed a batterer intervention program and provided direct services for Hispanic men in Taos, New Mexico.

Furthermore, Professor Arguello has held adjunct faculty positions in various colleges and universities. She has also presented her work regarding cultural issues related to Hispanic families as well as her work on mental health and domestic violence at many conferences and workshops across the United States. She also serves on the New Mexico Mental Health/Behavioral Health Planning Council. Finally, Professor Arguello has served as the Taos County Coordinator for the American Red Cross (ARC) as well as first disaster responder for the ARC nationwide. Currently, she was funded a grant by the New Mexico Behavioral Health Service Department to implement an Assertive Community Treatment Program for the severe and persistently mentally ill population in her community.

About the Contributors

David Chenot, PhD, MDiv, LCSW, is an assistant professor in the MSW program at California State University–Fullerton. Previously, he developed the Title IV-E program and offered instruction in the MSW program at California State University–Bakersfield. Professor Chenot earned his PhD at Case Western Reserve University. Prior to entering academia, he was a social worker for many years in public child welfare services and, subsequently, a supervisor in a county public mental health agency. Professor Chenot's research interests include the retention of social workers in public child welfare services, resilience among vulnerable children and families, and spirituality in social work practice.

Jean Kruzich, PhD, is an associate professor and co-chair of the administration concentration at the University of Washington School of Social Work. She teaches courses on leadership, program management, organizational assessment and change practice, and collaborative community-based program evaluation. Professor Kruzich's research has focused on the influence of organizational and community environments on marginalized populations, including elderly and youth with mental health challenges. She received her PhD from the University of Washington and her MSW and MPA from the University of Minnesota.

Nancy Timms, MA, MSW, LMHC, has been a social work supervisor for child welfare services in rural Washington State since 1997. She serves frequently as an instructor at the Children's Administration Social Worker Academy and, in 2000, received the Governor's Recognition for Innovative Practice Award. Prior to her child welfare professional practice, Ms. Timms worked for 15 years in community mental health as a crisis/solution-focused brief modality therapist.

Supporting researchers for more than 40 years

Research methods have always been at the core of SAGE's publishing program. Founder Sara Miller McCune published SAGE's first methods book, *Public Policy Evaluation*, in 1970. Soon after, she launched the *Quantitative Applications in the Social Sciences* series—affectionately known as the "little green books."

Always at the forefront of developing and supporting new approaches in methods, SAGE published early groundbreaking texts and journals in the fields of qualitative methods and evaluation.

Today, more than 40 years and two million little green books later, SAGE continues to push the boundaries with a growing list of more than 1,200 research methods books, journals, and reference works across the social, behavioral, and health sciences. Its imprints—Pine Forge Press, home of innovative textbooks in sociology, and Corwin, publisher of PreK–12 resources for teachers and administrators—broaden SAGE's range of offerings in methods. SAGE further extended its impact in 2008 when it acquired CQ Press and its best-selling and highly respected political science research methods list.

From qualitative, quantitative, and mixed methods to evaluation, SAGE is the essential resource for academics and practitioners looking for the latest methods by leading scholars.

For more information, visit **www.sagepub.com**.

Printed in the United States
By Bookmasters